A LIFE IN PARTS

BRYAN CRANSTON

SCRIBNER
New York   London   Toronto   Sydney   New Delhi

Scribner
An Imprint of Simon & Schuster, Inc.
1230 Avenue of the Americas
New York, NY 10020

First Scribner hardcover edition October 2016

SCRIBNER and design are registered trademarks of The Gale Group, Inc., used under license by Simon & Schuster, Inc., the publisher of this work.

For information about special discounts for bulk purchases, please contact Simon & Schuster Special Sales at 1-866-506-1949 or business@simonandschuster.com.

The Simon & Schuster Speakers Bureau can bring authors to your live event. For more information or to book an event, contact the Simon & Schuster Speakers Bureau at 1-866-248-3049 or visit our website at www.simonspeakers.com.

Interior design by Jill Putorti

Manufactured in the United States of America

10 9 8 7 6 5 4 3 2

Library of Congress Cataloging-in-Publication Data is available.

ISBN 978-1-4767-9385-6
ISBN 978-1-4767-9388-7 (ebook)

Some names and identifying characteristics have been changed.

Photographs on pages 5, 208, 221, and 276–77 courtesy of Sony Pictures Television.
Photographs on pages 9, 11, 19, 36, 82, 148, and 260 courtesy of Bryan Cranston.
Photograph on page 184 *Malcolm in the Middle* © 2001 Twentieth Century Fox Film Corporation, Monarchy Enterprises S.a.r.l. and Regency Entertainment (USA), Inc. All rights reserved.
Photograph on page 271 courtesy of Jeffrey Richards Associates, photograph by Evgenia Eliseeva.

For Kyle and Amy: We made it. A life worth salvaging.
For Robin and Taylor: You made it a life worth living.

One man in his time plays many parts.

—William Shakespeare, *As You Like It*

A LIFE IN PARTS

Walter White

She stopped coughing. Maybe she'd fallen back asleep. Then suddenly vomit flooded her mouth. She grasped at the sheets. She was choking. I instinctively reached to turn her over.

But I stopped myself.

Why should I save her? This little junkie, Jane, was threatening to blackmail me, expose my enterprise to the police, destroy everything I had worked for, and wipe out the financial life preserver I was trying to leave my family—the only legacy I *could* leave them.

She gurgled, searching for a gasp of air. Her eyes rolled back in her head. I felt a stab of guilt. Goddamn it, she's just a girl. *Do something.*

But if I stepped in now, wasn't I just delaying the inevitable? Don't they all at some point end up dead? And poor dumb comatose Jesse, my partner, lying beside her. She's the one who got him on this shit in the first place. She'd kill them both, kill us all, if I stepped in now and played God.

I told myself: just stay out of it. When he wakes he'll discover this tragedy—this accident—on his own. Yes, it's sad. All death is sad. But he'll get over it in time. He'll get past this like every other bad thing that's happened to us. That's what humans do. We heal. We move on. A few months from now he'll barely remember her. He'll find another girlfriend, and he'll be fine. Fuck it. We all have to move on.

I'll just pretend I wasn't here.

But I am here. And she's a human being.

Oh God. What have I become?

And then, somehow, as she was fading, she wasn't herself anymore. I wasn't looking at Jane, or Jesse's girlfriend, or the actor Krysten Ritter. I was looking at Taylor, my daughter, my real daughter. I wasn't Walter White anymore. I was Bryan Cranston. And I was seeing my daughter die.

From the moment she was born in 1993—a bit premature, shy of seven pounds, impossibly beautiful—I felt an instant, radical, unconditional love that redefined love. I had never allowed myself to imagine losing her. But now, I was seeing it. Clearly. Vividly. She was slipping from me. She was dying.

That was not the plan. When I do the homework for such a delicate scene, I don't make a plan. My goal when I prepare isn't to plot out each action and reaction, but to think: What are the possible emotional levels my character could experience? I break the scene down into moments or beats. By doing that work ahead of time, I leave a number of possibilities available to me. I stay open to the moment, susceptible to whatever comes.

The homework doesn't guarantee anything; with luck, it gives you a shot at something real.

It was real fear that gripped me—my worst fear. A fear I hadn't fully expected or come to terms with. And my reaction is there, forever, at the end of that scene. I gasp, and my hand moves to my mouth in horror.

When the director, Colin Bucksey, said, "Cut," I was weeping. Deep racking sobs. I explained to the people on set what had happened, what I had seen. Michael Slovis, our cinematographer, embraced me. My castmates, too. I remember in particular Anna Gunn, who played my wife, Skyler. I hugged her. I must have held on for five minutes. Poor Anna.

Anna knew. As an actor she has a fragility at her core, and she often had a hard time shedding her character's emotions after shooting difficult scenes.

That will happen in an actor's life, and it happened to me that day. It was the most harrowing scene I did on *Breaking Bad*, and really . . . ever.

It may seem odd. It may even seem ghoulish. To stand in a room packed with people and lights and cameras and pretend I'm letting a girl choke to death. And then to see my daughter's face in lieu of that girl. And to call that work. To call that your job.

But it's not odd to me. Actors are storytellers. And storytelling is the essential human art. It's how we understand who we are.

I don't mean to make it sound high-flown. It's not. It's discipline and repetition and failure and perseverance and dumb luck and blind faith and devotion. It's showing up when you don't feel like it, when you're exhausted and you think you can't go on. Transcendent moments come when you've laid the groundwork and you're open to the moment. They happen when you do the work. In the end, it's about the work.

Every day on *Breaking Bad* I'd wake up about 5:30 and have coffee, take a shower, get dressed. Some days I was so tired, I didn't know whether I was coming or going.

I'd drive the nine miles from my condo in Nob Hill to Q Studios, five miles south of the airport in Albuquerque—ABQ as the locals call it. I'd be in the makeup chair by 6:30. I'd shave my head anew. Knock down the nubs. It didn't take too long for makeup. By

7:00 a.m. we'd see everyone: the other actors, the crew. Then we'd start rehearsing.

The allotment was a twelve-hour shoot. Plus a one-hour lunch. So a normal day was thirteen hours. It was very rare that the day was shorter. Occasionally, it was longer. Some days went seventeen hours. A lot of it had to do with whether we were on location.

If it was just a minimum day, we'd wrap at 8:00 p.m. Then I'd grab a sandwich and apple for the road. I didn't want to take the time to stop. I'd call my wife, Robin, from the car. *How are you? Yeah, long day.* I'd see how she was doing. I'd ask about Taylor. I'd still be talking to her when I walked into the house. I'd say goodnight and then have that sandwich while looking over what we were doing the next day. I'd take a hot bath with a little glass of red wine. Then I'd hit the sack.

But even before the drive home, every night after we finished, I'd go in the hair and makeup trailer and take two hot, wet towels that my friends in the makeup department had presoaked, and I'd drape one over my head and I'd wrap the other over my face. I'd sit in the chair and let everything soak off, feeling all the toxins drain away. I'd sit until the towels went cold against my face, leeching myself of Walter White.

That day I saw Jane die—that day I saw Taylor's face—that day I went to a place I'd never been, I opened my eyes and stared through the scrim of the white towel into the light above. I'd put everything, *everything*, into that scene. All the things I was and all the things I might have been: all the side roads and the missteps. All the stuttering successes and the losses I thought might sink me. I was murderous and I was capable of great love. I was a victim, moored by my circumstances, and I was the danger. I was Walter White.

But I was never more myself.

Son

My parents met like most people do: in an acting class in Hollywood.

My mother was born Annalisa Dorthea Sell, but she was always called Peggy. Peggy was an impulsive girl, fun-loving, a flirt. In her youth she had a genuine innocence about her. She was one of those blond, blue-eyed cuties always told she ought to be in the movies. And so after a two-year stint in the Coast Guard and a failed starter marriage to a man named Easy, she left Chicago for Los Angeles, the land of empty promises, and she flung herself into auditions and acting lessons.

The litany of states where my dad, Joseph Louis Cranston, grew up was so long I could never quite remember them all: Illinois, Texas, Florida, California, New York. As a kid, I imagined that he hailed from a family of grifters. Only outlaws could be so . . . rootless. Being the new kids in school every few months, my dad and his brother Eddie were often picked on, so my grandfather taught them how to fight. Not street brawling, but the acceptable method, in the boxing ring. The Cranston boys had the gift. My father earned a boxing scholarship to the University of Miami. He fought up and down the East Coast—in and out of the ring. In all my early memories, my dad was scrapping with someone or something.

And he could tell a story.

The handsome pugilist and raconteur and the blue-eyed flirt fell for each other in a hot flash. It's easy to do that in an acting class. And after a couple of years, they tied the knot at the Little Brown Church in the Valley on Coldwater Canyon Avenue in Studio City. My mother became a 1950s wife: everything she had she threw behind her new husband and his goal to become a movie star.

They bought a modest tract home and followed the script. My brother, Kim, came first in 1953, then me in 1956, and finally my sister, Amy, in 1962.

We lived in Canoga Park in a single-story home at 8175 McNulty Avenue, close enough to Hollywood in physical distance, but a world away: the Valley—maybe best known for its lazy-tongued, sunbaked drawl. Seasons in the Valley were subtle. In the warm months, when the air pollution level was deemed dangerously high, our outdoor activities were restricted. We had smog days rather than snow days. We'd lie on our backs making smog angels in the yellowed grass.

Mom was an Avon Lady, a volunteer at the Braille Institute for the blind, a Tupperware representative, a team mom for our Little

League, and a member of the PTA. She hand-made our Halloween costumes every year.

Dad was our coach in Little League. He loved baseball. So I loved baseball. And I do to this day. I went to a Dodgers game with Dad when I was four or five. The Dodgers had moved from Brooklyn to LA, but they didn't yet have a stadium, so they played at the Los Angeles Memorial Coliseum for four seasons, from 1958 to 1961. The Coliseum was built for football and track and field, so the dimensions were strange for baseball—an enormous right field and a shallow left field—like Fenway Park in Boston. They put a high screen over the left-field fence in the Coliseum. To get a home run, a batter had to clear the screen. Even though left field was short, that screen was dauntingly high. Forty-two feet. Fenway's world-famous Green Monster is thirty-seven.

A player named Wally Moon, who hailed from the cotton fields of Arkansas, developed a knack for hitting home runs over that net. He'd switch his swing to an uppercut and whack it so high you thought he might punch a blue hole in the smoggy cloud wall: *home run*. People took to calling those soaring hits *moon shots*. I'd watch the ball hang in the sky—a pop-up, really—for a moment of breathless suspense, and then elation. Glory. That captured my imagination: swinging for the impossible, shooting the moon.

Even after the Dodgers moved to their permanent home at Chavez Ravine in 1962, and even after things at my house started to fall apart, I knew I could depend on the smell of fresh-cut grass, Vin Scully's dulcet voice calling the game on the radio, and the clean symmetry of the baseball diamond. The sense of hope you could dare to have with runners at the corners and no outs.

My dad would take us to the movie and TV sets where he worked as an actor. Once he surprised us with something inside a trailer hitched to our car. He opened it up and we peered into the dark, dung-scented metal box. A donkey! I remember that donkey so well. His name was Tom. My dad let it roam around our backyard for a time. All the boys and girls in the neighborhood came over to admire him and to go for a ride. We had him for a while. Maybe a month or two. And then he went back to wherever he belonged. Bye, Tom. Nice knowin' ya.

My dad also brought home props for my brother and me: infantry helmets and badges and uniforms. Later I realized he must have "borrowed" them and then returned them the following week. Props on a set are tracked carefully; they're not toys. But for us they were great treats.

When my dad brought prop guns home, we loved to play war. All the boys in the neighborhood were always battling the Germans or the Japanese or the American Indians. We didn't really understand history or war or why these people were our enemies. That's just the way things were.

And then one day an announcer came on TV and said, "We interrupt this program to bring you a special report." Every time I heard that for years to come, I clenched.

Walter Cronkite was on the screen, somber. "From Dallas, Texas, the flash, apparently official, President Kennedy died at one p.m. Central Standard Time." I remember how Cronkite took off his glasses. He wasn't a stoical journalist anymore. The mask came off. He was just a man, overcome by the size and shock of the loss.

There was a gasp and then a panic. My mother was weeping and clutching herself. And then she was locked in on the phone, as if my brother and I had disappeared. The adults couldn't get enough news. My dad came home, solemn, and the neighbors stopped by. They needed to tell each other it was going to be okay. I don't know how much I understood, but I felt the gravity of it. And now we had a new president. Lyndon Johnson. He talked funny. I don't know that I'd ever heard that deep of a Texas drawl. And I thought his wife had a strange name.

Our parents were devastated. We were learning life and death and fear and grief and succession. We didn't know what to do. A neighbor kid declared: "We are not playing with guns anymore." We loved guns, but we tossed them aside, imagining that we could somehow alter the course of things with our gesture. It didn't last long. The urgency diminished and normal life resumed. It was a new normal.

The Outlaw Frank James

Whereas I was a goof as a kid, my brother Kim had a serious streak; he was introspective. He was smarter than me, not as athletic. But we were aligned in almost every other way. Brothers in every sense. And we both inherited the acting gene. Kim became my first director. He wrote and mounted the McNulty Avenue Garage production of *The Legend of Frank and Jesse James*, then cast me as Frank James. For Jesse, he looked next door to the Baral household. The Barals had five boys, and my brother chose Howard, the middle child, to play the heartless outlaw. Kim cast himself as the sheriff, several victims, townspeople, the coroner, and a newspaperman. I'm not sure why he didn't cast others—there were plenty of kids in the neighborhood. Maybe he wanted them to pay their nickel like everyone else.

We draped white sheets over storage boxes, and they became snowcapped mountains. We fashioned a blue plastic tarp into a raging river. A stuffed alligator snapped at our heels. Alligators abounded in the Old West. Of course the denouement was a fateful shoot-out. We were boys, pretending to kill each other, playing with glee and abandon.

My first venture as a professional actor was a family production, too. My dad wrote, directed, and produced a series of ads for the United Crusade, which would later change its name to the United Way. I guess invoking a blood-soaked religious war wasn't the vibe they were going for as a charity. My dad cast me as the lead. I was seven. The story went I was playing baseball with friends on a sandlot when a foul ball rolled into the street and I gave chase. Look out! I got hit by a car, put into an ambulance, rushed to the ER, and put into a head-to-toe body cast. Weeks later the cast came off, and I started physical therapy on the parallel bars and in the pool to learn how to walk again. In the last scene I held hands with a woman pretending to be my mother as we joyfully walked out of the hospital. Healed.

I remember shooting every one of those scenes. I remember

feeling that there was something special about what I was doing. Maybe it was just the attention. But I think it was something more. A sense that I was part of something greater than myself.

Son

I especially loved acting for my dad. He was a big man in my eyes— barrel-chested with striking black hair that gave way to distinguished salt and pepper before he turned forty. He always seemed so tall to me, but as he aged, I realized that he was just shy of five feet nine at his high-water mark.

My dad wanted to be a star. No doubt. No compromise. Nothing else would do. He wanted the home run. But there were bills to pay. When he wasn't working as an actor, my dad wrote scripts and did some directing and dabbled in businesses. Over his lifetime there were a lot of businesses. He started a company that offered a video assist to help golfers perfect their swing. He opened a recreational trampoline center and then a bar and coffee shop. He had plans for a catamaran cargo ship company. He ran a magazine for Hollywood tourists called *Star's Homes*. At one point, he operated a tour of Liberace's gilded house.

The man did not lack for ideas. He approached each venture with vigor, but seldom found success. He had more ambitions and brainchildren than business acumen. His failures mounted and ate at him. And yet he never gave up. That was instructive. He kept at it.

His was the typical actor's life—uncertain employment, a little kismet, lots of hard luck. As a child, I never really felt the difference when the family was flush or flat broke. But my parents sure did. We got a brand new car one year. A while later, we sold it, and got an old car. A little elbow grease and it's just like new! Another year, my parents (really, my dad) decided to go to the great expense of installing a built-in swimming pool in the backyard. Everyone in the neighborhood came to our house that summer, and we laughed and swam until our fingers were shriveled and our bloodshot eyes cried uncle, and then we beached ourselves bellies-down on the warm concrete and recovered.

The following summer my mother told us that we wouldn't be able to swim because we couldn't afford the chemicals. As a result, our pool turned a murky green, like a pond somewhere in the deep woods.

My dad did have some moderate success as an actor. He was featured in several TV shows, a handful of films. He cowrote the script for *The Crawling Hand,* a movie about an astronaut whose dead hand goes on a rampage targeting beachgoing teenagers. He also cowrote *The Corpse Grinders,* a trash flick that was part of a triple-feature release (which also included *The Embalmers* and *The Undertaker and His Grisly Pals*) still fondly recalled by drive-in purists.

He acted in an incredibly fake and delightfully cheesy movie called *Beginning of the End,* a low-budget sci-fi film made in the late fifties by the great Bert I. Gordon—aka "Mr. B.I.G."—who specialized in "giant" movies that he made by superimposing images onto his films. For this one, Gordon filmed real grasshoppers, then unconvincingly superimposed them onto the action. You know the classic story: an invasion of angry, voraciously hungry, giant man-eating grasshoppers created at an experimental farm in Illinois.

Joe Cranston plays a soldier stationed as a lookout on top of a skyscraper. Grasshoppers are attacking the city. Don't they always? You never see them descending on a field of wheat. When my dad reports to his superiors over the two-way radio, he is still peering through his binoculars. "Eastern sector clear," he says. Just then, the quivering antennae of a giant grasshopper appear behind him. Cut back to headquarters: the officers are listening to Dad's report, his voice emanating through the speaker on the wall, "No sign of them here." Then a bloodcurdling scream. "Noooo!" Dad was a goner. Great stuff.

If my dad was featured in a show or movie on TV, neighbors would drop by the next day to report how they felt about his work. "I liked the production value, but all the actors were turkeys." "The beginning was great . . . but the end was a fiasco."

That was my first brush with celebrity. And critics. There was always a *but.* Everyone felt entitled to voice his or her opinion. As an actor, you were fair game.

My dad didn't seem to lack for confidence. And yet the endless stream of *buts* got to him. When things went south, he griped and fumed and resented others he felt were unworthy of their success. He was better than that actor. He worked harder than this other guy. So much of the world made him mad. You never knew what was going to set him off.

I remember riding in the front seat of my dad's car with my brother late one afternoon, and a guy driving a hot rod cut him off. Dad slammed on the brakes and straight-armed my brother and me to keep us from flying through the window. We were in the rusted car that had replaced our new one. My dad gave chase, honking, and at a stoplight he pulled up alongside the spiffy car and rolled down his window and started yelling. The man said, "What are you going to do about it, old man?" This guy was young—much younger than my dad. "Pull around the corner," my dad said, "and I'll show you what I'm going to do about it."

They turned the corner and parked behind some stores. Stay here, my dad instructed my brother and me. We were terrified, clutching each other. My dad got out of the car. The other man got out of his car. He was tall and well built. Much taller than my dad. But my dad marched right over to him and punched him in the face. The guy hit his car and fell to the ground, his nose a bloody mess.

My dad came back to the car and got in. "Don't mention this to your mother. It'll just make her worry." Kim and I twisted around to peer out the rear window as we drove away. The man was holding his face. His face was covered in blood. My father had done that. That was my father. The fighter.

The violence wasn't reserved to random motorists. My father and my mother fought, too—careening, blistering fights that occasionally left us children cowering in our rooms, out of the line of fire.

Things were already shaky by the time my dad took over the lease of the Corbin Bowl, a bar and coffee shop attached to a bowling alley on Ventura Boulevard in Tarzana. The occasional appearances on TV weren't enough to sustain a family, and so he had a vision for the bar: something cool and sophisticated with nightclub singers. The coffee shop would bustle during the daytime while the club ruled the night.

It didn't turn out like that. My grandmother manned the cash register. My mother worked as a fry cook and waitress. Kim and I bussed tables and washed dishes after school. Even my five-year-old sister did her part, bringing water to the tables. My dad managed the bar, but he was often away. Maybe at an audition. Maybe at a clandestine rendezvous.

My brother and I were aware of the fragility of the situation, if not the fine details. We waited in knotted anxiety for our dad's reappearances and the inevitable fights that ensued.

We looked for respite whenever we could get it. The movies were our favorite escape. We went to the coffee shop nearly every day after school, and at 3:00 p.m., if we'd done our homework, we went next door to the Corbin Theater to catch an afternoon screening before we had to be back to the coffee shop to help with the evening business.

Our favorite flick was *Cat Ballou*, a Western spoof about a prim schoolmarm who sets out to avenge the death of her father and becomes a notorious outlaw. Lee Marvin had two roles—the legendary gunfighter Kid Shelleen *and* gunslinger Tim Strawn. It tickled us to recognize the same actor in two roles. Nat King Cole and Stubby Kaye played a kind of a Greek chorus and crooned "The Ballad of Cat Ballou." My brother and I both had wild crushes on Jane Fonda. She was tough and beautiful. We went to see that movie every day as long as it played. We knew every word, every micro facial expression, every gesture. We'd go home and take a bath, and before bed we'd act out the scenes, playing different characters, singing the songs at the top of our lungs: *Cat Ballou, Cat Ball-ou-ou-ou. She's mean and evil through and through.*

Over two years we saw all kinds of movies at the Corbin. *The Glass Bottom Boat. Oh Dad, Poor Dad, Momma's Hung You in the Closet and I'm Feelin' So Sad. The Graduate.* I was eleven. Too young for *The Graduate.* But I loved it. I related to Dustin Hoffman's character, his confusion. He was trying to figure things out. That's how I felt, too. I was just starting puberty, just starting to awaken to the allure of girls, and I was enchanted and nervously excited by the idea that an older woman could seduce you, would *want* to seduce you. Dustin Hoffman's character watching in awe as Anne Bancroft pulls her stockings onto her beautiful legs? The taboo image stayed with me wherever I went. Until that movie, I thought there was some kind of law that you had to be with someone your age for the parts to fit.

Corbin Bowl was a dud. My dad had to bow out after a couple years; he was crushed. My parents grew even further apart.

There was a period of weaning off. He started to show up at home less and less. And then not at all.

Two years later, we went to a courthouse with my mom. She wore her best dress and a lot of makeup. Despite her coiffure and pretty façade, her mood was tense and downbeat. I think she told us she was the witness to someone's divorce. I don't remember exactly when we learned it was hers. Sometime later.

We saw my father in the cold marble courthouse hallway under the fluorescent lights. We hadn't seen him in two years. I remember his dress shoes and then his face close to ours when he knelt down to say hello. And then moments later, in a blur of violence, he slugged a guy. Boom. Man down. Blood splattered.

"Jimmy! Jimmy!"

It turned out Jimmy was the husband of the woman my dad stole and would soon marry. Her name was Cindy. It all happened so quickly. Maybe it took two minutes. Two minutes. And then my dad was gone. I wouldn't see him again for a decade.

Flea Marketeer

I remember lying to my friends and neighbors, the Baral boys, when they asked me, "Where's your dad?"

"Oh, he's been working every day but he comes home at night and wakes us up and we play for a long time." I think they believed it. Even I started to believe it.

For a while my dad had been a ghost. And then he was gone. We were never told why. In fact, we were never told anything. That's just what happened. Move on.

For the longest time I thought my sister, Amy, who was too young to understand what was happening, was luckier for sliding through that period relatively unscathed. But now I realize that she missed all the happiness and stability of the time before things fell apart—the Christmas lights, the outings, and the games we'd play as a family.

Because we had known the good times, I think my brother and I felt the loss more acutely. My father's waning presence, his chronic absence, his disappearance. Now he was just a memory.

He was the love of my mom's life. In his wake she grew angry. She began tending to her resentment like a private garden that was more real to her than any living thing. Where once she was vibrant and accessible, now she was overtaken by depression and inertia. Once caring and present, now she was sullen and melancholy and remote. She began to drink. Slowly at first, and then not slowly. She started with wine. Boxed wine. Wine in jugs with the little finger hole. I saw a lot of those empty jugs.

She would perch at the kitchen table draining her glass and complain to my brother and me: Your father. Ugh, your father. He *needed* to be a star. And he wasn't a star. And that's what drove him crazy.

She'd sometimes turn to me and say, with a sneer of bitterness and pain: You look just like him.

What was she going to do? Since there was now zero money coming in, she needed to find a pathway to income. Mom was a natural pack rat, so the obvious avenue was to sell off some "assets." Her plan was to pack up her '56 pink Cadillac (probably a holdover from one of our "up" periods), and drive to the Simi Valley swap meet to sell whatever she could. Every Saturday night, Kim and I would pack the Pink Lady, as my mom had affectionately dubbed her car, to the roof. And every Sunday morning, before sunrise, we'd somehow, someway stuff ourselves in, too, for the twenty-five-mile trip.

Kim and I were charged with unloading the car and arranging the eclectic items for sale on blankets. We made tidy rows while Mom went scouring for bargains from other sellers. About the time we finished setting up our wares, Mom would return with armloads of other people's junk for us. Not for us, exactly, not for our personal use, but to resell at a profit. We carefully integrated the new haul into our own.

When Mom found out that there was another swap meet opening up on Saturdays in Saugus, in Santa Clarita, we added that to our itinerary. We now spent the whole weekend at swap meets. We were in the junk business. Once we sold off our own items, we became fully dedicated to hawking other people's goods. The garage that Kim and I had once used as a stage for creative expression was now creating an expression all its own. Junk filled the space from floor to ceiling. It wasn't just the garage. The house was now unrecognizable to us. Everything was stacked and crowded and askew: slightly used bedding and secondhand clothing and radios with broken speakers and ratty furniture and tarnished table settings. There were dolls with one eye missing and tattered magazines with their covers torn off.

I came to abhor clutter. I still feel uneasy when things around me are in disarray.

But my mom pressed on. In spite of her growing desperation and despair, there was something valiant about her tenacity. I think she really did believe the swap meets would save us. But in the end, the numbers wouldn't add up. After a while, the bank told her that we were going to lose the house. And then we did.

Professor Flipnoodle

I got adequate grades, but the teacher comment section of my report card was always filled with ominous statements: *Bryan needs to apply himself. Bryan is often goofing around and disruptive. Bryan spends too much time daydreaming.* I so clearly remember hearing these comments reworked and recited back to me as admonishments whenever my parents disapproved of my behavior. If I were a kid today, I'd probably be diagnosed with mild ADHD. Back then, the only descriptor for my condition was: Bryan needs to pay more attention.

So, now entering fifth grade, what was different? Maybe I looked to school as a haven away from the chaos at home. Maybe school was a safe place where I could focus my energies. Whichever. My grades rose, and so did my spirits. Suddenly I was popular; I was invited to parties and asked to run for student-body president. I was a good athlete—not great, just good, but I harbored the dream that one day I would become a major league baseball player.

I also dreamed of Carolyn Kiesel, a torturously cute classmate. She wore her dark brown hair in an adorable cut that framed her petite features. Rather than telling this sweet girl how I felt or striking up a conversation, I put some of the tasty paste we used for arts and crafts in her hair. Naturally, that made Carolyn angry with me— which was . . . all right by me. I understood *anger*; it was *affection* I couldn't wrap my head around. Having Carolyn yell at me was at least better than having her not notice me at all. Eventually I realized I needed to find another way to tell Carolyn I liked her. Maybe next year when we were both mature sixth graders.

I was very fortunate to have two wonderful mentors in Mrs. Waldo and Mrs. Crawford, my fifth and sixth grade teachers at Sunny Brae Elementary. Neither of them was finger-wagging or textbook. They wanted their students to find their own ways to express themselves, and they encouraged me to explore performance. I learned that there were other ways to do a book report besides sitting down and writing the tired old: *Huck Finn*, Mark Twain's most acclaimed work, tells the story of the travails of a young man as he leaves his hometown seeking adventure, blah, blah, blah. None of that. I could *act* it. I could *be* Huck Finn. Or Professor Flipnoodle.

Professor Flipnoodle was the lead role in our school play, *The Time Machine*; Flipnoodle was the machine's wacky inventor, who traveled back in time to seminal, teachable moments in history. Two years earlier, the school had done the same play, my brother in the lead role, and I was blown away by his ability. When Kim donned the character's fire-red curly wig on the stage, he became a different person. I remember sitting in that audience and knowing with piercing clarity that I wanted to wear that wig, too. At last, my audition arrived. I can't remember the details, but I must have been good. I got the role. The wig was mine.

Two performances were scheduled: one in the daytime for the student body and teachers, and one at night for the parents. I chipped away at the text and memorized it. I was confident that everything would fall into place. Doing a play was like an oral book report, just longer.

With the red curly wig as my talisman, I breezed through the afternoon performance, winning applause and cheers. During a break, a castmate and friend, Jeff Widener (a convincing Davey Crockett), shared an idea, a note he thought would be a funny addition to the evening performance.

"Hey, Bryan, wouldn't it be funny if instead of saying, 'After delivering the Gettysburg Address, President Lincoln will return to the White House,' you said, 'President Lincoln will return to the White Front.' Wouldn't that be funny?" In the sixties and seventies, a department store chain named the White Front was as ubiquitous in Southern California as Target is today. I laughed and agreed, sure, substituting White Front for White House would be funny. But saying that would ruin the play. My response was emphatic, serious. No. Conversation over.

But now I was paranoid. I couldn't have been aware of the term *mantra*, and yet that's what I employed. I hammered these words into my head with grim determination. *Don't say White Front, don't say White Front.*

Hours later, I got up on that stage and performed my heart out. This happened before my dad punched the guy in the courthouse, but I don't remember him being in the auditorium. I knew my mother and brother and grandparents were out in the darkness, however, so I was filled with pride and adrenaline. I came to the part of the show dealing with the strife of the Civil War, and in a tone of supreme authority I pronounced that "after delivering the Gettysburg Address, President Lincoln will return to the White Front."

Silence.

I realized what I'd done instantly and stopped. Did they hear it? Maybe they didn't. Maybe God stepped in and corrected my word at the last second and saved me. I sheltered in the brief moment of silence and hope. But then came the laughter. The sound ricocheted off the walls and ceiling tiles like bullets. Men were doubled over in hysterics. Kids on stage were so overcome that snot was coming from their noses. Carolyn Kiesel was on stage, too, crying with laughter—which extinguished any hope of currying favor with her from my afternoon's *perfect* performance.

Everything came to a standstill exept my breathing. I stood there panting. I felt numbness in my face. A few years before, I'd had some teeth pulled, and afterward, as the drugs wore off, the world trailed by me in slow motion. Speech was distorted, faces misshapen. On stage, at that moment, I was reliving that sensation. Plus panic. I messed up something bad. Real bad.

I looked backstage and there was my beloved Mrs. Waldo. She couldn't contain herself, either. She was laughing so hard that she could barely muster the strength to wave her hand in a circle. She was signaling to me to continue the play. But I couldn't. I was frozen.

I suppose it lasted only a couple of seconds, though it felt like an hour. Eventually the roar quieted to some softer laughter and tittering, and I sensed I could continue. But what to do next? Plow forward? Go back and correct my mistake? I decided on a do-over. I said the line again. As written: "After delivering the Gettysburg Address, President Lincoln will return to the White House."

Suddenly the room was loud again with laughter. It was almost violent. The line now had a history, like a favorite joke; all you had to do was allude to it and people started to lose control.

I was no longer stunned. I was angry. I SAID IT CORRECTLY! I couldn't understand why the audience wanted to continue to punish me. It felt mean. The meanness of it struck me to the core.

I thought about walking off the stage—but somehow I knew that would make things even worse. Eventually the room settled down enough to start again. Fool me once. This time I plucked out a line that came after the now charged, loaded words *White House*. I pushed through the play with a hasty but precise pace, imagining everyone anticipating my next mistake so they could have another good chuckle at my expense.

Finally, mercifully, it was over.

I was upset. I was inconsolable. The worst part was that I had to endure the throngs backstage thanking me for an evening they would not soon forget.

That night set me on a course for many years to come. I became introverted, unsure of myself. And one thing I knew for certain: performing was not for me.

Suitor

Simon and Garfunkel's "Mrs. Robinson" was trilling from the record player, and Carolyn Kiesel was just a few feet away, looking beyond pretty. Perfect.

She'd warmed up to me over the last year. Perhaps she'd even forgotten my Flipnoodle debacle. I'd stopped putting paste in her hair and learned to talk to her like a real person. And she'd responded. She was sweet and generous at an age when nerves and hormones often overruled those qualities. I thought maybe she even liked me. So I'd made a plan.

I fingered the Saint Christopher medal in my pocket. Saint Christopher was the patron saint of travelers and mariners, and many surfers strung the medals around their necks for protection against the rough seas. For us in Southern California, the medal was a symbol of a man and his desires. Back then you gave it to a girl when she agreed to go steady with you, and she wore it as a pendant. Mine was going to Carolyn.

It was a leap. I felt something between us, but what if I was wrong?

My dad was gone. The White Front night shone like a specter behind me. I was quiet and unremarkable and shy. Why would she want me?

I hesitated. I debated. I tried to summon my courage and confidence.

As I hovered over a bowl of chips in agonizing conversation with myself I only semi-understood what was happening as the new kid in school, a skateboard dude with blond wavy hair, ambled up to Carolyn. *Where have you gone, Joe DiMaggio, a nation turns its lonely eyes to you. Woo woo woo.* Suddenly, Skateboard Dude asked Carolyn if she wanted to go steady. She smiled. She said yes. Their faces moved together and they kissed. They . . . *kissed.* They kissed right before my eyes. Just a few feet from me. *Hey hey hey.*

They kissed as if I weren't there.

Hey hey hey.

Farmhand

Most people in a divorce situation are forced to sell their houses in order to tabulate assets and divvy them up. We didn't have that problem. The bank took our house. Banks do that when people stop paying their mortgages. Men came and put a large sticker outlined in bright red on our front door: a proclamation to our friends and neighbors, our community—a scarlet letter.

I saw the looks on our neighbors' faces, somehow both judgmental and pitying. We were disgraced. Worse, we were forced to leave what comforts remained of our home. I had been under the impression all this time that we owned our house. I came to understand that the word *own* is often used loosely.

Amy and our mother went to stay with my paternal grandmother. My mom was still in love with my dad, so by moving in with his mother she thought she'd have a better chance of seeing him and perhaps even winning him back.

Meanwhile, one week into the school year, Kim and I were yanked out of John Sutter Junior High and shipped off to live with our maternal grandparents, Otto and Augusta Sell, both immigrants from Germany. Otto was a baker by trade, but now in retirement he had a small parcel of land where he farmed and raised some scant livestock. They lived in Yucaipa, California, in the foothills of the San Bernardino Mountains. A quaint little rural town, but to us it was the boondocks.

My grandparents' one-bedroom house was located right around the three-thousand-foot elevation level. Snow dusted the town several times a year. The lone attraction in the area was farther up the road at Oak Glen apple orchards—day-trippers would find a petting zoo, a kiddie amusement park, and the big draw: homemade apple pies, strudel, fritters, sauce. Pretty much anything made from apples.

Yucaipa was ideal for my grandfather, less so for my grandmother, but then it was the sixties, and they were Old World: the wife did as the husband pleased.

Neither could have been pleased to take on the role of surrogate parents to two boys in turmoil.

We were kids from the suburbs of Los Angeles. We bellyached: What are we going to do on a little farm?

The answer came quickly. Work.

Every day except Sunday we were expected to contribute sweat equity in exchange for room and board.

Our new next-door neighbor Danny Teeter had an egg ranch—a few acres of chickens cramped in small cages. Our day started there. We soon learned that setting a clock wasn't necessary due to the cacophony of *cock-a-doodle-doo*s at dawn.

Until that time, *chicken shit* meant someone who was scared to lie down in the street and let kids jump their bikes over him with a homemade plywood ramp. But now it had a whole new repulsively toxic meaning. A vividly pungent smell that haunted my clothes and hair hours after I'd left the coop. Breathe through your mouth, Bryan. I did that for a while, but then some kid at school told me that when you smell poop, actual tiny particles of that poop are getting into your nose. If that were true, my mouth-breathing solution to the chicken shit problem meant that I was actually *eating* poop. I went back to nose breathing.

Apart from being neck-deep in chicken shit, Danny was a good guy. He had Kim and me sell flats of eggs on weekends to daytrippers as they journeyed up the hill to the apple orchard. But the job Kim and I loved most was egg collection. Nearly every day, after school and after homework, Kim and I would hop the fence to Danny's property and eagerly go to it. We drove flatbed Cushman electric carts up and down the aisles of the coops, two hundred feet long and just wide enough to accommodate the cart. Three chickens were housed in a twelve-inch-by-sixteen-inch cage. The cage's floor was built with a slight incline so that when a chicken pushed out an egg it would gently roll toward the front of the cage and come to rest against a curved stop. Kim and I collected eggs from both sides of the aisle and deposited them into the flats on the front of the electric carts. A flat held thirty. We were taught to stack them about eight flats high. The cart held about six stacks. A lot of eggs.

When we reached our limit we'd drive to a cool, temperature-controlled room to unload. From there, each individual egg went through a washer—we thought of it as a mini car wash. The machine took the egg on a conveyor belt ride though pressurized cool water. No hot or warm water. You didn't want to promote the process of decay. And then soft bristles scrubbed the fecal matter and urine off the shell.

One of us would place the eggs onto the conveyor while the

other watched each one pass by a high-watt lightbulb, looking through the gossamer shell for blood spots, which indicated a fertilized egg. People don't like to see blood spots in their frying pans when they make a western omelet in the morning. Go figure. Each fertile egg was taken out of the washer and placed in a flat under a warming lamp. Soon it would be transferred to the hatchery to help regenerate the coop with new chicks.

Once all the unacceptable eggs had been removed (there were some truly amazing freaks of the egg world), the remaining inventory was separated by size and placed in a cardboard container. Finally, we'd fill padded shipping boxes with the delicate cargo and place them all in a large walk-in cooler.

Twice a week, at five in the morning, we'd awaken to the combustive rattle of a diesel-engine truck arriving to pick up our eggs and take them to market. That sound gave me such a sense of satisfaction. Work I had done was of value in the world. People would be fed by my hand.

Grandpa Otto was a good neighbor, unfailingly friendly and helpful to those in need. To thank him, and as a bonus for our labor, Danny gave him chickens whose best laying days were behind them. Grandpa took them with delight.

We'd monitor the hens to see which still had it in them to lay with some consistency. The old, the feeble, the infertile: they weren't so lucky.

There is a correct way to kill a chicken. Otto taught us. Grab it by the legs with one hand, collapse the wings with the other. Then secure the legs and wings with one firm hand. Next, lay the chicken on the block of a tree stump. Don't let go. Pick up the hatchet with your free hand. With one clean, strong stroke, drop the blade onto its neck.

The head will fall to the ground and the hatchet will be wedged into the block. Let go. Hold the chicken's body with both hands over a blood bucket until a couple of pints of warm blood have drained away. The chicken doesn't know it's dead just yet. The central nervous system will respond to the sudden loss of a brain with jerking and shaking. Steady. Once the blood is drained, toss the carcass into the dead-chicken tub.

Grandpa had already killed several chickens that day with a deftness and a stoicism that left us in silent awe. This is how it's done, boys!

Neither Kim nor I wanted anything to do with murdering chickens, but we knew we were going to be expected to pull our weight. We stood there, impassive but steeped in dread. We had no choice. We had to absorb Grandpa's lessons and do the deed ourselves.

Thank God Kim was older, so he was up first. It never crossed my mind to call him out for being nervous. I knew: I was next.

Kim grabbed his chicken correctly, let out a short, terrified breath, closed his eyes, and swung the hatchet. Instead of landing on the chicken's neck, he hacked right into the comb. A chicken's comb is like human hair; getting it severed feels like getting a haircut. This was one rough haircut. Kim let go of the chicken in shock, but its comb was still fastened to the chopping block by the hatchet. The animal knew this wasn't just another day of pecking seed. It flapped and clucked and sent its feathers flying in distress.

"Oh, for crying out loud!" Otto said and pushed Kim out of the way, grabbed the animal, pulled the hatchet out of the comb, and decapitated the chicken with one chop. He drained its blood and tossed it onto the tub of other dead chickens. Easy peasy.

Kim balled his fists and willed himself to do it again and do it right. He succeeded. A few times.

Kim had proven himself. Now it was my turn.

I filled my lungs with air that I hoped also contained minute particles of courage along with chicken poop. I understood that this was some kind of test. If I passed, I would be welcomed into manhood. I used to pity our friends and neighbors, the Baral boys, having to endure the rigors of memorizing passages from the Torah in preparation for their bar mitzvahs. Now I envied them. Reciting Hebrew was a cakewalk in comparison to this rite. I aggressively reached down and grabbed my first victim. The bird squawked, but I paid no attention to its discomfort; I was too concerned with my own.

I remember saying a silent *I'm sorry* to the creature. I was its executioner. Dead hen walking.

I hooked my left hand around one of the chicken's spurs, the sharp underdeveloped opposing digit that comes out of the back of the ankle. It dug into the flesh of my hand. I wasn't going to let that slow me down. I quickly gathered the wings and legs in one hand. I yanked the hatchet out of the stump with my free hand and plopped the chicken's head in its place. I was focused. No way was I going to wince and shut my eyes and miss my target as Kim had on his first attempt. No way.

The chicken struggled to free itself from my grasp. Not a chance. I raised the hatchet well above my head and brought it down with a ferocious swing. The head plopped lifelessly to the ground. Clean. Dead. I'd done it. And I'd buried the blade deep into the chopping block.

No time to revel in the glory. Once the head was off, the animal's central nervous system sent out emergency signals, and the carcass convulsed. I held steady, watching the dark red stream of blood drain into the nearly full blood bucket. But the violence of the shaking surprised me, and soon one of the wings was loose from my grasp. As I struggled to get the wing under control, the other one worked free. Blood was still flowing. I wasn't about to let it drip outside of the bucket, and catch a furious "What da hell!" from my grandfather. I pressed the bird downward. Not a drop of blood hit the ground.

But its wings flapped mightily, plunging deep into the bucket, sending streams of blood upward. Suddenly blood was in my nostrils, ears, and mouth. Oh God. I wore it. I tasted it. I drank it. But I didn't let go, by God. I should have, but I didn't.

I had blood in my eyes, so I couldn't see. I tossed the carcass in the direction of the bucket where its brethren lay. I missed. The moment it hit the ground, the bloody, headless creature rose to its feet and ran around the yard, ricocheting against whatever obstacle it encountered.

I tried to wipe off my bloody face, but there was blood on my hands. Kim later told me he stood in awe, switching his gaze from me to the chicken, the chicken to me. One bloody mess to another.

The chicken finally collapsed, and I hung my head while Kim rinsed me off with a garden hose. No way Grandpa was going to let me use the only indoor bathroom to clean up. That was reserved for Grandma. Kim and I were relegated to the outhouse. (Grandpa even tried to teach us how to separate our waste for fertilizer. Good times.)

Later that night I had to relive the "blood boy" experience as Grandpa, now finding the event very amusing, told the tale—with some embellishment—to Grandma. She was less sympathetic than I had hoped. I remember her laughing heartily. Everyone laughed. I guess it must have been funny.

Paperboy

After a year of collecting eggs and killing chickens, my brother and I were whooshed out of the country and reunited with our mother and sister at 7308 Owensmouth Avenue in Canoga Park, a house in need of either a retrofit or a wrecking ball. On the plus side, it was big. To offset the cost of leasing the whole place, my mother rented two small cottages in the backyard and two rooms inside the house to strangers. The renters were middle-aged single men on the low ebb of their luck. They all used one toilet in the back of the house, but had to find other means to shower. We never knew and never asked.

However, one man insisted as part of his rental agreement to be allowed to take a bath once a day in the only bathroom in our house. Every day at 3:00 p.m. we were required to unlock the access door to the bathroom from the back hallway to allow "Mr. Clean" to come in and bathe, shave, and do whatever he chose to do in there for an hour. This meant we had to make sure we didn't need to pee during that hour. If we did, we'd have to walk two doors down to the library to use their facilities.

The boarders plus my mother's full-time employment at the photo counter of JC Penney covered most but not all of the monthly nut. My brother worked at our next-door neighbor's western apparel store. I took on a number of odd jobs. We both chipped in.

In junior high, I had a job—a con job, really—distributing a throwaway rag, the *Canoga Park Chronicle*. First, I was supposed to stick people with the paper. Then I was instructed to knock on their doors to collect the fee. Shock of all shocks, not many people cared to pay $3.10 a month for a paper they neither ordered nor wanted. The few nice folks who did pony up only felt sorry for me.

I canvassed every house in the square mile of my territory. I lost track of how many times I heard: "Stop delivering that damn thing. It pisses me off every time I have to pick it up off my driveway and throw it in the garbage."

"Okay," I'd say, more desperation in my voice than brightness, "let's just have you pay the last month as a cancellation fee."

"I never ordered it, jackass!"

Trying so hard to give people something they clearly didn't want was eroding my confidence and spirit. Every day I wanted to quit. And the amount of time it took to complete my deliveries was cutting into my master plan to achieve a C average at Columbus Junior High.

I decided that I'd only deliver the paper to the nice people who sympathized with my plight. The rest of the papers I jettisoned into a Dumpster near my house. I'd stroll casually up to the receptacle, look around to make sure there were no witnesses, open the lid, and quickly throw all my papers inside. Then I'd walk away nonchalantly.

No one was any the wiser . . . until they were. Apparently, businesses that paid for the Dumpster didn't appreciate my disposal habits. They called the newspaper, and I suppose it wasn't too hard for my bosses to find the culprit in the case of the missing papers. My boss called my house and excoriated me. I remember he used the word *stealing*. Several times. And then he fired me.

I stood in the kitchen with the receiver in my hand for a while after he hung up. I was racked with shame, and more than that— surprise. I knew my actions were underhanded, but I don't think I fully understood that they constituted thievery.

Sneaky Pete

I was the kid who always looked for the shortcut, the scammer, the trickster. I was the mischief maker. If there was a way to shirk responsibility, I'd find it. Somewhere along the way, my family nick-named me Sneaky Pete.

And especially during my teenage years, I lived up to the name. In woodshop class, the teacher asked me what I would like to make for my final. I was feeling estranged from my mother, so I decided to try to bridge the gap by building her a chessboard tabletop, one of a half dozen approved projects. Though I was devoid of much talent in the woodworking department, the piece came out pretty well. I bought professionally lathed legs, attached them to the top, and voilà! I presented the finished product to her. *Hey, Mom. I made something for you.*

The look on her face. She was elated. I hadn't seen her so happy since my single-digit years, before my father left. I hadn't been receiving a lot of praise or nurturing, so genuine appreciation and marvel at what she perceived to be my skill and craftsmanship was pure joy. Joy all around.

One day I walked into the living room and she was proudly show-ing off the table to a friend, running her hand along the legs like a game show hostess displaying the grand prize. *Bryan made these*, she exclaimed. So beautifully designed. *My son*, she said.

I was about to interject with a clarification that actually I'd only made the chessboard, but the friend was impressed, which made my mom even more jubilant. I was caught somewhere between smiling and throwing up. I wanted to say: I didn't make those legs! Look at them. They're perfect! They could *only* have come from a profes-sional mill. How could she not know that? I told her I made her a chess table. I assumed that she would understand that meant I made the table's *top*. But I couldn't bear to correct her. She wasn't happy very often—for the rest of her life, really—and I didn't want this little run to end. So, from that moment on, I just nodded when anyone asked if I made the table. She kept that thing for years and every time we had a guest, she'd wax on about my craftsmanship. I'd just nod and smile, starting to get comfortable with my lie.

Throughout high school I got sneakier and sneakier. I somehow connived to obtain two student-ID cards; both pictured me, but my alter ego was named Bill Johnson (I picked a name I could easily remember). My idea was that if I got into trouble, I could throw the authorities off Bryan Cranston's scent by handing them Bill Johnson's ID card. Bryan was in twelfth grade, Canoga Park High class of '74. But Bill was class of '75, a junior. I didn't want any confusion. I considered every detail.

I belonged to no school clubs or organizations, but on photo day my best friend, Sergio Garcia, and I inserted ourselves into a good many group shots. There we were among the Knights and Ladies. And standing tall with the proud members of the Chemistry Club. We were also handsome cub reporters on the *Hunter's Call*, the school paper. The other kids actually took part in something; they learned about science or journalism or . . . I don't know what the Knights and Ladies learned about. But I was just there to pose for a picture. It was a goof, a joke, and all the other kids thought it was funny, but behind the joke was the truth: I was a guy searching. Showing up for the wrong things. Not showing up for the right things.

And in fact in my senior yearbook I am missing from the row of students with last names beginning with *C*. At some point, I drew an arrow to the place I should have been pictured and wrote in all caps: *WHERE AM I? RIP-OFF!*

WHERE AM I?

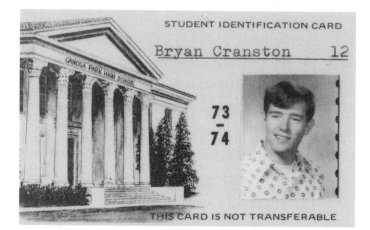

Beast Feeder

I picked up a job a few blocks from my home, preparing the Sunday *Los Angeles Times* for delivery. Boring. But on the plus side, I got to work with Reuben Valdez. Reuben was an excellent athlete, with a great personality and a smile that made him popular with girls. I, on the other hand, didn't make the baseball team, and I had a crooked smile. I was unremarkable and shy. I liked working alongside a beam of light like Reuben. Maybe some of his light would rub off on me.

We arrived at our jobsite, an industrial garage unit, at 3:00 a.m., and the unmistakable scent of newsprint hit us before we even rolled up the metal door. We went to work assembling all the sections of the paper that had been dropped off at the door. Then one of us fed the beast, an ancient paper-folding machine with an assembly line of rollers and a wrapper; the beast made a horrible crunching sound as it bent the thick paper and tied it with string. The guy who wasn't feeding collected the finished products and stacked them for our boss, Leroy Waco, whose name was pronounced with a long *A* like the city in Texas, but of course we called him "Wacko."

At dawn, when we were finished feeding and stacking, we'd stuff Leroy's car. He'd go off to deliver, and I'd walk home in an exhausted stupor.

Leroy was busier than a one-armed man flinging newspapers from a stick-shift VW Bug. Actually, that's exactly what he was. The guys at the paper called him the one-armed bandit. He had lost his right arm. (I never asked how.) He'd slip his left arm through the steering wheel and rest it on the shifter. When he approached a customer's home, he'd slow down, put the car in neutral, and pull his arm free, steering with his knees. He'd grab a paper and then hurl it toward a porch or driveway. He never, ever missed his target. He had the elegance, precision, and timing of a Gold Glove shortstop turning a double play.

Occasionally when we were ahead of schedule and the papers were wrapped and ready to go, I would ride shotgun. "Coming up!" Leroy would say. That was my cue. Wedged into the passenger seat, I'd prepare to toss a paper out my window. We'd slow to a crawl. "NOW!" Out it went. I did not have a fraction of Leroy's skills. I hit a lot of trees. A lot of gutters. "Goddamn it, kid," Leroy grumbled. He called both Reuben and me "kid." I don't think he ever knew our names. We'd come to a stop, and I'd run out and put the paper where it belonged.

It didn't take long for Leroy to reconsider my role. "Just keep a steady supply of papers for me to grab when I'm ready," he'd say with a sigh. Just feed the beast.

Housepainter

When the beast-feeding finally got to me, my friend Jeff suggested I work for his dad, a housepainter who needed help on the weekends. I'd met Jeff in the West Valley Division of the Los Angeles Police Department Explorers, a branch of the Boy Scouts. He was Native American, and his last name was Redman, and he was able to joke about it. He was cool and streetwise, with a strong mischievous streak. His dad, Jim, was a man of few words.

On our first day together, a Saturday, Jim picked me up at 6:00 a.m., and we rode in silence to an industrial building, a job he'd already started. When we began, he tossed a rag to me and said, "Soak that in turpentine and keep it in yer back pocket. Any time you make a mess, clean it up right away. It'll be your best friend."

"Okay," I said. Made sense.

We finished day one at dusk. I was beat. And uncomfortable. By the time Jim picked me up the next morning, I had developed a mysterious rash on my backside, raw and itchy and irritating as all hell. On the drive to work, he noticed me scratching my sore left ass cheek.

"What's the problem?"

I told him that I didn't know, but something probably bit me or else I was having some kind of allergic reaction. I glanced his way and caught a slight smile crossing his lips. We sat in silence for a while—easy for men to do. But why would he be smiling? Then it dawned on me. He told me to keep the turpentine-soaked rag in my back pocket. It was the turpentine! That bastard did it on purpose!

I didn't say anything. I took it as some type of initiation. But I did find another location to stash my turpentine rag.

One day after quitting time, we didn't go straight home. Instead, Jim drove to a far-flung neighborhood. In the alley behind a row of tract houses he slowed to a stop and got out of the truck. I wondered where he was going but didn't say anything. I had become accustomed to his taciturn ways. He peered over a fence and then came back into the truck cab. He handed me a lunch-sized brown paper bag and told me not to open it. "Just take it up onto the bed of the truck. When you're up there, look over the fence and you'll see a swimming pool. Toss the bag into the pool, then come on down and get back in the truck."

The task seemed simple enough, and I knew why he asked me to do it instead of doing it himself. The years of physical labor had beaten him up pretty badly. He had limited mobility in his arms.

I began to ask what was in the bag. "Just go on," he said, and I did as my boss instructed, hopping into the back of the truck and peering over the tall fence that separated the homeowner's property from the alley. I saw that it was an easy fifteen feet to the pool's edge, so the throw had to be at least that. Better to be long than have it land on the deck or a chair. I flashed back to how disappointed one-armed Leroy had been after I'd butched it with the newspapers. I couldn't mess this up. I weighed the bag with my hand and determined that it was heavy enough to toss underhand, like a horseshoe. I gauged the distance several times, thinking it all through, and finally Jim got impatient. "What the hell are you doing up there? Throw the goddamn bag."

I took a deep breath and I tossed it high into the air. It felt good. It looked good. It WAS good! Right in the middle of the pool. Swoosh. YES! I quietly pumped my fist and scampered down and into the truck's cab. As Jim drove off I waited for an explanation. When that wasn't forthcoming, I asked. He nodded and smiled. "Inside the bag was dried India ink," he said. When the paper got saturated and fell apart, the powder would expand and bloom and spread throughout the pool, finally settling on the plaster siding and bottom and permanently staining it. The owners would have to drain the pool and sandblast the entire surface to remove it. That's why he told me not to open the bag. It would have stained my hands. He explained that he'd painted that house nearly a year ago. He'd tried again and again to get them to pay, but no dice. This was his way of closing the account.

On another occasion, Jim picked me up and we went to a small market that opened early. He grabbed a couple sodas, a few packs of cigarettes—the man could smoke—and six whole mackerels. An odd selection of groceries, but as I had come to know Jim . . . not that odd. I didn't even bother to ask.

We drove to an unoccupied two-story modern in the Mount Olympus area off Laurel Canyon in the Hollywood Hills. We parked on the street in front of the house and Jim told me to grab the ten-foot ladder. He retrieved the hidden key from the planter near the back door and marched upstairs—I instinctively knew to follow. He pointed to a spot in the middle of the upstairs hall. I opened up the ladder on exactly that spot. He told me to climb up and open the air conditioning's intake grill. I did. The filter plopped out of its resting place and I handed it to him. As I steadied myself about eight feet off the ground, I heard crinkling. I looked down and saw Jim removing the wax paper from the mackerel.

He calmly instructed me to throw the first one inside the AC ducting in one direction as far as I could. I threw it and we heard it slide fifteen or maybe twenty feet. He handed me another cold dead fish, this time telling me to send it down a different duct. I threw three fish in three directions. I replaced the filter and reaffixed the intake grill's clasp. We methodically moved to the downstairs intake and repeated the steps. Three fish—three directions.

We returned to the truck and drove for a while in silence. When I couldn't stand it anymore, I asked what it had all been about. "No other fish stinks like mackerel when it rots," he said. They'd only expunge the smell by replacing all the air conditioning ducts and compressors. The whole system. It was another nonpayment situation. I asked if he ever tried small claims court. He smiled wider than I'd ever seen him smile. "We just did."

Explorer

My dad liked that the name Kim Edward Cranston sounded like *King* Edward Cranston, but when my mother suggested that they just name him King, Dad countered that it would be too hard for my brother to live up to that name, and it might confuse people. They might think it was our dog. *Here, King!* So, Kim it was, and Kim it remained for about a dozen years.

Kim always felt he got short shrift in the name department. Kim was a girl's name, he'd say. Edward, his middle name, was slightly better, but I think he hated his options there, too: Ed, Eddie, Edward. Blah!

In high school he became Ed, the least objectionable of the bunch.

Ed joined the LAPD Explorers, a training ground for future police officers, after career day at Canoga Park High. In those days every high school, especially ones like ours in lower-middle-class areas, would host visits from service providers to get kids to start thinking about their lives after twelfth grade. I'm not sure exactly what drew Ed to the program, but I know what drew me. The first year my brother was in the Explorers, he took a trip to Hawaii. The following year he went to Japan. I was marking time at odd jobs while my brother sent postcards of white-sand beaches and torii gates. I stared a long time at those images, steeped in envy.

I joined the minute I reached the minimum age of sixteen. I had no designs on a career as a cop; I just wanted to travel the world. But in order to join the Explorers you had to go to the LAPD Academy for eight Saturdays in a row to study police work. Explorers were asked to man parade routes, help with minor traffic control, issue bicycle licenses, and participate in searches for evidence at crime scenes, among other duties.

Our West Valley Division was the cream of the crop. The big reason was Sergeant Roy Van Wicklin, Van to everyone except new recruits; you had to earn the right to call him Van. He'd been a paratrooper in the army in World War II, and he brought a soldier's discipline to the Explorers. He was squared away. And he was tough, but only because he cared so much. He arranged for his division's newbies to go through a Hell Weekend prior to the start of the regular academy with the rest of the division's recruits. We studied police procedures and codes, drill formations. We trained like animals: eat, train, sleep, repeat. The older recruits made it extra hellish. It was a bitch. The consolation was knowing the shit you were taking, you'd get to give back to next year's new crop.

Sergeant Van Wicklin set up a special trip to the morgue for us every year. *Special.* My ass. So many guys came up with lame reasons why they couldn't make the trip: homework overload, my grandma needs me to walk her across the street, explosive diarrhea.

Those of us without the brains or the balls to make an excuse took the bus over together. I looked around and saw all the guys smiling tightly. Every one of us felt deep dread, though none of us showed it. Wouldn't be manly.

The smell of formaldehyde—like pickle juice and aftershave— made my eyes water. We walked by a long row of bodies draped in white sheets. They seemed like zombie spectators settled in along a parade route to watch terrified teenagers shuffle past. I caught sight of a man's bluish foot sticking out from beneath a sheet. Looking around, I realized that all the bodies had one foot uncovered, toe tag dangling—a way for the technicians to quickly locate the corpse they were looking for. Whatever these people had achieved in life, whatever they had seen or suffered, was reduced to a toe tag. That was the inevitable fact.

In another room, two men wearing rubberized jumpsuits casually chatted as they worked. Music played from a tinny transistor radio. They barely registered our presence. One was tending to a new arrival, a body in full rigor mortis—natural muscle stiffening that occurs shortly after death. We saw the technician snap the body's extremities. We'd learn this part of the process was called breaking rigor. They released the muscles, preparing the body for the next step. No explanation could change how savage it seemed. It was hard to accept that bodies didn't feel anymore.

The other man was washing a female body with a sponge and soapy water. I was sixteen. The only thing I wanted in life was to see a naked woman. To my great misfortune, this was my first. Well, outside of *Playboy* magazine, and accidentally seeing my grandmother stepping out of the shower.

Whoever she was—midtwenties, pretty—I wondered what her name was, how she died, whether her family was overcome with grief. A shuddering, overwhelming compassion moved through me.

BLAM! One of my fellow Explorers hit the ground. He'd fainted. Out cold. People rushed to his aid. He'd be all right. The technicians shared a smile.

A doctor was describing the protocol at the morgue, but his voice became background noise, like the teacher's drone in a Charlie Brown cartoon. It wasn't until we were almost out of the room that I noticed the song that had been playing on the transistor radio. The Everly Brothers hit "Wake Up Little Susie." I'd never hear that song the same way again.

If breaking rigor and body washing was the warm-up act, then an autopsy was the main event. We watched a doctor cut a clean line through a man's chest with an electric saw. At another table, a physician peeled back a woman's scalp. Body cavities were opened. Fluids escaped. Organs were gently removed for study. Down went a couple more of my friends. They were carried from the room. Two others left so they wouldn't have to be carted out. I focused on my breathing. My great chicken-shit epiphany crossed my mind, but I chose mouth-breathing in the end. If I breathed through my nose the formaldehyde would nauseate me. I wasn't going to go down like my fallen comrades.

At some point I was able to get beyond my physical responses and focus on the mystery at hand—the essential mystery. An autopsy is ordered only when the cause of death is not absolutely certain. There were discoveries to be made. What happened? Bodies were complex riddles to be solved.

Once the doctors had collected all the evidence, they put the body back in the condition they found it, more or . . . less. They poured all the fluids and plopped the organs into the cavity and sewed it up. I saw how professional these people were, and how serious a duty it was to attend to the dead, and yet this was their job, and they needed to desensitize themselves, to be slightly workaday about what they might have once found gruesome; which, of course, was the point of the visit to the morgue. If I took the law-enforcement path, I would have to learn to shut down and not let blood and guts and death affect me.

But did I want to be desensitized?

At that moment, what I wanted or did not want in the long haul was irrelevant. The whole reason I'd joined the Explorers program in the first place was so I could see the world, and sure enough, when summertime rolled around, I got to go on a monthlong trip to Europe. The entire cost, including airfare, food, and travel was something like six hundred bucks. That was a fortune to me then, but the idea of seeing the greater world beyond Canoga Park and the confines of my mother's house was all the motivation I needed. I socked away every dime I could.

Police departments in Germany, Austria, Switzerland, France, Belgium, and the Netherlands hosted our group: twenty teenage boys accompanied by a few policemen chaperones. We slept in military barracks or police auxiliary halls. You put your sleeping bag on a cot, and you were home.

My first trip abroad, my first time being around people who spoke different languages; they sounded almost moonlike to me. But we didn't have much time to fraternize; every detail of our days was accounted for. We were guests at lunches and functions and took tours of police facilities, even Interpol. In the evenings, we were unshackled from the itinerary. Each night we got the lecture: Be back at 2300 hours. Be careful. Don't do anything stupid. Don't go to bars.

We went straight for the bars.

One night in Austria, I paired off with two guys a little older than me, both more aggressive and confident. They were resolute, they were dogged, they were on a mission: their virgin years were about to be over. It was time.

Like they had some teenage boys' version of sonar, they made a beeline for an Old World house close to the center of Salzburg. A red light gleamed from an impressive wall sconce. This was the beacon! This was the promised land!

I stood in the foyer as the two boys haggled with the proprietor using hand gestures and broken English and agreed on a price. Meanwhile, I made the lame excuse that I forgot to bring money and gave the universal sign for empty pockets.

My buddies went upstairs with their chosen companions, and I shrugged and took a seat and stared at my shoes. I think this had been my plan all along. I hadn't had the courage to make that night *the* night. My friends had boldly met their agenda. No hesitation. And there I sat, glum, berating myself, then giving myself a pep talk. Those guys were braver than me. But I bet neither of them had ever beheaded a chicken!

When I looked up, a woman in a minuscule blue dress was standing over me, hands on hips. She waved me to come with her. I fished out the few bills I had to show her: *I don't have enough.* She took the money and grabbed my hand.

In the room, she indicated I should take off my clothes. *This was happening.* I undressed slowly. She handed me a sealed condom. I struggled to open it for a bit too long, and she snatched it back, opening the package and putting it on for me. I was already erect— more nervousness than excitement. She lifted her dress. She wore no panties. What was the point? She lay down on the twin bed and brought me down on top of her and pulled me into her. I saw her breasts. *I've got to touch her breasts.* I went for it. Soft and—WAP. She slapped my hand, hard, clearly indicating *You don't have enough money for that.* Just get it over with.

And soon, it was. There'd been no fireworks. No tenderness. No talking. We never exchanged names. I'd had no idea what I was doing. It was just this stranger and me at this particular moment in time. As uncomplicated as it could be. She wasn't expecting anything from me. She wasn't disappointed. She felt nothing. For her, it'd been an utterly forgettable moment. But it was a moment I'd never forget. Though I admit I couldn't conjure her face under a threat of death.

I got up and got dressed. She got herself together and she was gone. She left the door open behind her.

It turned out nearly half the guys in our group went to whorehouses that night—including my brother; we lost our virginity on the same night, an odd coincidence that we never bring up. From that point on, it was the hooker tour. Most of the kids' parents had given them money. *Enjoy your trip!* In Paris, Brussels, Amsterdam, whenever we were allowed any free time, it was the same patter. What's that? The Louvre? That's nice. Why don't we get going so we can experience some interactions with the locals and help circulate money to the people? Help the economy by supporting small business.

Back home I discovered that the Explorers wasn't just about foreign relations. I discovered I had real aptitude for police work. As I neared the end of high school I realized that's how you forged a career. You alighted on something you were good at and then you bored into it.

I applied myself to the Explorers and excelled in physical and scholastic achievement: running, obstacle course, sit-ups, push-ups, relay course, and marching drills. I learned that a 211 was a robbery and a 459 was a murder. Code 1 was get there when you can. Code 2 meant get there quickly. (Lights.) Code 3 was get there immediately. (Lights and siren.) Code 7 was grabbing a bite to eat. A 10–100 meant you were on a bathroom break. (A bit of police argot the film business borrowed; it's part of the lexicon on set.) There were codes for all kinds of things. I memorized every last one, along with proper procedure on securing evidence, when to approach a crime scene, crowd control.

I graduated first in my class of Explorers. Number one out of 111 kids from all over the city. Number one! Had I ever been number one at anything? The die was cast. I'd learn to shut down my feelings and do the job.

I say I was first. I was first with an asterisk.

In the final testing at the police academy, I aced the scholastic stuff.

And then came the physical component. I breezed through the obstacle course and scored one hundred, the maximum, in jumping jacks and sit-ups. All I had left to do was polish off the push-ups. Every Explorer was given a buddy to do the counting to assure accuracy. My buddy was another West Valley recruit named Vince Serratella. Vince was a good guy. He was a friend. After I counted out his sixty or so push-ups, it was my turn to knock off a hundred and get a perfect score. I had done one hundred push-ups a few times before in training. It wasn't easy, but it was doable, and I was confident going in. I was in peak shape. I was sixteen years old, determined to finally achieve something.

At about push-up seventy-eight, I was laboring and fatigued, but still pretty strong. When I hit eighty, Vince called out: "Ninety!"

What? I was initially confused, thinking that Vince made a mistake, but after a few more push-ups I realized what he was doing. Ninety-two. Ninety-three. He was cheating for me. Only a handful of the 111 recruits accomplished one hundred push-ups, so ninety was noteworthy. The instructors and other Explorers rushed over to cheer me on. I could feel the crowd thickening around me. The group began to count down in unison.

I ground out the last few, my whole body burning, my mind racing about what I should do next: Should I continue and finish it the right way? Or should I just go along and pretend I'd really done the full count? I was still undecided when Vince cried out: One hundred! My classmates surrounded me and cheered. Vince clapped me on the back. I was a hero. And I was glad not to have to do ten more push-ups.

At the same time, I thought, *I could have done ten more.* I was exhausted, but not completely spent. I might have done something great. Now I'd never know. I quickly let myself forget Vince and got lost in the moment. But as I was getting congratulatory punches on the shoulder, deep down I knew. I hadn't earned it.

Security Guard

I was only nineteen, and the LAPD's minimum age requirement was twenty-one; plus the police department's pay scale was better if you had a degree. So I enrolled at Valley Junior College as an administration of justice major, a fancy name for police science.

On the side, I got a job as a Protect-All security guard. I worked in a gated community called Bell Canyon, an exclusive area in a ritzier section of the San Fernando Valley. I waved to residents as they passed by the automatic entry gate, and checked in guests and delivery people. I worked the night shift, so there were very few guests and almost no deliveries. In essence, my job was to sit in a roomy, climate-controlled guard booth and get paid to do my homework and sip coffee.

I had a pocket notebook with the Admonition of Rights printed on the front cover. On the back, I scribbled a rating system I'd devised for my security jobs. X was bad—one time only. XXXX meant a great place to work. I gave Bell Canyon an XXX.

And I did my job well—so well, in fact, that I got a visit from my fully uniformed and armed supervisor. He said he was pleased that I was always at my post and never called in sick. He had zero complaints against me, and he was impressed that I'd volunteered to work nights and that I did so without grousing. He wanted to reward me. How did I feel about a promotion? "What about moving out of this dreary place," he said, waving his hand dismissively at my booth. "How would you like to see some real action? Real criminals. The cops are called in almost every night. And"—he gave a slight pause for emphasis—"you get to carry a gun."

He smiled at me, excited. I smiled back, uneasy. I looked around. I kind of like it here. I do my homework. I listen to Dodger games on the radio. No one bothers me.

I didn't want to leave a good thing, but I didn't want to insult my boss.

"Does the promotion come with a raise?" I asked.

It did. Twenty-five cents an hour. I calculated. That would bring me to a grand total of $4.10. The extra quarter would have been nice, but I didn't want to carry a gun, and I was incidentally surprised that assuming the immense responsibility of carrying a weapon only earned you twenty-five cents more.

I politely declined, feigning disappointment at the amount of the raise. "Oh, uh, well I suppose there are a couple other posts I can offer you," he said, taken aback by my crippling lack of ambition.

He assigned me to an event at the Century Plaza Hotel on Avenue of the Stars. I was stationed at the back entrance. All the action was in front. The back was much quieter, more intimate. An occasional limo rolled up and out spilled a publicity-shy celebrity.

Nothing happened, nothing happened. And then suddenly— Alfred Hitchcock. I recognized his portly silhouette immediately. Security personnel whisked Mr. Hitchcock through the back entrance, and the limo doors were taken care of by the driver and valet. I wasn't sure what my job was even supposed to be. But, hell, it was Alfred Hitchcock. I resolved to politely greet him when he left. An hour after he arrived, people around the back entrance started buzzing, and I sensed that someone was making an exit. Mr. Hitchcock emerged and made his way to the waiting car, and I rushed ahead of him so I could open his door. When I got close, I softly asked, "Did you enjoy your evening, Mr. Hitchcock?" I waited for him to bestow upon me some bit of sage wisdom I'd always cherish.

Lunging for the limo, he turned slightly toward me and said, "AAAAAAAAAAAARGH!" He waved his arms chaotically as if to shoo away a fly. He dove into the backseat. I stood there stupidly for a while. And then I went back to my post.

That was my first brush with a Hollywood legend. Since I was going to be a policeman, I was pretty sure it was going to be my last.

My other reward for being such a great booth guard was a posting in a grocery store called Hughes Market on Highland and Franklin, a transient corner in Hollywood that was rife with crime. I gave Hughes a quadruple X rating in my notebook. My job was to man the two-way mirrors strategically placed high above the store and catch shoplifters.

My mother had always had light fingers. Whenever we'd go into the produce section of a supermarket she would help herself to a piece of bulk candy. She loved those individually wrapped chocolate-covered caramels. Or she'd casually snap off a sprig from a bunch of grapes, popping them into her mouth as she shopped. My mom taught us it was okay to "sample," that the markets factor samples into the overall cost. When I was a kid, I would always take a caramel. My brother, too—because it wasn't stealing, it was sampling. We never took big items, and never too many: one was acceptable, three was not. But if, for example, we spotted a bag of Toll House chocolate chips that had already been opened, we'd help ourselves to fistfuls. They couldn't sell the bag now anyhow! I became so accustomed to the candy samples that whenever I walked into a grocery store, I'd crave something sweet. That Pavlovian response went on for years.

I vividly remembered looking up at those mirrors in stores and wondering if anyone was behind them. Now I finally learned the answer, and the answer was me.

My dark aerie, in an attic high above Hughes, had an L-shaped catwalk. The ceilings were low so I had to crouch, but the view was expansive. The mirrors protruded so I could even observe the meat counter beneath me. Little stools were set up, and I'd sit and wait and watch.

I was good at spotting thieves long before they stole. I was never wrong. It wasn't that I possessed some preternatural powers of perception. Once you know what to look for, thieves are pretty conspicuous. People who shop are busy: they're scanning their lists and examining labels, doubling back for that item they forgot. People who steal look around and down aisles furtively. Shoppers move quickly. Thieves have a slower pace. They're trying to be careful. I learned to detect the telltale signs. The most telling of the tells was when people looked up at the two-way mirror. *I wonder if anyone is there.* And I was sitting there in the dark whispering: *Yes, I'm here!*

People stole constantly. They would take *anything*. Lightbulbs, coffee filters, a whole pineapple. One guy stood in the pet supply aisle and pocketed four or five leashes. Dog leashes? You're going to risk getting arrested for dog leashes?

By law, a thief had to be outside the store to be caught. If you confronted a guy inside the store, he could point to the cold cuts in his pocket and say, I didn't grab a basket, so I just put it here for the moment while I was looking for something else.

Oh, I put salami in my pocket all the time!

I had a little microphone at my station behind the mirrors, and when I spotted a thief, I needed to alert the manager. We had a code. At the precise moment the thief was crossing the threshold of the store, I spoke into my microphone, and my voice blared out through on the intercom: Fred, the coffee is on in the front. Or: The coffee is on in the back, Fred. The front or back told Fred where to look for the culprit, front door or back door. The manager then rushed to the relevant door and detained the shoplifter outside the store. I made my way down and said, "I witnessed you stealing such and such," and then walked back to the manager's office and waited for the cops to show up.

It was ridiculously easy. Per six-hour shift, I could catch up to ten people. Sometimes I'd have more than one thief in the store at the same time, and I had to decide which one I was going to follow. "You have packages of soup mix in your jacket."

"No I don't."

"Just show us you don't have them, sir."

And the guy would say, "All right, all right." He'd open up his jacket, and what do you know? Soup galore.

There were no big-ticket items at the store, so it was all petty stuff. But you had to detain them and call the police because otherwise they would come back night after night. Once you got caught, you were in the system. If we caught you again, there was a cumulative effect, and that meant an arrest and potentially jail time.

Hughes Market carried huge roasts wrapped in cellophane. They could run up to a foot and a half long. One time I saw this couple in their late teens, grungy, probably runaways, loitering in the meat section. The guy was doing that telltale glance-over-the-shoulder while the girl shoved a giant slab of meat down her pants, down the length of her thigh, and headed toward the back door. The roast was so long she couldn't bend her knee, so she was limping, dripping a trail of bloody roast juice in her wake. My cue. Fred, the coffee is on in the back. The manager detained them outside, and I went down and confronted her. She got this sheepish look on her face and glanced around as if maybe she were thinking about running and then let out a sigh of concession and pulled the roast out of her pants. I did the paperwork and waited for the police to show.

I was doing my job, and yet I couldn't help feeling sorry for these two. They had to be hungry.

Minister

Catalina Island is twenty-six miles off the coast of Long Beach. We always knew the exact distance because the hit 1950s song "26 Miles" by the Four Preps still came on the radio every now and then: *Twenty-six miles across the sea / Santa Catalina is a-waitin' for me / Santa Catalina, the island of romance, romance, romance, romance.*

They said it four times for a reason.

While attending junior college, during summer breaks, my brother and I got jobs on Catalina. He drove a taxi, and I landed at a company called Island Baggage, which did big business in the days before some logician invented wheeled luggage. Once the boats docked on the island, Island Baggage would offer to cart the bags as the vacationers walked off their sea legs with a leisurely half-mile stroll into town. Thirty-five cents a bag. A different color tag for each hotel. I loaded up all the bags on Cushman golf carts and then distributed them to the various hotels. It was a summer fantasy come to life, being outdoors and scooting around the island all day long in the company uniform: shorts and flip-flops. Shirt optional.

Schlepping luggage may not sound like the height of romance, but Island Baggage jobs were coveted because we had first crack at the pretty girls as they filed off the boats in their summer dresses and short shorts. "Let me get your bag for you. No charge. Want me to show you around?"

"You live here?"

"Yes, my brother and I are on the island for the summer. Do you have plans for tonight?"

I'd come out of my shell a little, and the freewheeling atmosphere of the island in the seventies made it easy to be with someone new weekly. Girls on vacation were so different from girls at home during the school year. Don't you want to get to know her first? Sure. But the weather is warm, there's an ocean breeze, and she's wearing a bikini. What else do I need to know? I fell in and out of love several times over the course of a summer.

Getting a job on Catalina was no problem. The hard part was finding a place to stay. Enter Reverend Bob. During our second summer on the island, Bob invited my brother and me to rent a room in his condo for a dollar a day. He had a nice place, and the price could not be beat.

Bob Berton was a forty-year-old guy with an island tan and a toothy smile. He organized and ran the Miss Santa Catalina Beauty Contest—mostly as a way to attract more lovely young women to Avalon, the only incorporated city on the island. The pageants made him a bit of a polarizing figure, but my brother and I thought he was great. He didn't drink or do drugs. He was just a harmless lady lover.

Bob was called Reverend because he was an ordained minister with the Universal Life Church. He wasn't religious, but he had fashioned himself into the go-to guy for anyone in Southern California who wanted a nontraditional wedding. He made God a good time.

He came to me one day and told me he'd made a mistake. He'd booked two weddings. Same day, same time. One was there on the island. One was in the Valley. "You need to marry them," he said.

"What? Me? Have you forgotten who you're talking to?"

He fleshed out some of the details, but still I was lost. "I couldn't possibly officiate a marriage. Don't you have to have a license or something?"

Bob said, "I'll ordain you, and you can marry them."

"As in legally married? No, Bob, I really can't do this."

"You're theatrical. You can do it. And it pays $175 for two hours work."

Cash has a way of creating bravado. One hundred seventy five bucks was more than I made in a week. Despite my apprehension, despite my insecurities, I was in.

Bob slipped an official document into his IBM Selectric, typed in my details, and, whoosh, out it came: my application for registering as a minister in the Universal Life Church. Bob had me sign it and explained that it went to the secretary of state of California and it would get a rubber-stamp approval. "By the time you send in the marriage certificate, you'll be registered. Good to go."

He handed me a book. "Here's Khalil Gibran. People like this passage: 'For the oak tree and the cypress grow not in each other's shadow' and so on and so forth. Here is the marriage certificate. Fill out groom's name, bride's name. Fill out location, witness one, witness two. Fill it all out and we'll send it to the secretary of state." He handed me the address of the wedding, and his car keys. "Have fun!"

I got on the morning boat to the mainland, hopped in Bob's VW van (he had parked it at the terminal), and off I went. I arrived at the address Bob had jotted down for me. Could this be right? I was at the Van Nuys airport, a busy regional airstrip for private planes.

I wandered around the airport, dressed in a Hawaiian shirt (I thought I should dress up for a wedding), shorts, and flip-flops. It was midsummer, so I had a sunburn—I called it a tan—and my hair was shoulder length and strawberry blond. I spotted a couple that looked dressed for an occasion. "Hey are you guys getting married?" They nodded, confused. "I'm, uh, the minister." They looked me up and down. The bridal party appeared to be having second thoughts. I assured them that they were in good hands. "It's going to be a memorable day! This is your day! I'm going to take good care of you!" I was trying to convince myself more than I was trying to assuage their concerns. "Where are we going to do this?"

The groom smiled and looked up. "We're getting married in the sky, bro."

We boarded a six-passenger plane. I knew I needed to take control. I started getting assertive, suggesting the best seat assignments. "I'll sit up front with the pilot. Then come the bride and groom. Maid of honor and best man in the last row. All set."

I asked where we were headed. The groom told me that we were going to fly around and that they wanted to start the ceremony once we got a clear view of the Hollywood sign. We took off, and before long we were doing loops over the sign. We could start any time. My cue.

I took a deep breath, twisted around in my seat, and began to yell out so that I could be heard over the twin engine props. "STAND TOGETHER, YET NOT TOO NEAR TOGETHER, FOR THE OAK TREE AND THE CYPRESS GROW NOT IN EACH OTHER'S SHADOW!" The bride and groom were holding hands, looking at me with moist-eyed sincerity. I was a nineteen-year-old kid, and they were looking at me as if I were the pope. I wanted to honor the faith they'd bestowed in me. I wanted to honor the solemnity of their commitment and make the performance believable. I wanted to do a good job. I started to improvise. "COMMUNICATE," I screamed over the hum of the engine. "IT'S EXTREMELY IMPORTANT. I CAN SEE YOU LOVE EACH OTHER. CHERISH THAT LOVE. WHEN TIMES ARE HARD, THAT LOVE IS YOUR BEDROCK. IN SICKNESS AND HEALTH. RICHER OR POORER."

I could see the best man and the maid of honor leaning forward, straining to hear. "REPEAT AFTER ME. WITH THIS RING I THEE WED." The yelling didn't seem to diminish the power of the moment. They were nodding and crying.

As I progressed, my confidence grew. By the end of the short ceremony I felt like a reverend. I yelled, "BY THE POWER VESTED IN ME BY THE STATE OF CALIFORNIA AND THE UNIVERSAL LIFE CHURCH, I NOW PRONOUNCE YOU HUSBAND AND WIFE . . . " I paused—momentarily forgetting what came next—oh, right! "KISS HER, BRO!" He did. I turned around in my seat, facing front again, and exhaled. The pilot gave me an approving nod.

I performed several more marriages through the years. Most of my couples were overbookings from Bob. But I married some friends and relatives, too. I married my cousin and my uncle. Not to each other. It was fun, not weird.

Some people didn't care for the pomp and circumstance of a formal wedding. Some people wanted a party rather than a church ceremony. I did a cowboy-themed wedding. I married a couple knee-deep in the water off Catalina, getting pushed around by the currents, trying to keep my footing as I soliloquized. I married a couple as an Elvis impersonator. Years later, when my brother agreed to marry a dear family friend from Britain, Julia, so she could stay in the country legally, I presided over their union wearing a bunny-rabbit costume left over from Halloween. I was the Reverend Bucky O'Hare.

I'd say: "For the oak tree and the cypress grow not in each other's shadow. —Kahlil Gibran."

"Love is patient, love is kind. It does not envy, it does not boast. —Corinthians."

"And if you can't be with the one you love, love the one you're with. —Stephen Stills."

When I married a couple of friends, Sandy and Steven, I did my whole oak tree and cypress thing, and then I said: "This love radiates through them so clearly and strongly, because you only get married once." I paused. They looked at each other and then back at me. Everyone knew they'd both been married before. I continued, "You only get married once . . . in a while." Wild laughter from my congregation.

I married a Korean couple. They stood before me with bowed heads and grave expressions. They were petrified. They weren't expecting the fun, secular service I had in store, so I had to adjust to suit their seriousness. The Universal Life Church would marry anyone, gay (only symbolically back then), straight, young, old, conservative, liberal . . . it didn't matter. It was ahead of its time, progressive and inclusive, and all without a blood test, so I could have married siblings and I wouldn't have known the difference. I occasionally wonder if some of the couples I married are still together and it suddenly dawns on them: "Holy shit! Honey, I think Walter White married us!"

Student

Not having any experience or guidance, I chose nearly all my classes within my major during my first year in junior college: Criminalistics and Police Systems and Practices and such. I did very well. I was sailing right along.

So I was surprised when my counselor looked down at my transcript, shaking his head, and told me I needed electives. I was planning to transfer my credits to a four-year university the following year, and I thought I had to be completely nose to the grindstone: all criminal procedure all the time. My counselor told me no, in fact, admissions offices would want to see a well-rounded curriculum.

All right. I gazed up to a large board above my head: ELECTIVE COURSES. Listed alphabetically. Abacus for Beginners. Archery. Acting. Wait—I thought of my traumatizing turn as Professor Flipnoodle and sighed. But it was just an elective. And it could be a good time. I signed up for two classes: Intro to Acting and Stagecraft.

The first day of class was a typical September day for the San Fernando Valley: hot. The small classroom was crowded with kids and painted entirely in flat black. I felt like the walls themselves were a heat source. I learned later the black walls were purposefully neutral. The artistry of the work would supply the color.

I looked around. Girls outnumbered boys, maybe eight to one. I didn't mind that. The next thing I noticed was that the girls in acting class were *much* better looking than those in the police science courses. I didn't mind that at all.

The teacher handed out two-person scenes for us to perform. "You two do this one. You two take this." I happened to be standing next to a cute brown-haired girl. By virtue of proximity we'd be acting partners. I smiled nervously at her. Nothing. I cast my eyes down on the paper.

I turned my attention to the scene. The opening description read: *A couple is making out on a park bench.*

I glanced up at the girl and then quickly back to the paper. Son of a bitch, she was really pretty. I read the first line again just to make sure I read it correctly. *A couple is making out on a park bench.*

I barely remember what the scene was about, and I have no clue what play it was from. I only recall that the boy was to break from the embrace and try to explain to the girl why they should start to see other people. I knew with absolute certainty that if the boy in the scene were somehow able to see the girl who was playing his girlfriend, he would never, ever break up with her.

As I reviewed the scene I kept darting glances at my acting partner. She was busy chatting with a friend and hadn't yet looked at the text. I worried that when she discovered our shared mission she would be dismayed that I was the leading man.

She finally got around to focusing on the script. And she did the same thing I did after reading the opening sentence . . . looked up. I pretended to be gazing in the other direction as she assessed me. I glanced back and gave her a casual smile—no wholehearted grin. That would be too much. To my surprise she didn't grimace or frown or show any sign of displeasure. She just cocked her head slightly to one side and pursed her lips. I guess you'd call it a pondering look. Technically, it was a neutral gesture, but I found it *so* sexy. I took her noncommittal glance as a major victory.

Was I supposed to really kiss her? Really? I went to the teacher and whispered, "It says that the couple is making out . . . should we really, uh, make out, or just pretend to do it?" A valid question, I thought.

The teacher didn't think so and dismissed me: "You're not in high school anymore."

Message received. I had to go for it. I was emboldened by the teacher's answer. My heart quickened as I watched an hour of other students' scenes. At last, my partner and I were called upon. The stage was set, just a bench; the rest was up to us to imagine.

We sat down and I dropped my script on the floor. I'd pick it up when I needed it. I hoped she could handle what I was about to do. Ready or not here I come. I started to turn toward her—but she beat me to the punch. She kissed me wildly. Her hands roamed all over my neck and my chest and my legs. She thrust her body into mine, moaning with pleasure. I was delirious. I surrendered to our shared lust, rubbing, tapping, kissing—wait, what? Tapping?

Yes, my upstage thigh was definitely being tapped. The girl was rubbing my body with one hand and tapping me with the other . . . but why? Was she performing some kind of dexterity test? Like patting her head and rubbing circles on her stomach at the same time? Whatever she was doing, she was amazingly adroit at it. A pro. And then it occurred to me: the scene! We have to do the scene!

She was telling me, tapping me, as subtly as she could that it was up to me to start the dialogue—*my* character was supposed to pull away—not hers. I finally pushed away from her, took a gulp of air, and said . . . nothing. I forgot my line. I lunged for the papers on the floor and desperately looked for the opening line, but I was looking at page two.

Before the kiss, I'd easily memorized my first line, "Beth, we need to talk . . . about us," and left the script open to page two where I was to follow up with a long explanation. Only I didn't count on having those first few words completely vanish from my brain because of all the kissing and rubbing and tapping.

I recovered. The scene started to take off. Before I knew it, it was over. Strange how time seemed to speed up. The teacher gave us some notes. I heard nothing he said.

At the break I casually approached my acting partner, who was smoking a cigarette. She exhaled a long plume of smoke, and I worked up the courage to say, "That went really well."

"It got off to a rough start," she replied.

"Yeah, sorry. But after that, I thought it went pretty great. We rebounded."

"I guess we did." She gave me a little smile.

Clearly we were simpatico, a potential match if ever there was one. Her kiss was all the clarity I needed. I went in for the close: "We should have lunch sometime."

She looked confused. And then she looked at me as if I were a lost puppy. "Oh," she said without affect. "No." Seeing that I was still in the dark, she added, "I have a boyfriend."

What? But you just kissed me as if I were the most desirable man on earth. You grinded your pelvis into mine and moaned as if you couldn't get enough of me. That's what I thought of saying. Instead, I feigned indifference. "Hey, that's cool. You know, whatever."

Indifference was my go-to whenever I felt vulnerable. I was not mature enough to be honest and show surprise, even though that was my feeling. Utter shock. I felt like I was the victim of a practical joke. Her lips pursed again, this time it was more *sorry* than sexy. She might as well have patted me on the head and told me I reminded her of her little brother. But I remained inscrutable. No sign of surprise or disappointment or confusion.

She walked away.

She wasn't into me. I mean not *at all*. She was *acting*. She was given the task of pretending to be hot for me and that is what she did. I had to sit down. What just happened?

A month later I wouldn't remember her name. But she left me with something I'd never forget: I learned that you could so fully inhabit a character that you could fool others, move others. With talent and commitment, you could seduce or terrify. You could make someone feel utter hate or desolation or compassion or even love.

Biker

Ed passed his entrance exams easily. The next step was to start the training academy and pick up his gun and badge at the Orange County Sheriff's Department.

At twenty-two, he was fully legal. He was a man. And yet he wasn't sure what he wanted in life. When he got the call from the sheriff's department to confirm his acceptance, he hesitated.

I was also tentative about what to do next. My junior college experience gave me one orderly year of studying police science, and one year of emotional chaos in acting classes. I had enough credits to transfer to a university. But now I wasn't sure what my field should be.

If I stayed the course and chose the path that aligned with my aptitude, was I embarking on a life of compromise and regret? If I threw it all away and jumped into acting, was I being impulsive? Foolish? I'd seen what became of actors like my father. That all-or-nothing approach to stardom exacted a heavy toll. I knew an actor's life would be hard. It could even be tragic. My father's failure as an actor had contributed to the implosion of my family. He wanted success more than anything, and it eluded him. Maybe because he wanted it so desperately.

I didn't know why he left. I had ideas; ego and alcohol were factors. But trying to boil it down to one reason was a loser's game.

He left. That was all. He pursued a life without us. I was mature enough to accept that ours was not a unique condition. But I think his absence was what left me struggling in those years, grasping and Sneaky Pete-ing. I was still lost.

And I didn't really have anyone other than Ed to talk to about how I felt or about what I should do with my life. Who knows where our dad was? And by that time my mom was drinking steadily. She was there, but not really there at all. By now she was remarried to a drinking buddy named Peter, and they'd moved to Fresno, dragging Amy with them. In subsequent years, they pinged over to Massachusetts and then down to Florida, where they bought a motel. It didn't work out in the end. Terrible idea, really. No matter her physical location, my mom was flirty and coquettish, sashaying around the house singing Peggy Lee's anthem of loneliness, "Is That All There Is?"

I had my brother. And we were on our own. And we were at a crossroads. We had talked about doing a big trip for a while. Why not now? Why commit to a job in the sherriff's department when we could see the country? We could be free. Would there ever be a better time to go?

It was 1976. The Bicentennial. The pageantry was extensive:

fireworks and Spirit of '76 public-service announcements made by men in Founding Father costumes and tall-masted ships in the nation's large harbors. Small towns painted their fire hydrants red, white, and blue. The Vietnam War was behind us at last. It had been three years since Nixon had tried to make our country's loss more palatable with his Peace with Honor speech. They stopped the draft the year before my brother came of age. He'd had to register and his number was low, in the single digits. Had he been one year older, he would have gone.

Jimmy Carter would soon be president-elect. And despite the occasional gas shortages and high inflation, the country was starting to feel less fraught with strife than it had felt during the war. With the Steppenwolf road anthem "Born to Be Wild" playing in our heads, we blasted out of California on motorcycles for parts unknown. Duration unknown. Everything was unknown.

My Honda 550cc was loaded, my saddlebags and scoot boot filled with the essentials: a sleeping bag and pup tent, a mess kit and camp stove, a change of clothes and all-weather gear. I had a full tank of gas and $175 in my pocket. Ed's bike had a bumper sticker on its rear end: "I'm Hot to Trot."

It only took a few days to get the hang of life on the road. Ed and I developed hand signals to indicate our needs. Gas, food, sleep, mechanical issue, whatever: we had a signal for it. Since we had no money to spare, we were sleeping under the stars most nights. In the country we'd find a cozy patch of grass and bed down. But most cities prohibited sleeping on open land, public or private, so on weekdays we'd seek peaceful sleep at churches, synagogues, and temples. If we happened to hit a town during a weekend, when houses of worship were otherwise occupied, our search shifted to schools.

One evening in Yuma, Arizona, we were in a middle school playing field, lounging in our sleeping bags and heating up some

Ovaltine on our miniburner as a nightcap. Born to be wild. All of a sudden four or five police cars burst into view. Having the background in police procedure, we were out of our sleeping bags with our arms stretched out wide before they'd gotten out of their cars. They surrounded us, guns drawn, barking orders. Ed and I glanced at each other. We calmly complied and lay prone on the ground, model suspects. With one knee in our backs, officers patted us down while others carefully searched our bikes and belongings. One officer sifted through our powdered beverage hoping to find narcotics. To his dismay, he found only Ovaltine. We were clean.

On the road we couldn't make plans because everything was always changing. Everything: where we were, how we felt, what we thought about, the weather. Riding in a car, you're a passenger. You're shielded by glass and metal, protected from the elements. On a motorcycle, you feel it all, moment by moment: the soft breeze at dawn, the warmth of the early light, the bugs, the heat, the dust, the thick smell of desert blooms and the scent of dirt after a rain. The road beneath you. The elements. You have to be present so you can react and adapt to whatever you encounter. That felt like freedom.

When we were broke and severe weather made it dangerous or just plain uncomfortable to be outside, we stayed a few times at homeless shelters. One night, as a storm threatened, we sought refuge at the Star of Hope Mission in Houston, Texas. We locked our bikes together to a post and covered them as best we could, hoping the storm wouldn't drown them.

Inside the shelter we learned that the protocol was to bolt the doors for the night and require all of us homeless men (temporary or otherwise) to listen to some proselytizing. Normally, I was open to those moved to speak about their faith, but the guy at this shelter was a fear-mongering zealot, delivering the news about how God would damn to hell anyone who drank or did drugs. I found his threats offensive and laughable. It was ridiculous that people had to be subjected to this kind of fire-and-brimstone speechifying simply because they needed a place to sleep for the night.

After the dark sermon we were led upstairs in single file and told to strip naked and turn in our clothes for the night. We handed our garments to an attendant, who gave each person a numbered tag to claim them in the morning. The attendant put the clothes of about one hundred transient men into a walk-in closet and locked the door shut. Great. I'd probably never see those pants again.

Next was a parade to the showers. Every man was given a bar of soap—more like a tab—and a hand towel intended to serve as a bath towel. We took turns pulling the chain on a half dozen shower heads. The tepid water drizzled over us, washing our bodies clean of sins, or at least some road grime. Dropping off the towelettes in a drum on our exit and the excess slivers of soap in a bucket, we were shown to a hall where fifty-some-odd bunk beds were arranged in tight rows. It looked like an internment camp. We were assigned our bunks. Younger, able-bodied men on top; older and infirm men got the preferred bottom.

One hundred men sleeping in the same room. One hundred men who happened to have the worst eating and drinking habits in the country. A cacophony of belching and farting. The smell of gas, stale alcohol, fumes from festering wounds left untreated, and years of poor hygiene that no shower could ameliorate. Most were hardcore smokers, with deep hacking coughs to prove it. Decay permeated the room. I thought back to my morgue experience. Which was worse, the smell of formaldehyde or this? I was hard-pressed to say. I looked over several rows of bunks to my brother. The lucky bastard got a bunk by a window, which he'd cracked open just enough for the cool breeze to lull him to sleep.

I tried to sleep with the covers over my head. Good luck. I prayed for dawn to show itself, and when the first signs of light came through Ed's window I jumped out of bed and was first in line to get my clothes and get the hell out of there. The attendant from the night before sleepily took my chit and opened the vault. He handed me my clothes, and oh God. While I'd awaited the morning, my relatively clean clothes had been wrestling with everyone else's filthy duds in the sealed enclosure. I had no choice but to put these deliriously toxic things on. I was desperate to get outside to my motorcycle. But not so fast.

First: breakfast. In our putrid state we were marched into the mess hall and seated on long communal benches, a tin plate and cup set before each man. We were served a plop of porridge, a package of melba toast, and coffee. I tasted a speck of porridge. Looked like Spackle—tasted like Spackle. The coffee too matched my expectations. It was the hue of scorched butter. The taste reminded me of my childhood habit of putting coins in my mouth—that slightly bitter, metallic flavor, with an aftertaste of rust.

I looked several feet down the bench to Ed, who was grinning. He'd been watching me from Spackle to rust. His grin made me smile, too. Then I looked across the table and saw a dour face staring back. The fellow leaned forward and whispered, as if we were in a prison movie planning our escape and couldn't risk drawing the attention of the guards. "Hey, ain't ya gonna eat that?"

"No," I whispered back. "You can have it." I slid my food over to him. His toothless grin said thank you.

When we escaped the clutches of the Star of Hope, Ed and I went straight to a Laundromat to wash the stench from our clothes. I wasn't sure they could ever be clean again. In spite of our stench, we felt freer than ever after our night in captivity. And more exhausted. Before sunset that night, we pooled our meager funds and got a cheap motel room, somewhere in east Texas, and I collapsed instantly, feeling dead.

After that, we agreed—no more shelters. From then on, we slept at schools, churches, parks, golf courses, and historical sites. Late one night we found a park that seemed remote, tossed our sleeping bags over a fence, and bedded on the grass, faces up to the open sky above. In the morning I awoke to a *plop*. It was dawn and I didn't see anyone around so I lay my head back down. *Plop*. There was another one. I turned my head and saw an egg rolling down a hill toward me. A bird? When it rolled to a stop I saw that it wasn't an egg: it was a golf ball. In the darkness we had bedded down on a fairway. We grabbed our sleeping bags and waved to the puzzled golfers as we scaled the fence.

We arrived in Little Rock, Arkansas, after dark on a weeknight and set ourselves up on a perfect patch of grass by the back door of a church. We'd be up and out by sunrise before anyone was awake.

In the middle of the night, a car woke us up as it drove onto the loose gravel driveway. Its front tire stopped within an arm's reach of us. In the pitch black, I could see Ed's fear. I lay frozen, too. The door creaked open and we saw two black shoes crushing the gravel beneath them. Another man got out of the passenger side and followed the driver into the church. They were murmuring to each other, trying to be stealthy. They didn't want to get caught. We couldn't make out a word. Were they there to rob the church? I glanced at Ed. He reached for the all-purpose knife he was carrying, the only weapon we had. It was possible they didn't see us. We were in dark sleeping bags in the shadows, and we'd parked our bikes elsewhere. We waited in silence. The church's back doors flung open and we saw one man walking backward. Then we saw that he was pulling something on a flat dolly. A desk? A couch? No. It was a casket! We remained silent, terrified. The men opened the back hatch of the sedan and slid the casket in. Suddenly, they were pulling away; the gravel crackled and popped beneath their tires like gunfire.

Would they come back for us? Should we run? Remain still? Did they need more bodies? We were half asleep and barely sane. We finally calmed down enough to devise a plan: we wouldn't leave, but we'd stay awake, on guard. We'd remain alert.

We woke at dawn. So much for alert. We looked around and realized that, due to fatigue and darkness, we'd camped behind a mortuary. We hurried to wrap up our sleeping bags, and a few people came out the back door and asked us to come inside for some coffee and donuts. We joined them in the kitchen, and they told us they'd seen us the night before. "We sat in the car for a minute trying to figure out how to make our delivery without waking you guys last night. We whispered so we wouldn't disturb you."

Only when we were beyond road-weary did we spring for a dirt-cheap motel. Once, in rural Louisiana, or maybe it was Mississippi, it was pouring, so we drove our bikes right into the room with us. The next day we backed them out. Amazingly, we didn't draw the ire of the manager. For that matter, our filthy bikes didn't much affect the general cleanliness of the room. A real five-star situation.

We had no problem finding temporary jobs as we traveled. We'd bus tables at a diner for cash, or we'd get jobs at that venue ever in need of sober workers: a carnival. When we were living with our grandparents and killing chickens, Ed and I briefly had after-school jobs at a nearby carnival. We worked a game-of-chance "joint" (the carnie name for "booth"). I held a fistful of darts and exhorted passersby, "Hey, come on over and take a chance." One time I even accidentally punctured my own hand with a dart when a girl I knew from school came over to say hello.

So we sort of knew our way around a carnival, and we got a job during what was called *slaw*. (I don't know why exactly—maybe from the word slaughter?) It was how the carnies described closing down the carnival at that location. We dismantled the whole place top to bottom and stacked it on trucks. The Tilt-a-Whirl, the Wild Mouse, the Ferris wheel, and the joints all had to come down. It was hard work, but decent pay. I think we got $8 per hour. Cash. Enough to get us to wherever the road took us next.

Suspect

We arrived in Daytona Beach just in time for a Thanksgiving feast with our maternal cousins the Tafts. They lived in a big house at 715 North Halifax Avenue; the intracoastal waterway was basically their backyard. Of the seven Taft kids, Ed and I felt the most kinship with Fredrick—Freddie—a handsome, skinny, blond, girl-crazed, fun-loving knucklehead, and a local man-about-town. He convinced Ed and me to sing at a local nightclub for fun. We actually won a few first-place prizes. Mine came for singing Elvis tunes. Freddie pushed me out of my shell. Before him, I don't think you'd have seen me on stage singing "Heartbreak Hotel."

Our cousins were gracious hosts, but Ed and I didn't want to overstay our welcome, so we found a cheap place not too far away from them on Oleander Avenue, conveniently located next door to a 7-Eleven. During the day we picked up odd jobs. We worked at a co-op natural-foods store, dividing up bulk food like honey, peanut butter, and oats to be sold. We didn't get paid, but we got food at cost. And we got jobs at the local minor league stadium for the

Montreal Expos' spring training, selling programs and hats and pictures and stuff that people didn't want. On hot days Ed and I would get at the top of the stairs and yell "ICE COLD HATS!" We had a routine, and we'd have ballplayers turning around and watching *us* in the stands as if they were a stage.

At night, we easily found jobs as waiters at the Hawaiian Inn Polynesian Restaurant and Showroom. It was there we met Peter Wong, a man we would come to hate.

A little man in every sense, in stature and in spirit, Peter was incongruously loud. His screaming went on without end. He was the Hawaiian Inn chef, and if an order came out wrong from the kitchen, he'd go crazy on the servers. Loud enough for the whole restaurant to hear, he would bitch and shriek about your complete worthlessness and stupidity. He was a culinary dictator, ruling his kitchen with an iron wok.

Except with women. Around women he blushed like a schoolboy. The male waiters came to an understanding with their female shift partners each night: I'll do any other dirty work, so long as you deal with Peter.

Imagining all the different ways we might murder Peter Wong became a group pastime. Personally, I thought it would be fitting to create a new dish in his honor, made with savory spices, fresh vegetables, and slow-cooked, thinly sliced chef. I'd call it Moo Goo Gai Peter.

Other than Peter, life at the Hawaiian Inn was good, profitable, and spicy. It was the 1970s, pre-AIDS; if you caught something, you could easily get penicillin. So the consequences of sexual liberty seemed minimal. Practically everyone you met had had crabs at some point. It was almost a badge of pride. Wild parties and drunken sexual encounters were common.

We spent many nights gathered in a large booth at the ABC bar just down the street from the inn. We played liar's poker and drank, and were cavalier with our tip money. Still, Ed and I saved most of what we made, and planned to soon get back on the road. When the season was over, the restaurant scaled back to fewer hours and fewer workers, and we took off.

Once we were gone, something happened. Peter Wong, the chef that everyone wanted to kill? Someone did.

Just days after Ed and I left on our trip up the East Coast, Peter disappeared. Vanished. He'd been gone a week when the police came in to talk to the few remaining waitstaff. Did anyone know where Peter might have gone? Check the dog track or jai alai pavilion, everyone said. He was an inveterate gambler. No one socialized with that creep. The cops pressed on. "Did anyone ever mention a desire to harm or kill Mr. Wong?"

Everyone went silent.

Finally, a waiter raised his hand and said yes.

The cops asked, "Who?"

"Everyone."

Our coworkers at the restaurant regaled the officers with tales of the man's repugnant personality in vivid detail. We all thought about how we'd kill him. Why were they asking?

"Because," the detective said, "he was found dead. Murdered."

Silence.

Then came the second bombshell question: "Is there anyone no longer employed here who also talked about killing Mr. Wong?"

Some in the group exchanged looks. "Yeah, the, uh, well, the Cranston brothers. They took off on their motorcycles last week."

"That's right around the estimated time of death of Mr. Wong," one officer said. The officer took descriptions of our persons, our bikes, our approximate destination. Everyone cooperated.

Our cousin Freddie later told us that the authorities put an all points bulletin out on us—but then canceled it two days later when they found out what had really happened.

Peter always carried a thick wad of cash. Apparently he was flashing it at the dog track and he showed it to the wrong hooker. She lured him to a house where he was jumped and killed. His body was found in the trunk of an abandoned car, bludgeoned to death, cashless.

A gruesome way to die, and I felt awful . . . that I didn't feel awful.

Vagabond

We made plans to rendezvous with girls. We even pinpointed and triangulated the locations of our recent paramours on a map for maximum efficiency. The little dots represented free places to stay, eat, and rekindle relations. We called it the GIDGT, the Geographically Incredibly Desirable Girlfriend Tour.

We rode through Georgia and the Carolinas up to the northeastern states, headed for Maine. We were happy to be traveling again, happy to be unmoored from the encumbrances and worries of humdrum, normal life.

Being on the road simplified things in some ways, but complicated them in others. There's no complacency on the road. We always had to be aware. We became experts at recognizing potentially dangerous situations. Still, for every danger, there was a delight. Every face you see is a new one. Adventure and surprise are right around the next corner.

Around the Carolinas, we encountered a group of bikers at a truck-stop diner. They were doing the same kind of aimless, indefi-

nitely long trip as we were—they were just a lot dirtier. Their hogs
rattled and spewed choking exhaust out of the tailpipes they'd modi-
fied to ensure maximum decibels as they twisted their throttles. We
rode dependable Hondas that comparatively made no sound. They
sat back in their seats, while we sat upright. They had "ape bars"
reaching for the sky to hold on, we had our arms at a comfortable
horizontal level. We rode with windscreens—they had to pick the
bugs out of their teeth; we did Coke and Sanka while they did pot
and cocaine.

So when their leader came over to inspect our bikes, we were a
little . . . nervous. We could tell right away he was a ball-buster. And
his look was so on the nose that if you were to cast him in a movie,
people would say: too cliché. Torn leather pants, thick leather belt
with a skull buckle, leather vest and jacket, leather bracelets and
necklaces. The man liked his leather. He had the hair of a rock-
and-roll wannabe. He reeked of the road and snickered at our bikes
and packs. Snickering was acceptable—much better than a fist to
the throat. He gained instant, albeit measured respect for us when
he noticed our California plates. "Whoa. You ride all the way from
Cali?" Yep, we said proudly. He nodded his approval. The interview
portion of our introduction was going surprisingly well. Then our
rough-and-tumble friend asked, "You got bitches?"

A pause. Had I heard him wrong? "What's that?" I said.

He repeated, "You got bitches?"

Ah ha, I didn't hear him wrong, he just asked us if we had bitches.

My uneasiness made me get risky with my new friend. "Well, my
brother and I argued about this . . . I thought *he* was responsible for
bringing the bitches, but he insists it was *my* mistake . . . so, here we
are on the road with no bitches."

He stared at me blankly, no inkling that I was fucking with him.

It was a stupid move on my part. He took his time and assessed our situation . . . just stared. Did I screw up? Were he and his posse about to beat us to a pulp? He got real serious and hyperfocused, despite his obvious inebriation, in order to bestow upon us a valuable life lesson. He said, "You gotta get yourselves some bitches. My bitch is in there right now." He pointed to the truck-stop diner. "She's making cash giving head to truckers, while I just had me some steak and eggs . . . *steak and eggs!*"

She sounded like a keeper. I turned to Ed and he said, "We gotta get us some bitches."

"Right away," I replied. "Like in the next town!" We thanked the motorcycle Zen master, hopped on our bikes, and left quickly. We were on the road, living wild—for us. But compared to other anarchic road warriors, we were squares, and always would be.

Our GIDGT was going according to plan, sort of. We were making our way up the Eastern Seaboard, but as per our habit, we were running behind schedule. Our aim was to make it out of New England by late summer. The fall in New England is beautiful if you're by the fireside sipping apple cider. Not so great on a motorcycle. We didn't make it to New York until October.

A lot of important things happened in 1977. Apple Computers became a company. Elvis gave his last concert and took his last breaths. The Son of Sam murders were solved. My brother and I arrived in New York for another historic event: my Los Angeles Dodgers were taking on the perennial powerhouse New York Yankees. The 1977 Bronx-Is-Burning World Series. And we were there. Ed and I had to go. But of course we had no tickets, and we were running low on money. So we figured we had to sneak in . . .

to Yankee Stadium . . . during a World Series. All balls—no brains. The greatest thing about youth is that you're not yet battle-weary, so you'll try anything.

We locked up our bikes near the YMCA in Midtown where we were staying and hopped on the subway to the Bronx. We arrived at Yankee Stadium. You can have something described to you a thousand times and still be unprepared for what it's like in life. Pre sky boxes, pre corporate sponsorship, Yankee Stadium was a giant energy machine—full of loudmouths and troublemakers and dyed-in-the-wool fanatics. It was a monolith, and you could feel its history, its majesty. We were in awe. We had to find a way in. We sniffed around to assess our options. We couldn't see any way to climb a fence or steal into a service entrance. Security and police were everywhere. We were just about to sulk back to the subway when some guy with cartoonish buck teeth whispered, "Youze wanna get inta da game?" We had him repeat the sentence just to hear his lyrically thick accent.

"Sure," we said. "But how much?"

"My cousin's da ticket take-a at gate tree," he said. "Ya each put a twenty under deez old tickets, an yer in."

He handed us a couple of used tickets. Ed and I looked at each other. Are we doing this? We nodded to each other and lined up at the cousin's gate. We saw cops on the other side of the turnstiles watching happy ticket holders enter the stadium. Our hearts pounding, we slipped the bogus tickets to the cousin with our twenties folded underneath. When he felt the bills in his hand he just said, "All right all right, enjoy da game." And just like that we were in.

We found two seats behind the Dodger dugout along the third base line. Heaven. A few outs into the game an usher reminded us that we didn't actually have seats. We resigned ourselves to pinging around the stadium, getting kicked out of seat after seat for the rest of the game. We zeroed in on two empty seats about ten rows behind the Yankee dugout. We made our way there, pausing to check our fake tickets to give our neighbors the impression that we were in the right place, before slipping into our temporary seats. The first half inning was just ending. We wondered how long it would be before another usher would give us the bum's rush.

It never happened.

We watched the entire game from those fantastic seats. What luck. Well, with two exceptions. The Dodgers lost that game—they'd go on to lose the series. And at one point a New Yorker right behind us, a die-hard Yankee fan, didn't approve of us rooting so enthusiastically for our team. He gently reasoned with us by brandishing a knife and threatening us through gritted teeth, "Sit da fuck down and shut da fuck up or I'll stab youz in da fuckin' backs!"

For the rest of the game, we became Yankee fans.

Winter was closing in, so we scuttled plans to go farther north and headed back to Florida. We decided to ride south on the Blue Ridge Parkway, which runs from Virginia through to North Carolina along the crest of the Smoky Mountains. The ride is beautiful on a motorcycle—unless it's rainy, foggy, and cold. That's how Ed and I found it. Stuck on a serpentine, slippery road without the payoff of a nice view, we were miserable. The rain was pelting so hard it was a miracle we saw the PICNIC AREA ONE MILE AHEAD sign. We hand signaled to each other. We needed to find shelter. We turned off the parkway and glided down the road to a small clearing near a running creek.

The picnic area was basic: four corner posts and a modest roof sheltered a table. We drove our bikes inside, rearranged the table to accommodate the bikes and pup tents. Our fancy digs for the night. We opened up one of our carburetor valves with a screwdriver to trickle out fuel for our camp stove, and we heated up some water to dissolve two chicken bouillon cubes for supper. We shared a couple of rye crackers. And then after dinner there was gin. As in gin rummy. Ed and I got so good at knowing each other's strategy that the games would go on for hours. Thank God, because the rainfall was relentless. All we had was time.

Eventually, we brushed our teeth and scrubbed our faces of road grime and retired to our tents. Tomorrow we would continue our sojourn south. I climbed into my sleeping bag and cracked open my one literary companion on the trip: a thick anthology of plays I'd included when we packed up our Hondas back in California. I'd so loved my acting classes in junior college that I thought if I was going to be an actor, I'd better start reading. I'd better start learning. I had just finished Arthur Miller's *Death of a Salesman*, which I loved. I was just starting Henrik Ibsen's *Hedda Gabler*. I got a few pages in before I felt the pull of sleep.

The next morning was like the day before. Rain. Looked like we would have to spend another night. On the plus side, we wouldn't run out of drinking water, the main ingredient in Top Ramen, Sanka, Postum (a powdered malt beverage), instant hot chocolate, and, of course, bouillon soup. Add to that a bag of raisin and peanut mix, and rye crackers. Or the saltines we'd stuffed our pockets with at roadside cafés—and we had a veritable feast.

Day three: more rain, steady rain, no sign of any other soul. We thought about leaving and finding the next town to check into a motel but realized that could be ten or one hundred miles away. No GPS in those days. We didn't know exactly where on this beautiful goddamn Blue Ridge Parkway we'd landed. We'd have to wait it out. Our routine continued: meager meals, followed by some calisthenics to keep us loose, conversation to keep us sane, gin to keep us interested, and reading to pass the time.

Day four: the same.

Day five: the same.

I stared out at the rain, mesmerized by its constancy—the utter lack of change. I grew up in eternally blue-skied Southern California. I'd never seen rain like this. Thick streams of water cascaded off the roof in columns. They looked to me like bars on a jail cell. I slowly stuck my hand out to disrupt the flow—momentarily breaking the bars. But I pulled my hand away and the bars were back. I felt stuck. I felt like a prisoner.

Did I really want to be someone who jailed others? Police officers did so many noble things. But was that who I was? I didn't know. I didn't know who I was supposed to be.

I was becoming dark in my thoughts. I was road worn. Fatigued. Was I losing my mind? I was extremely hungry, and worried about running out of food. Ed and I had fewer conversations. What was there to talk about?

I turned to my book of plays. I sank deep into *Hedda Gabler*, reading by the daylight filtered through the rain clouds. The entire drama unfolds in a single room. But though I was stuck at that rest stop, the play didn't make me feel more claustrophobic. The opposite. It set me free. I forgot about where I was. I forgot time. When I got to the last page I was straining to make out the words. My only light source was a street lamp fifty feet away. It was night.

I was astonished. I hadn't noticed the change from day to dusk to night. How could I have missed that? I was so completely absorbed in the play that the story took me away.

As I lay there drifting off, I had a feeling. It cast out any shred of ambivalence about what I should do with my life, how I should be. I knew at that moment, lying inside a sleeping bag in a pup tent under a shelter on the Blue Ridge Parkway in Virginia: I was going to become an actor.

After being pelted by a week of ceaseless rain, my active mind had shut down and, at the risk of sounding overly—who cares? It's true. Somehow my heart and soul had opened up. I saw my future. I saw it so vividly it was as if I'd had a conversation with my older self. At that precise moment I conjured a credo that would guide me for the rest of my life: *I will pursue something that I love—and hopefully become good at it, instead of pursuing something that I'm good at—but don't love.*

When I awoke the next morning—day seven—the skies were clear. A sign? Maybe. It felt that way. I rode away from that shelter knowing exactly what I was going to do.

Lifeguard

Ed and I returned to Daytona Beach, broke again. We got day jobs on the pool decks of hotels. Officially I was a *lifeguard*, but my first order of business wasn't rescuing flailing swimmers. Instead, I was charged with keeping the pool and deck spotless and selling suntan lotion. This was at the oddly named Alaskan Hotel, a box of white-washed stucco and thin walls, featuring cheap fixtures and cheaper food. And me: a ginger-haired idiot posing as a lifeguard. I wasn't in a position to save my own life.

Mostly I hawked Sub Tropic oils and lotions by the caseload. Though it wasn't as desirable as the Hawaiian Tropic brand sold at other hotels, Sub Tropic paid for the pool cleaning and maintenance at the Alaskan. In return, Sub Tropic got exclusive rights to sell its products on the premises.

After selling oils to pale tourists dreaming of a perfect tan, I'd sell them an aloe vera concoction to soothe their nasty sunburns. I negotiated a deal that paid me 50 percent of whatever I sold—only commission, no hourly wage—so I tended to focus on selling rather than swabbing the pool deck. Every three days, my supplier would count the remaining inventory of bottles unsold, and I'd owe them their cut in cash—Sub Tropic got the other 50 percent. He'd then restock my supply for the next three days.

Here was Sneaky Pete again: working, planning, conniving a way to increase profits poolside. At the end of each day I would pick up the half-empty bottles of lotion and oil abandoned on the pool deck, and I'd bring them to the subterranean room where the filtration system was housed. Once a week, under the cover of darkness, I would empty all the lotions into one big bucket and all the oils into another—regardless of the brand or SPF rating. Then I would clean the empty Sub Tropic bottles I had collected and make them look like new. Next, I'd use a funnel to fill the Sub Tropic bottles with the amalgamated liquids, thus creating my own inventory, which I then sold. I kept 100 percent of what I made on these doctored products. I thought I was pretty clever. Sneaky, but clever.

Rainmaker

I gave the pool my daylight hours—crack of dawn to dusk. At night, it was all theater.

My epiphany on the Blue Ridge compelled me to stop by the Daytona Playhouse to see if I could help out backstage. I just wanted to be a part of the production. Ray Jensen, the artistic director of the playhouse and the director of the soon-to-open musical, *The King and I*, asked if I had ever acted before. I timidly shrugged. Yes? I was going to add, "Not that much," but before I could open my mouth, he said, "Great, how would you like to be in *The King and I*?"

The part was mine! But, wait, what part? Ray said, "The Kralahome, the King's prime minister and right hand." He handed me the script and said, "We rehearse in an hour. Try to memorize your lines by then." I looked at him dumbfounded. He laughed. "I'm kidding. You have a week."

I learned my lines in no time, and my castmate, Louis Rego, assisted me with my extensive makeup. He applied purple eye shadow to my lids and the bronze body makeup everywhere else, in an attempt to turn an Irish and German kid Siamese. The makeup went a long way toward convincing me that I could pull off the performance. I was intimidated and nervous about doing a full-fledged production, in a musical no less, but for some reason I'd been given this opportunity. I was not going to waste it.

After early performances I would remove the purple eye shadow, but it left a distinct pink hue on my eyelids. I drew a lot of attention (including some unwanted romantic advances) as I went around town with my eyes painted pink. I consulted Louis for advice. He told me to put a layer of Vaseline on my lids prior to the makeup. That would allow me to wipe it all off after the show without leaving any color behind. Perfect. I did as Louis instructed.

In a very physical performance under the hot stage lights, near the end of the play, the Vaseline began melting into my eyes. Apparently, I had applied too much. I tried to wipe it away but the damage was done: my eyes were stinging and burning and everything on stage was a blur, though I could make out the shapes of people and objects just enough to fake my way around. I gave a disastrous performance. Or that's what I thought. At the end of the play when the king was dying, the Kralahome was bereft and I knelt down by his majesty's side to recite a few mournful last words. Vaseline tears streamed down my face, forming a small puddle on stage. As I struggled to concentrate, from the darkness of the audience I could hear sympathetic murmurs. Did I hear people crying?

At the curtain call, my applause was much bigger than it had ever been. After the show, audience members and cast congratulated me on a great performance. No one knew that I was using a PEV (Performance-Enhancing Vaseline).

Later that night, I thought about what it would be like if I could elicit that kind of reaction in people by really feeling the emotion, truly experiencing the pain of the character—allowing real tears to flow or relishing real affection or getting overtaken by real anger or feeling real *anything* on stage.

I'd gotten a taste of what it was to be an actor: a real actor with a real audience. I gave something to the audience, and they fed off me. And then I fed off them. I could feel a kind of hive mind at work in the darkness of the theater. A symbiosis. A connection. I didn't have any craft. And I didn't have a vocabulary to describe it then. But I felt its power. And I wanted more.

After *The King and I*, I acted in *There's a Girl in My Soup*. And then Ray Jensen asked Louis and me to produce Tennessee Williams's play *The Night of the Iguana*. We agreed. Let's see what producing is about. About three days before we opened, Ray Jensen quit. He'd been embroiled in a fight with the board of directors and tempestuously walked out.

With nowhere else to turn, the board asked Louis and me to take over. Louis was more experienced, and he thought it best if he called the show and handled the technical aspects, while I stepped in as creative director. I had three days to put the finishing touches on the play, which centered on a defrocked priest, Shannon, who'd ended up in subtropical Mexico and was coming to terms with his failures.

The play was about self-imprisonment, how we can be trapped by our own decisions, our own inadequacies. I thought about how I'd felt jailed by the rain on the Blue Ridge Parkway. What if we could make it rain on stage? I was imagining a gossamer wall of water, a wall you could see through but couldn't fully penetrate. It was perfect for the story.

I talked to the construction guy and we devised a plan to fashion a system so that rain could hit the roof and then cascade down to form a curtain between the actors and the audience. The water would flow into a trough hidden downstage, which would lead to a basin outdoors. We figured out a way to do it cheaply, without inflicting any damage on the theater.

We took it to the theater board and described how it could safely be done, but some complacent board members weren't comfortable with such a "crazy" idea. "We don't need to do that," they said.

"We don't *need* to do anything," I argued. "None of us *needs* to be here. But we're here to tell the story the best we can for our audience. Otherwise, what's the point?"

I fought for it and eventually won. It rained on stage. It wasn't just a visual trick, it supported and amplified the story. Our audiences loved it. They gasped in awe.

A year before, I was a police science major. Now I was demanding rain. And getting rain.

As the Playhouse's season was ending, my brother heard about parts in the chorus of the annual Summer Music Theater. I auditioned with a song I knew well from my nights at the Aku Tiki: Elvis Presley's "Return to Sender." Not your typical audition song for musical theater, but it was all I had in my hip pocket, so I gave it a shot.

Ed and I both made the cut. (In retrospect, I don't think the local talent pool was that deep.) We were offered the summer gig. It paid $75 per week. Terrible money, even back in 1978. But we weren't doing it for the money.

The lineup was *Two Gentleman of Verona*, *Pirates of Penzance*, and *Damn Yankees*.

I loved *Damn Yankees*, of course, because it was about baseball. In the cast was a talented but reckless actor, Kevin McTeague, who played the role of Mr. Applegate, aka the Devil. The role was fun and wicked and powerful. I coveted that part.

One day, McTeague disappeared. We heard he'd split with a girlfriend to parts unknown. I thought maybe I would throw my hat in the ring. Maybe I could play Mr. Applegate. But I never followed through on my impulse. I was just a kid. I'd barely made the chorus; I'd be foolish to think I had a shot at the part. I wasn't ready.

For the first time, I felt the pang of wanting more than I had, more than I was given, more than I'd allowed myself to think was possible. Someday I should play that role, I thought. Maybe even on Broadway.

Hypnotist

I met Michelle (Mickey) Middleton at the Daytona Playhouse. She was pretty, kind, talented, a couple of years older than me. I don't recall asking her out on a date, really. We were just part of a crew of theater rats who hung out together from the moment I walked into the playhouse. We all spent long nights working out scenes, and we shared pitchers of beer and oysters at the local bar, and we played in backgammon tournaments around Daytona. Backgammon was the craze.

We also stared into the blank slate of the future, nursing fantasies about what our lives would be like when we were real actors. We shared our hopes and goals. We were friends, and then more. I looked up one day and I had a girlfriend.

My cousin Freddie had learned hypnosis to try to help his mother cope with breast cancer, and he taught me some basic techniques. Not everyone is susceptible to hypnosis. If you're an open, emotional person, it's more apt to work on you. If you're guarded, not so much. I was hard to hypnotize; despite my effort and desire, I couldn't shut down my racing mind. But Mickey? A few seconds and sweet Mickey was *gone*. Lights out, Daytona Beach.

I became the hypnotizer and she was the hypnotee. We developed a visual cue and a verbal cue. The visual one was that I'd hold my hand in front of her and collapse my fingers into my palm to make a fist. By the time my fingers were in a fist, she'd be out. The verbal cue was that I'd count from the date of my birthday (the seventh) to hers (the twelfth). Seven, eight, nine, ten, eleven, twelve. By the time I said twelve, bye-bye.

Mickey was so susceptible that I had to be careful not to include our cues in casual conversation, and when I put her under, I made sure she was protected and out of harm's way.

Freddie taught me how to install positive suggestions in Mickey's psyche. If she was nervous about an audition, I would hypnotize her beforehand and plant affirmations. If she was worried about a family member's health, I would assuage her fears.

We also planted harmless and fun suggestions. Every time you hear Freddie's name, you must touch him. Sure enough, when she came out of hypnosis, each time she'd hear his name, she'd find some rationale to grasp Freddie's hand or wipe lint off his shoulder, having no idea why. Or, for example, we'd plant: When you hear the word *sandy*, you clap. And sure enough, when someone said, "The floor is sandy," Mickey would find some justification to clap her hands.

Clap. "Now where did I put the broom?"

Skeptics always said, "No, no, it's an act." But believe me, it wasn't an act. It wasn't a gag. I'd see Mickey go under, deep, and it was real and it was wild. If I remember correctly, there are seven stages of depth in hypnosis. Freddie and I practiced to see how far we could make Mickey go. Occasionally I would get nervous. She's at level six! I feared we couldn't get her back. But that never came to pass.

Hypnosis was a kind of an intimacy, I guess, a trust. And Mickey was a good girlfriend. But we were primarily a couple because Mickey wanted us to be a couple. That is not a knock on her, but a comment on who I was at the time. Even though I'd gained a nascent sense of what I wanted to do professionally, I was still immature.

The Daytona Summer Music Theater's season ended in August, and Ed and I resolved to head back to Los Angeles. We'd been on the road for two years, and it was time to go home. We had both decided. Law enforcement was not our path. We were both going to be actors. A few weeks before the journey west, I was trying to tell Mickey, I hope I see you sometime—vague, distant future talk. But she interrupted: I want to come with you. She was emphatic. I couldn't think of a good reason to say no. She also wanted to try to make it in show business. Who was I to say Los Angeles was off-limits?

Sure, I said. Come along.

Off we went. The three of us, Mickey on the back of my bike. We took six weeks and really saw the country on our return trip. We made it as far north as the beautiful, desolate Badlands of South Dakota and marveled at Mount Rushmore before arcing down in a southwesterly direction. Little goblins and ghosts dotted the streets on the day we arrived in Los Angeles. Halloween.

Mickey and I settled into a two-bedroom apartment in Van Nuys. My main focus was building my life as an actor. Mickey's suddenly was marriage, a house, a baby. She had incredibly precise domestic dreams and notions. There was a church choir component. She came from a Southern Baptist clan so tight-knit that when we moved west, Mickey's dad, who had been the president of Embry-Riddle Aeronautical University in Daytona Beach, asked to move his president's office to Embry-Riddle in Prescott, Arizona, to be closer to us.

After a couple of years together, Mickey wanted to get married. I wasn't self-aware or courageous enough to say whoa. Instead I said: You want to get married? Okay. Sounds good to me.

I don't remember what I was thinking as I watched her walk down the aisle. I know Mickey looked happy. I know I was nervous. But that's about all I can conjure up. I must have been a stranger to myself. I was just a kid, twenty-three years old, dressed in a very 1970s tuxedo, standing at the makeshift altar at her parents' house in Prescott, Arizona, a little town in Yavapai County, saying "I do" when what I really felt like saying was "I don't know."

Though I'd officiated other people's weddings, I don't think I grasped the depth and the consequence of the commitment I was making. The vows I spoke weren't empty. I cared about her. I even loved her. But in the end, I wasn't ready.

Estranged Son

The motel my mother and Peter bought in Florida didn't pan out. To no one's surprise, she and Peter didn't pan out, either. Shortly after they moved back to California, they split. My mom moved to a mobile home in Desert Hot Springs. Her hobbies included finding early bird specials, flirting with men, and drinking—she'd switched from wine to . . . anything. Once I went to visit her in her trailer, and she took three trips into the bathroom in the span of an hour. Each time she returned a little more inebriated. I went to the bathroom on a hunch and searched around. I finally lifted the lid off the toilet tank and peered inside. I saw a tall, thin plastic container filled halfway with a clear liquid. I picked it up and unscrewed the top and smelled it. Vodka. That's the kind of alcoholic she'd become.

My poor sister, Amy. With good reason, she'd run away from my mom when they were living in Florida. After dropping out of high school at sixteen, she was waiting tables, living in North Hollywood with our family friend Julia, the one who eventually married my brother to stay in the country. Amy got her GED, but it would take her several years to decide she wanted to go back to school and become a nurse.

Ed and I saw our mom sporadically, and we checked in on Amy and Julia in their little two-bedroom apartment as often as we could. But we were laser-like in our focus. We wanted to be actors. Ed changed his name again and enrolled at UCLA as a theater major as Kyle Cranston. I took the impatient route. I wanted to get to work right away.

Though our paths were different, our purpose was the same. And that spurred us to track down our dad. We hadn't seen him in a decade, but my paternal grandmother, Alice, was still alive, so he wasn't hard to find. I guess we could have tried earlier, but I think we'd assumed he didn't have any interest.

But now we had a subject. Men have to have a subject, a reason. If a guy said to me, "Let's have lunch together," I'd say, "What's up?" There has to be a reason. Women like to get together to get together. Men need a reason. Kyle and I had ours. We wanted to get into acting. We wanted his help. I think subconsciously we really wanted to reconnect with him, but we were scared to admit that.

Kyle and I decided that a reconciliation dinner at Grandma's was the best idea; Grandma could be a buffer. And her presence did put us all at ease. We bantered. We discussed the business. My dad was glad to help, glad to have some neutral topic on which to focus.

Though we never talked about it directly—men of his generation didn't talk about things—I think he felt a tremendous, heavy guilt about how he'd left. He just kept saying over and over again, "It was a bad time." My brother and I would try for years after that to reopen the subject, but we'd never get much more than that. For my father, the past was the past. It was painful, and it could teach us nothing. So it wasn't worth dredging up. Eventually I realized he had gone as far as he was capable.

Still, I saw how he tried with us, his forced casualness, his eagerness to help with our careers (he introduced me to my first talent agent, Doovid Barksin), and I felt the regret we all had about the unrecoverable chasm of lost time, the ten years he'd been gone, recede a bit.

We played racquetball. It was good to have an activity and something to hit. There was just the *thwack* of the racket and the hard *boing* of the ball and the focus and intensity and driving rhythms. There was winning and losing. I'm sure we said a lot in those games without ever saying a word.

Paul Bratter

When you first start out in the business, you have to expend a lot of energy. Hustling isn't complicated. How much energy you put out dictates how much heat you generate. I decided to be a furnace. I felt the hotter I could get, the higher the odds of something catching fire.

I did psychotherapy. I did improv and stand-up comedy solely for the purpose of conquering my fears. It was the 1980s, the self-help era, and EST (Erhard Seminars) and Scientology were big in Los Angeles. I took what I could from those ways of thinking and discarded the rest. If I became too enthralled with one approach, one way of thinking, I knew it was time to move on.

I enrolled in a bunch of acting classes, and I soaked up everything I could. Some actors fall under the sway of one teacher, but I learned important lessons from so many: Ivan Markota, Warren Robertson, Harry Mastrogeorge, Shirley Knight, Bill Esper, Andy Goldberg, Mindy Sterling, Michael Patrick King, and legendary comedy teacher Harvey Lembeck. I guarded against becoming a great "classroom actor." Whenever I felt I was one of the best actors in a class, I left to find another one where I wasn't.

Some aspects of acting—philosophies and ideas and techniques—can be imparted in a formal environment. But the fact is that at its heart there's an element of mystery to any craft, and the mystery takes you inward. Writing, meditation, yoga, acting—it's about letting go. You can teach someone how to drive a car or throw a fastball, but it's hard to teach someone to let go.

The best teacher is experience. Find the educational in every situation.

I got the lead role (the Robert Redford role) in a production of *Barefoot in the Park* at the Granada Theater. I was Paul Bratter. A young woman from Nebraska played my bride, the Jane Fonda role, Corie. My costar was pretty and innocent and had a master's degree in theater. I was impressed and excited to work with her. But things went south quickly.

We were supposed to be newlyweds, mad about each other. But while rehearsing, she'd stand as far away from me on the stage as she could. I'd go over to her and grab her and kiss her and she'd turn her cheek. I was thinking: *Did I offend you? Am I not your type? If you're not attracted me . . . fake it. You're acting! Find something.*

The director, Bob Barron, said to the girl: "You're newlyweds. When he walks through the door after having been at work all day, what would you?"

"What would I do?"

"Yes."

"I would run to him and throw my arms around him."

"Yes! Do that!"

"Well, you didn't tell me to do that."

Most actors know instinctively to prepare. Part of that preparation is reading a script and studying a character and coming to the stage or the set with ideas. My costar didn't seem to feel that sense of accountability, but still, I wanted to find a way in.

It's tricky to navigate the romantic aspect of acting, to be open and vulnerable—even if you're in love with someone else in real life. Or even if you find the actor you're working with to be unattractive or repulsive. Whatever her reasons for not giving me much on stage, I wanted to try to make a connection. I was flirting, not intending to take it anywhere else, but I needed to see where she was vulnerable, where there was an opening. I needed her to see me, too.

I tried taking her to lunch. I complimented her regularly. My hygiene was set. I brushed my teeth. I spritzed myself with every cologne in the store until I finally found a scent I thought was irresistible. When that didn't work, I changed colognes. Nothing moved her.

I wondered: Is it *me*? I thought back on that girl in that college drama course, the one who kissed me wildly and without warning on the park bench, and I thought: *I wish I were doing this play with her*. She was all in. She didn't have any inhibitions. We're in love? Let's go.

I didn't know what to do. I called Ivan Markota, with whom I was studying at the time. He was an insightful, no-bullshit, tough guy kind of mentor. He'd know what to do. "I can't get in," I told him. "She squashes all her impulses. She's not open to me, and she's not telling me why. I'm starting to judge this girl. I'm starting to shut down. She's pissing me off, and it's starting to affect the play."

Ivan said, "Maybe she was taught improperly. There's nothing you can do about that. Just keep it simple. Look for one thing. Find one thing about her that you find attractive. Focus on that."

Fortunately she had very pretty blue eyes. I gazed into them. She became all eyes to me. It's true that sometimes I imagined them on a different face. On a different person. Even though I felt annoyed by the rest of her, I could pour some affection into her eyes.

Conditions improved marginally, but what I learned from that experience on *Barefoot in the Park* was how to work in suboptimal circumstances, how to try to make something from nothing. What not to do.

Cranston!

I was absorbed in building my foundation as an actor, but I needed a job to survive. I found it on the loading dock at Roadway International, a large trucking firm, near intersecting highways in Vernon, a depressing industrial city five miles southeast of downtown LA. It often seemed that the only residents of Vernon were homeless people.

I worked on a cement slab—a dock—loading and unloading trucks. The foreman only used your last name, screaming, Garcia! McVicar! Fitzpatrick! Cranston! I worked a ten-hour shift—graveyard, 9:30 p.m. to 8:00 a.m., with a half an hour for lunch. Brutal, but I got paid $14.50 an hour, which was excellent money in 1979. Our rent for a two-bedroom place in Van Nuys was $375, so three days of work and I was covered for the month. Plus it was primarily a weekend job, so I was available during the week to audition.

The job was tough. Everyone was angry, even the punch clock. I'd stick my time card into the machine; it wouldn't engage. I'd gently maneuver the card to just the right spot. Finally the machine would bark—*AAARRRRNNNTTT*. That first violent noise was my welcome each night, and it triggered a strong fight-or-flight response. Then the foremen would yell: CRANSTON, PICK IT UP, PICK IT UP, LET'S GO!

At first I buckled down, doing everything I was ordered to do and more. I figured that if I could outwork the others, I'd have a job as long as I needed it. I gave myself over to the physically demanding work. I reminded myself that working nights allowed me to be free to audition during the day. I was paying dues. That kept my spirits up.

We had scheduled fifteen-minute breaks every few hours. At one of the breaks, four of the union regulars (the nonunion guys like me were called "casuals") paid me a visit. They told me I was working too hard—too fast—and that I needed to slow down. I was confused. I explained that the foreman was up my ass already to speed it up. The regular who'd been appointed spokesman said, "Fuck him. We run this place. You need to slow down or we're going to have a problem. We gotta work here every damn day, you motherfuckers come in a few times a month. You work fast, it makes us look bad. That shit can't happen, understand? It's not your fault, but it *is* your problem. Slow. The. Fuck. Down. That's it."

Message received. I slowed the fuck down. I tried to set a pace so that the union guys and the foreman were both only mildly upset with me at all times. I cut it right down the middle.

"Cranston, get moving!" I learned to endure the foreman's yelling. "High and tight! High and tight!" That's how he wanted the cargo loaded. Fill every space. That job is where I learned how to load my dishwasher: high and tight. To this day, I'm the loader of my dishwasher. Please don't do it. I'll just redo it.

A lot of actors worked as Roadway casuals because of the pay. I remember working with Andy Garcia. I knew him only in passing. We were all so tired; it's not like any of us had a lot of energy to make friends. Besides, we were all covered up: steel-toed boots, jeans, hooded sweatshirt, gloves, and a bandanna to cover our ears, noses, and mouths from the swirling dirt and cardboard dust. All you saw were a guy's eyes. And some guys even wore clear plastic glasses to shield their eyes.

Somewhere beneath all that protective gear, I was elsewhere. They got my body, but I wasn't going to let them get my mind or soul. I think if I hadn't been absolutely determined to be an actor, I wouldn't have made it through. But I was determined.

CRANSTON! When the foreman yelled, I acknowledged I heard him. I nodded, but I didn't let him in. I just kept repeating a few lines from my inner script. I kept saying to myself: One day I will be able to call myself an actor. Not a part-time actor, but a real actor. One day. One day. One day.

I would fantasize: there's me driving onto a studio lot; there's me breaking down the beats of a scene on stage. I was cold and I was getting yelled at, and the energy of many of the guys was a dark energy. Most of those guys hated their jobs, and probably hated their lives. It would be so easy to be sucked into that despair. But I didn't allow that to come inside. It wasn't welcome. I wasn't going to let them clutter my brain. I had something real to hold on to.

Assistant to the Assistant to the Assistant

Someone was terrorizing the people of Chicago in 1980. He slithered undetected through the sewers, killing stray animals, the homeless, sewer workers, and the occasional wandering soul seeking privacy for illicit activities. Only one person understood the true nature of this horrible *thing*, a lone police detective named David Madison. He fought in vain to warn others that they weren't looking for a man, but a beast—a gigantic alligator with a voracious appetite. It sounded crazy, and the authorities ignored him at first. But when another citizen went missing, and another, Detective Madison was the city's last hope. He leapt into action, and he hatched a plan to kill the alligator with a cache of TNT. But what to use as bait? He'd use himself. *He* would lure the monster out of its dank lair. And sure enough, the cold-blooded killer appeared, betrayed by its hunger. The alligator tried to make David its tasty lunch, but the experienced cop had an escape plan. A manhole. He had wired dynamite to the bottom rung of the ladder; as the angry alligator made a lunge, David climbed out through the manhole cover and rolled away on the street above just before—*KABOOM!* Pieces of the leviathan's flesh, bone fragments, and blood spewed everywhere. David was fine—a bit bruised and cut up, but the beast was vanquished.

That was basically the whole story behind the movie *Alligator*.

I made the blood and guts stuffed into the cavity of the alligator. I didn't concoct the recipe—the special effects expert did—but I worked for him. Actually I worked for his assistant's assistant's . . . assistant.

I was originally hired by the production office for fifty bucks a day for fourteen hours of menial work. But when the special effects (SFX) department asked for a production assistant (PA) to be assigned to them exclusively, I raised my hand and showed my enthusiasm. With several fewer degrees of enthusiasm an SFX representative said, "Okay, you'll do."

The biggest thing was the alligator's blood. The assistant's assistant instructed me how to mix a concoction of cut-up chunks of foam rubber and red-dyed Karo syrup. (A thick sweetener made from corn and used largely in industrial kitchens, Karo has a blood-like viscosity.) We stirred up huge vats of the stuff, poured it into gallon-sized Ziplocs, and stuffed the stand-in alligator that was stationed in its final resting place in the real sewers of Los Angeles.

Boom went the alligator. We blew him up. Twice. And twice, the director, Lewis Teague, looked at our handiwork and said, "I need a lot more blood." So I made trips to several Smart & Final stores to buy out all the Karo syrup I could find. Finally, after about a week more of pulling apart foam rubber and stirring syrup and dye, we were done. The alligator was stuffed like a tick in a blood bank.

The spewing of copious blood and guts had never looked so beautiful. A fountain of viscera. After the explosion there were congratulatory handshakes for the SFX team. I wasn't part of that. I may have shaken hands with the assistant's assistant.

I did, however, have an encounter with the star of the movie. I'd grabbed a seat in a transport van heading from base camp to the sewer set, and a few others hopped on for a ride to another part of the set. The door slid shut, and I realized that I was sitting right next to David Madison himself, the actor Robert Forster. A genuine star. I knew him also from the massively influential *Medium Cool* and the Marlon Brando movie *Reflections in a Golden Eye*.

Our shoulders were *touching*.

I thought I was being smooth, but I guess he felt my stare on him and he said, "Hey, how ya doing this morning?"

To which I replied something like, "I'm . . . you know, I'm, yeah, good, yeah. How are you?" He said he was fine. He introduced himself and we shook.

"Nice to meet you, Bryan. What do you do on this movie?"

He was engaging me in conversation! And he used my name in a sentence! My first name. Not like the foremen shouting CRANSTON! I told him of my duties as a PA with the SFX department and he seemed genuinely interested, or at least he made me feel as though my job had real value. That's a nice quality in a person: making someone else feel valued—even if that someone is currently on the bottom rung. I made a mental note.

Nice to meet you too, Robert. Look forward to working with you again.

One day.

Mars Bar Spokesperson

When I was about twenty-three, I got a call from my agent with the breakdown of a Mars candy bar commercial. The setup was a young guy rappelling off a huge rock, while a snappy tune played in the background. The guy expertly drops to a landing and pauses to chomp into a Mars bar for energy and chocolaty goodness. You, too, can be young and adventurous . . . just start eating Mars candy bars.

I went to the first audition and they said, "Tell us about your mountain climbing and rappelling experience."

"Wow, where do I start?" I said. "I love going with the family to Mount Shasta to camp. You see, the best climbing is deep in national and state parks, where there are a lot fewer people, and it's easier to attempt more difficult climbs and rappels. Unfortunately, we're all so busy that I have to settle for closer mountains to get my thrills, and frankly, they're not as challenging . . . but it's better than nothing."

I had never been mountain climbing or rappelling in my life. Mountain climbing was, in fact, one of a few recreational activities that I had no desire to do. I love hiking in the mountains—but that's not what we were talking about. This was mountaineering, ascending and descending the faces of huge rocks. A mistake could kill you. And there I was, presenting myself as Edmund Hillary. But it worked. I received plenty of smiles and nods at the audition—good signs a callback was probable. The very last thing the casting director said to all the prospects was, "The clients would need to see you actually rappel off the three-story office building next door. How would you feel about that?" A few of the other actors in the room hesitated, a couple said, "Okay, I guess," and I said, "Cool, let's do it now!" Another lie. I knew that they weren't set up for rappelling at that time—so it was an easy, hollow boast.

I had a strong impression the callback was imminent, so I got to work. I called A16, an outdoor outfitter that catered to everyone from the day hiker to the seasoned mountaineer.

A guy named Chad answered. These guys are always named Chad. I asked if he could recommend an instructor for basic climbing with emphasis on rappelling. He said, "Dude, I'm your guy." We settled on $100 for a one-day, five-hour crash course, and since I knew the callback would come within a week, we arranged a time and place to make it happen ASAP.

I met Chad up at the Chatsworth Rocks, not far from my boyhood home. As I'd expected, Chad was blond-haired and spoke with a serious Valley-girl inflection. Did I want to put my life in the hands of a guy who said *tubular* and who was probably stoned out of his mind? Not particularly. But I wanted the job.

We hiked back into the rock formations with the gear in tow and stopped at a spot next to the face of an enormous boulder. Chad let the equipment drop and pointed to the top of the boulder—about forty feet high. "This stone is choice 'cause it's got some gnarly vertical," he said.

We circled around the back side of the rock and quickly ascended. We were soon about four stories up. Chad got busy tying off a thick climber's rope he called a "gold line" to a large boulder nestled roughly twenty-five feet from the edge of the forty-foot mother rock. Then he gave me complete step-by-step instructions and a lesson on all the equipment: carabiners and figure-eight descenders and belay devices. Once I got the jargon down, Chad had me go back to the bottom of the rock and watch him. He descended the rock effortlessly, springing off the face twice before floating gently to the ground. He moved with precision and sobriety and grace. Totally gnarly.

We hiked back up to the top of the rock. He then secured me to the line and carefully guided me through the steps again. Then he left to continue his tutelage from below, where he'd have a better view.

The transition from standing on a huge boulder to "walking off" and dangling by a rope forty feet off the ground is physically simple but psychologically complex. The proper way, per Chad: step off backward with one hand guiding the rope in front of you while the other regulates the descent speed from behind your back. Your body is perpendicular to the vertical mass of rock and you're facing the sky.

Chad yelled out encouragement and told me to get into proper position. I had to gather all my courage just to hear him. Following his instructions was a whole other story. Both of my hands were clutching the rope in front of my body. And my body wasn't perpendicular to the rock. Instead, I was dangling at the top of the boulder, my face so close to the rock I could kiss it.

Chad tried to assure me that I wasn't going to die. He told me how to correct myself. "Take your right hand off the rope and grab it from behind your back!"

"Okay," I said unconvincingly. I stared at my hand and mentally *commanded* it to move. It didn't. My extremities suddenly had a mind all their own. I felt a chaos spreading throughout my body. I was sweating. My breath was shallow. I was having a panic attack. I also realized that I couldn't hang from a rock all day—even that was becoming exhausting. So I stared down at my hand and gave it one more stern command to move around back. *MOVE, GOD-DAMN IT!*

Surprise! My right hand let go of its death grip, swung around back, and grabbed the gold line. Oh my God, it did it! The hand actually did it! Good job, hand. Welcome back to the team.

With my right hand now governing the amount of gold line I let out, I planted my feet onto the rock and began to push away from the face until I was a perfect right angle to that bitch. My confidence starting to return, I let out a little more line and backstepped down the rock toward the ground. Easy does it. Although my organs still felt as if they were forty feet above the ground, eventually I made it to the bottom. I took a few deep breaths, wiped the sweat off my face, and in a sickening flash I knew I was in trouble. I had a desperate feeling in my bowels.

I disconnected the harness and told Chad I needed to run back to my car. "Forgot something," I said. I was too embarrassed to admit what was really going on. I was having an intestinal emergency. I bolted and made it halfway back to the parking lot before I got the feeling I was about to be opened up like the chest-bursting scene from *Alien*. I found a relatively secluded spot and dropped trou. Getting down off of a forty-foot rock had caused a sort of internal avalanche.

"What did you forget?" Chad asked when I returned.

"Uh, I forget what I forgot."

I returned to the rock feeling . . . lighter. I scaled the serpentine path to the top with a bounce in my step.

Harness on, gold line in hand—left in front, right in back. I made my way down the rock, one steady step at a time. Done. Back up top again.

The third time down I was shrieking with joy like a child in a bounce house. The fourth time I was leaping off the rock and twisting into the air, doing a 360, then landing on the rock, light on my feet, as if I had been doing this for years. With the fear factor removed, I was able to move with abandon. I was able to enjoy the experience.

Two days later, I got the callback. Now was my chance to show them what I'd learned. The casting session was held outside the three-story building. I was up against four other guys. A random selection placed me third. The first guy took the elevator up to the roof, where a professional stuntman hooked up the harness. I saw him peer down, fearful. I knew the feeling. He took halting stutter steps down the face of the building to the ground—as exciting as three-bean salad at a picnic. The producers and director whispered to each other and shook their heads in dismay.

The next guy was up. They instructed him: Give it some energy! Have fun. He tried to outdo his predecessor by yodeling a few times, but his maneuvering on the rope was equally lethargic. The producers and director were now starting to panic. They sold this concept on the premise that outdoorsy fun equals Mars bars. If they couldn't find the right actor, they might have to scrap the whole commercial.

I knew what they wanted—what they *needed*. They looked to me. *You're up.* I said to them, "I see that the guys are rappelling using a double gold line through their figure-eight descenders. Is it all right if I hook up with a single? It's kind of like packing your own parachute."

They had no idea what I was saying. *I* barely knew what I was saying. Sure, they said. Whatever.

On the roof, I told the stuntman to allow me to thread a single line through the descender, but I asked him to watch me so that I did it correctly. "It's been a little while since I've done this," I said modestly.

Standing on the edge of the parapet wall, I peered down and asked if they were ready with the camera. They gave me the "okay" signal. I took three deep breaths. I smiled, waved to the crowd, and leapt backward off the ledge. After getting some significant air, I hit the middle of the building's face like a bull's-eye. I immediately reloaded my legs with a deep squat and pushed off, soaring high into a 360-degree turn and landing back on the building. One more big shove and I zoomed into the air before I alighted on the ground.

As I unhooked myself, I saw that the decision-makers were ecstatic. The other actors were deflated. Two other guys would go after me, but it didn't matter. The part was mine. I knew it.

Two weeks later, I received directions to the location where we'd shoot the commercial. I shook my head. Chatsworth Rocks, where just weeks before I had struggled with my confidence, argued with my hand, and lost my bowels. We're capable of so much. So much more than we know.

My accomplishment made me a little cocky. As we were getting ready to roll, I told the producers, "You're not going to believe this, but Chatsworth Rocks is where I first learned how to rappel."

Divorcé

About two years into our marriage, Mickey wanted to buy a house. We focused our search on Saugus in Santa Clarita Valley, off Interstate 5. The same town where my mom took me to swap meets to sell our belongings.

Mickey and I couldn't afford to buy in the San Fernando Valley, and even out in Saugus the most we could swing was a mobile home. Maybe not even a new mobile home. Maybe one that was "gently used."

There were a million questions. Are there any hidden fees? How much is insurance? The more we delved into the particulars, the more real it became. And the more real it became, the more uncertain I felt. All the mobile homes looked so, I don't know, *settled*. And then there was Saugus. It meant an hour commute each way—if there was no traffic. When you're spending that much time in the car, it's not like you're reading or learning a part. Driving is just driving. I suddenly felt as if I were trying to be a New York actor and weighing a move to Rhode Island.

Back in Van Nuys, I was splayed on my bed in the middle of the afternoon, and all of this was weighing on me. Saugus, the mobile homes, Mickey, our conversations about children. I was on track in my career, but nothing else felt right. Mickey was in the other room, and I called her name. She came in and sat down on the bed. I remember the sunlight streaming into the room. I remember lounging for a while, just looking at each other. I asked her: Is this what you want? I meant everything, all of it.

She said, Yes.

You want a home. You want a baby.

Yes, she said. That's what I want.

How could I deny that? Those were perfectly legitimate desires. I said, Can I ask you something honestly? You were ready for that when we met in Daytona?

Yes, I was.

That was four years ago. She'd been very patient.

And you thought I was a good prospect, the right guy, to have this happen with?

Yes.

Did you feel that when we first met?

Yeah, I did.

Before we even knew each other, you felt I represented the best possibility for you to have those things you wanted?

Yeah.

And I said: I think we made a mistake. I never had the courage to confront this. I was just going along with it all. That's not what I want. I don't want to have a baby right now. I don't have a desire to own a home. Because I know what that means. And I don't think I would be a good husband or father at this moment.

Maybe I was thinking of my dad's impulsivity. *Let's build a pool!*

Let's run a coffee shop and a nightclub! Maybe I was scared of repeating his mistakes. Whatever the reason, I knew I wasn't ready. I finally realized that I wasn't able to make a commitment.

I owe you an apology, I said. I was too immature and passive when we met to be able to do what I should have done, which was to say: I'm not ready. Let's not get married. I want something other than what you want.

She nodded sadly. She knew. If either of us had been honest, we would have gone our separate ways much earlier.

She was a sweetheart. No arguing. No bitterness. We were just mismatched.

Once we'd both confessed, a sense of relief washed over us, and we became closer than we had been in our two years of marriage. Even when she moved back home to the panhandle of Florida, we would talk on the phone. An hour, once a week, giving each other support and friendship.

She soon slipped back into her southern accent, and six months later she was married to a guy named Steve, who already had four girls from a previous relationship. Mickey got pregnant quickly. Suddenly, she had a big family. She got what she wanted. I was happy for her.

We lost touch over the years, naturally. We both moved on. Then, I was promoting a film in Florida several years ago and Mickey saw the interview and called the station. When I called her back, a man with a deep voice answered the phone. It was her son. A grown man. I'd forgotten how many years had passed.

And then Mickey got on the phone. We chatted briefly. Pleasantly. We were old friends—but when we said good-bye, it felt final. We were just kids when we were together, and that was a long time ago.

Dating Consultant

Newly divorced, I was living in an apartment in West LA and working for a company called Great Expectations, a precursor to dating sites like Match.com. People would come in for interviews and to record personal videos. They then would screen other videos, searching for a suitable mate. And I'd help them find a match.

It cost $800 to join. A steep price of entry. Potential customers would say to me: Eight hundred dollars. That's a lot of money!

I'd say, It *is* a lot of money. But can you imagine yourself going to a store and spending eight hundred bucks on a TV? That's reasonable. Now a husband? A wife? Somebody to love you? Someone to change your life. How do you value that in relation to a TV? More or less important? Going to a bar is a crapshoot. Waiting on your friends to set you up? Good luck. Do the math. How much are you spending in time and money looking for a partner?

Now the $800 sounded reasonable.

Easy sale.

Once I signed people up, I conducted their video interviews. They were usually stiff on camera. They'd say robotic things they thought they were supposed to say: I'm a Virgo and a high school chemistry teacher and I enjoy long walks on the beach.

No one wants to hear that.

I wouldn't turn on the camera until I felt the candidates were being themselves. I'd say: Tell me about that bracelet you're wearing. It's pretty. Were you a dorky kid in grade school? If you could meet anyone in the world, dead or alive, who would it be? Seen any good movies? What's the last great book you read?

If the person remained stiff, I'd tell him or her a joke and press a secret button to turn on the camera as he or she was laughing. I'd engage, disarm, and once the person felt comfortable, we'd be under way, and in a minute or two, finished. Most of the time without them even knowing we were taping. People were always more authentic if they weren't aware the cameras were rolling.

I loved that job. It got me off the miserable loading dock—plus, I got access to a fascinating variety of human beings. Dating can lay you bare, bring out your quirks and insecurities. I got to see it all, the whole palette of personality. I came to think of Great Expectations as a kind of acting class.

I was learning in my acting classes how to reveal and present the range of human emotions, which came in handy here. Finding love is about being open, letting someone see you as you really are—not some facsimile of what you think someone wants. I'd try to help people be themselves. In the process I learned what that meant.

Lover

I met her at an audition for some TV show whose name I can't remember. She asked me out there and then. She wanted to go out that night. *Tonight?* She was pretty, funny, quick-witted, and I found her assertiveness sexy. Yes, I said, let's go out. I met her at her apartment; it was a Friday at 7:00 p.m. I didn't leave until Monday at noon.

I've never been into drugs—I do drink now and then, nothing out of hand—but that weekend with Ava felt like what I imagine a binge or a bender must feel like. I lost track of time.

The idea of spending the weekend   that kind of weekend—with someone you just met wasn't unique back then. But it did take its toll. It's the myth of my generation: sex creates intimacy. It would take me several more years to discover that the opposite is true: intimacy creates sex.

And crazy creates great sex. From the beginning, Ava gave me clear signs she was not emotionally well. I remember going to a play with her at the old Schubert Theater in Century City. We'd had an argument at intermission. I figured we'd work things out after the play. As we settled in for Act Two, Ava resumed the quarrel. Not in a hushed tone, but at normal volume, totally unacceptable during a performance.

"We'll talk about this later," I whispered.

She said, "We'll talk about it NOW."

Half the audience heard that. I saw scornful faces all around us. We were close enough to the stage that the actors heard her; they continued tentatively with their dialogue. I heard a chorus of shushing. I shushed, too: a desperate plea. Ava blurted out: DON'T FUCKING SHUSH ME!

Everything stopped. The actors froze, the audience was aghast. My heart planted itself in my throat. Abject embarrassment and shame coursed through me. I left my seat and raced to the exit. I should have kept going, but I let her catch up with me outside, and our argument escalated. I don't know what it was. Maybe I was attracted to her unpredictability. The danger was sexy. But it was also dangerous.

Once, we were on our way back from a day trip, and we were at it again, naturally. As she drove up to her apartment, I suggested maybe it was best if I headed home. She slammed on the brakes and said, "Get the fuck out."

I got out and walked to my motorcycle, which was parked across the street. I heard the squeal of tires and turned to see that Ava had swung a U-turn and was headed right for me. I quickly ducked between two parked cars as she zoomed by, inches away from sideswiping the car in front of me. She screamed out her window, "Fuck you, asshooooole."

The first time I tried to break up with Ava, she collapsed in my apartment, her eyes rolling back in her head. She was having some kind of seizure. I quickly picked her up and went out to her car and managed to put her in the passenger seat. I drove her to the emergency room of a hospital not far from my house, and waited. I was scared.

After an hour, the ER doctor came out and asked me if I brought her in.

"Yes," I said.

"Are you her boyfriend?" I hesitated. Then I figured it was easier to say yes than to get into all the drama.

"Well," the doctor said, narrowing his eyes at me, "your girlfriend overdosed. We pumped her stomach, but I need to know what she took."

I told him that I didn't know. He thought I was lying. I wasn't.

I thought back to a night we'd gone out to a nice little restaurant on Melrose Avenue. I should have known then. We were celebrating, a birthday or a job or something. She made half a dozen trips to the bathroom; she was more agitated each time she returned. My condition is acting up, she explained. She did have a condition. Her body didn't regulate temperature very well, so she had a tendency to overheat and sweat. This had been corroborated by her mother, a nice woman I had met a few times, who was just as ignorant about Ava's drug use as I was. But now I knew.

Ava was released from the hospital a day later. She made me promise not to mention this to her mother or sister. I promised. I waited a few more days before finally, unequivocally breaking up with her. I was determined, and willing to take the blame for the failed relationship. I was prepared for any response: sadness, anger, bargaining, confusion. If she cried, yelled, or threw things, I was ready. I just wasn't prepared for the response she gave.

No.

That was it. Just, no. She calmly, unemotionally, said, "No, we're not breaking up."

In early 1983 I got a job on a new daytime drama for ABC called *Loving*, which was to shoot in New York. So, done. Not only did I land the job that would change the course of my career, I also got to flee a messy relationship. Hallelujah. I found a nice studio apartment on the Upper West Side, on Seventy-First, just a half block from Central Park, and I explained to Ava that I was going to live in Manhattan; better for both of us to just move on. She accepted that. Finally, we were no longer a couple.

But a few months after I moved, Ava followed. She subleased a friend's apartment in New York and contacted me and said she wanted to have dinner. I politely refused her invitation. I cautioned that reacquainting would not resolve our issues but exacerbate them. She lamented that her process of ending the relationship was not like mine. For her, the "cold turkey" approach was cruel. I'd left her dangling emotionally. How can you do this to me? she said. Didn't I mean anything to you?

Her words filled me with guilt. Maybe she was right. Maybe if I agreed to a casual meeting and showed no interest in a relationship, it would give her closure. Maybe being with her as just a friend would allow us both to clearly see boundaries and honor them. We'd meet in a public place. What could go wrong?

Halfway through dinner she went to the bathroom, and when she came back, she started blaming me for some strange thing. But she wasn't making any sense. It was like she was carrying on a conversation using every other word. And my confusion wasn't helping. The opposite.

Eventually she worked herself into a frenzy. The manager had already been on us for the volume of the conversation, and I begged Ava: Let's get out of here. She refused. When I tried to stand she put her hand on my shoulder and pushed me back down. She was small in stature, but her will gave her a scary might.

I looked around the restaurant and tried to appease the other patrons. "I'm sorry," I stammered.

She yelled, "Don't apologize to these assholes, you fucking pussy!" With that, she swept everything off the table: dishes, wineglasses, water glasses, vase, silverware—everything crashed to the floor.

It took one man to shove me out the door and two to get Ava into the street. I reached into my pocket and grabbed all the cash I had and handed it over to the guy who'd manhandled me. I knew it wasn't nearly enough to pay for the damage, let alone the food and wine, but I didn't know what else to do. I was embarrassed. I was livid. I exploded with anger. I grabbed her arm and physically forced her down the street, screaming at her, holding nothing back.

It worked. She shut down. Apparently brute force was the only thing she responded to. In fact, my burst of anger excited her, and she kissed me wildly. I am ashamed to admit it, but I got caught up in the moment. We were in public, ripping each other's clothes off. We had just enough sense to get to her apartment to finish the act. This was not a loving, tender moment—it was savage, sick, something out of the animal kingdom.

Afterward, I lay there, astonished by my stupidity. How had I ended up here again? I was trapped. It was my own damn fault, but still . . . trapped. I knew I had to do something radical. I apologized profusely. It's my fault. Completely. I'm so sorry. I just can't do this anymore.

She, of course, would not accept that. She would try to see me before or after work on the soap opera. She'd leave messages on my answering machine, alternating between desperate and threatening. On one message she pledged her love. We were destined to be together. The next, she vowed to have me killed.

ABC Studios on West Sixty-Sixth Street, where we shot *Loving*, was a very busy place. Cameras, props, and sound equipment were constantly shifting from set to set, while actors ran lines and reviewed their blocking before shooting their scenes. I was in our kitchen-set rehearsing with my TV family when for some reason my gaze was drawn to one of the large cameras getting into position for the scene. Ava. She was standing next to the camera, staring at me, arms folded, furious.

I froze, too stunned to even acknowledge her. She'd somehow gotten past building security and then onto the floor of the studio? Impossible. My castmates observed my reaction and followed my sight line and understood this was not a welcome visitor. I believe it was my friend Susan Walters, who played Lorna on the show, who told our stage manager, Brooks, to call security. The exact sequence of events is foggy now. I only remember that within minutes, Ava was whisked away, her name put on a "no access" list.

I was deeply troubled that she'd just shown up at my workplace, but I found it even more worrisome that she'd left peaceably. This was not her modus operandi. If she wasn't intending to make a scene, why did she go through all the trouble to sneak past security? On my walk home that day, I stopped cold in the middle of the sidewalk. It suddenly occurred to me that she'd gone to the trouble because she wanted me to know that she could get to me any time she chose to.

I started walking again—fast—darting looks over my shoulder. She could have been anywhere. I approached my apartment building, crouching behind cars. I dashed inside and up to my apartment and locked, chained, and bolted the door.

I took a breath, put my things down, and pressed play on my answering machine. A couple personal calls, one from my manager, then Ava's low, unmistakable voice. It sent a chill up my spine.

"That's how easy it is, Bryan. So simple. You think I can't get to you anytime I want?"

I guessed right. Terrifying.

She continued: "You think I can't have someone take you out? Wrong, asshole. You led me on. You told me that we were going to have a life together. I bend over backward for you and this is what you do? This is how you treat me?! Motherfucker. You're dead. You're fucking dead. You'll never know when, or where, but I've fucking got you. You're dead."

I stayed in my apartment all night, sleepless. The next day I was nervous and scared. And truth be told, I was embarrassed. I was a young, strong man; how could I be afraid of a woman who barely stood five foot two? My viewpoint may have been immature and myopic—but the feeling was real.

I didn't hear from her for a few days. I relaxed a little. One night as I walked into the apartment, the phone rang. Forgetting what had become my routine—screening all calls and responding to messages later—I picked it up.

"Hello, Bryan."

I shuddered. She suggested we meet. I told her that seeing each other wasn't healthy for either of us. A pause. In the silence I sensed her coiling, getting ready to strike. "Do you think you can just ignore me, motherfucker? You can't just fuck me and dump me on the side of the road."

She planned to have me killed, she said. My body would never be found. If it were found, it would be unrecognizable.

I was a cornered animal. But I spoke slowly, emphatically. "Ava," I said, "if you don't stop this and leave me alone, I'm going to tell your mother."

It sounded so juvenile, but I knew it would get her attention. Ava and her mother adored each other. They were very close. But Ava's mom was completely in the dark about the stalking, the drug use, the instability. Ava would die if her mother found out. She would keel over.

Silence on the line. I knew I had her.

"I've kept the tape of all the phone messages you've left on my machine," I continued, "and if you don't stop this right fucking now, your mother is going to hear them all."

Except for the ambient street noise in the background from the pay phone, I heard nothing. I said, "If you stop, I won't send the tape to your mom, but *only* if you stop. Do you understand?"

Silence.

The quiet became unnerving. I said, "Ava? Do you understand? If you stop all of this, right now, I promise not to send anything to your mother." A long pause. "Ava, are you still there?"

A slow, guttural, deeply resonant sound came through the receiver. It started low and built into a high pitch. Something resembling a war cry.

"I. Want. That. Tape."

"Ava, listen to me. If you stop right now, I will never send the tape to your mother. I promise."

"I WANT THAT TAPE, MOTHERFUCKER! I WANT THAT TAPE!"

"Ava, you're not listening to me. If you just stop I won't—"

"I'M COMING TO GET THAT TAPE, YOU COCK-
SUCKER."

"Ava, just calm down, okay? Ava?" Silence. "Ava? . . . Ava, are you
there?"

Nothing. Silence.

Finally: "Hello?" The soft male voice surprised me.

"Hello?" I said. "Who is this?"

"Ben," was his reply.

"Ben? Who are—are you with Ava?"

"Who's Ava? I'm just trying to use the phone. It was dangling off
the hook."

Oh. Shit.

She was on her way. And I knew she wasn't bluffing. I paced
my apartment in terror. I contemplated leaving. But she could have
called from the corner and it was possible that I'd run into her on
my way out. She might have a gun. It was entirely possible, maybe
even probable. What to do? My fear paralyzed me. I had recorded
proof of her threatening to kill me. That is a crime. I could have
called the cops. I should have. I really can't explain why I didn't. But
I wish I had.

I just kept pacing. She would have to gain entry into the
building—but anyone could breach the door's buzzer system. Push
several buttons on the entry panel of any New York apartment
building and someone will buzz you in. I needed a weapon. I went
to the kitchen to find my best option, a knife, but wait, the door! Did
I lock it? I quickly double-checked, and yes, the door was locked.
Thank God she didn't have the keys to my apartment. I sat down
and waited it out.

The sound of the buzzer sprang me to my feet in panic. She was
here. In seconds she'd ascended the three stories and was pounding

on my door. Each pound was like a hammer. Would she beat the lock off the door? I had no idea what she was capable of. I could envision the veins in her neck bulging as she was screaming, "Open the door, motherfucker!"

My body was now pressed into a tight ball, on the floor, at the foot of my bed. And I was rocking, muttering to myself, overtaken by fear. Ava was kicking the door and screaming obscenities and threatening to kill me.

I squeezed my arms around my legs, making an even tighter ball. Then slowly, very slowly, I felt something that surprised me. I was calming down. I was separating from the fear. I was moving past fear into a quiet resolve. I rose and walked to the door. I unlocked it.

Ava was still screaming as I opened the door, her face flushed red. Seeing me didn't bring her any relief. I grabbed her arm and brought her into my apartment. I saw no weapon but then again I wasn't looking for one. In truth, she could have been armed, and I would not have noticed or really cared. I was on another plane. The fear had broken and given way to pure anger and an eerie stillness. I was controlled and determined. Once we were in the room together, I adjusted my grip on her body to hold her shoulder firmly with my left hand, and her hair at the back of her head with my right hand. Her screaming continued but I was no longer hearing words, just a cacophony of high-pitched sound. I walked her over to the lone brick wall in the apartment.

I slammed her head against the brick wall. Months and months of fury rippled throughout me and gave me an almost superhuman strength. But I was also surprisingly calm. I slammed her head against the wall with a metronomic consistency. Clumps of hair and bits of skin and brain matter stuck to the brick. Blood formed on the wall and then began dribbling to the floor.

The screaming had stopped, of course.

I remained calm. I was released from fear and anger. I wasn't glad or relieved or filled with satisfaction. I felt nothing. I let go of her and the body slid to the floor.

Dead.

I stood still. My eyes closed. There was silence. Sweet silence. I was numb. Then I heard a faint cry . . . a whimper, really. I couldn't tell where it was coming from. My eyes flashed open. My breathing was rapid and shallow. My stomach convulsed in a dry heave. I was sweating and shaking uncontrollably. My body was revolting.

It was only then that I realized I was still tightly wrapped in a ball on the floor at the foot of my bed. I looked at the brick wall. No blood. Ava's body wasn't in a heap on the floor.

It didn't happen.

Thank God. Oh, thank God, I didn't do that. It was a dream—but it wasn't, it couldn't have been. I wasn't sleeping; I was more awake than ever, and feeling every particle of anger and dread. How then could I explain what I had seen? What I had done? Ava was still outside my door in the hall. I could hear her. But something was different. Something had changed. And it wasn't just me.

I began to recognize other voices in the hall. I stood up, but immediately felt sharp pains streak through my body: my legs, arms, neck, back, head—everywhere. I'd been holding myself so tightly that I was cramping. I breathed through the pain and made my way to the door to listen.

The police were in the hall. Her vitriol was now distress. I heard two strains I had never heard in her voice before: defeat and surrender.

The police took her away without ever knocking on my door. A couple of neighbors had called about the disturbance and told the NYPD that she was not a tenant. That was all the police needed to remove her from the premises as a trespasser. The last thing I heard from Ava as the elevator door was closing was a deep, mournful wailing, like a mortally wounded animal.

Nothing happened in that apartment, but everything had changed. I understood clearly, without question, that I was capable of taking a life. I understood that given the right pressures and circumstances, I was capable of anything. I think that's true of all of us.

I understood the fragility of everything we think is solid and true. That was humbling. It shook me to my core.

I never saw Ava again.

When I heard many years later that she had died, I hoped she had eventually found some peace.

Bystander

Those with the means to flee Manhattan had fled. The rest of us were miserably sweating out the heavily oppressive August humidity and heat. I was more miserable than most. A week earlier, I'd stopped by a salad bar to pick up a healthy lunch, and I'd also picked up a parasite—a tapeworm. I was taking antibiotics to kill the microscopic beast, but after a week of severe stomach cramps, I wasn't so sure I wanted to live, either. I couldn't venture too far from a toilet. Fortunately my doctor's office was around the corner from my apartment.

My doctor was Dr. Constantine Generales. I was equally comforted by his name and proximity—near my apartment, directly across the street from the famous Dakota apartment building. As I was approaching the corner on Seventy-First to head north on Central Park West, I heard a loud *BANG!*—the nasty sound of metal and glass, instantly recognizable as a car crash. Instinctually, I ran to the corner. A woman was pointing. I saw a man lying just street-side of the row of parked cars. I was the first one to him. He looked up at me with panic in his eyes. I muttered, "It's okay," though I had no idea whether it was going to be okay. It didn't look good. Shattered glass was everywhere. His body was severely mangled. He obviously had broken bones. Blood was spilling out from under him. I yelled back to the woman to go inside and call 911. Stunned, she hesitated, and I yelled the instruction again. She fled toward the building's lobby.

I checked to see if the man was still breathing. He was. He had dark hair. He was in his late thirties, older than me, but not by much. I cradled his head in my hands to keep it off the asphalt. I looked down and noticed my hands were covered in blood. I looked up and spotted another bystander in the street directing oncoming traffic away from us. The injured man was staring directly at me, pleading with his eyes for help. I started to feel woozy—my stomach condition, the excessive heat, the blood on my hands, and this stranger looking to me to save his life. A large crowd was gathering. "Did someone call an ambulance?" I yelled.

A doorman shouted, "It's on the way!"

The man was now starting to convulse. His color was disappearing. I was losing him. "It's all right. You're going to be all right. The ambulance is almost here." I yelled to no one in particular, "Did anyone see the car that hit him?" A quick scan of the bystanders indicated the answer was no. "Did it stop?" Again, no one responded. I guess it didn't matter at that moment. I was just searching for answers.

All of a sudden someone's hands were replacing my own on the wounded man's head. I felt another person help me up. I turned to see that paramedics were there and assisting both of us. I was escorted to the sidewalk and asked if I felt okay. I probably answered yes, though I had no idea how I was. I remember the paramedic touching my hands a lot. Later I realized he must have been trying to wipe off the man's blood.

I was now reduced to a spectator myself, which struck me as unfair. I was cast aside to watch like every other pedestrian. An odd feeling. I'd made a connection with the man. I had been his caretaker. I needed to stay involved. Also, I needed to find the driver and make him see what he had done.

I turned to the doorman and asked if he saw what happened. "No," he said, "I was inside. I heard the noise and came out. I just can't believe he'd do that."

"What do you mean? Do what?"

The doorman muttered a name I don't remember and raised his chin at the man in the street. "He lives in the building. I heard he was sick . . . but I never thought he would kill himself."

No one saw a vehicle hit him—because there was none. For the first time I noticed the car that was parked right next to the man lying in the street. Its entire roof and windshield were smashed in—from above. How could I have not seen that before? I just assumed the glass came from the phantom vehicle, the vehicle that had threatened the life of this man whom I had come to know intimately, and yet never knew at all. I looked skyward at the building behind us on the southwest corner of Seventy-First and CPW. It was tall, maybe twenty stories.

"He lived up on fourteen," the doorman said.

Everything completely shifted at that moment. When I thought this man had been hit by a car I was eager to help, concerned about his life. When I realized that he was committing suicide, I felt that he had lied to me. Of course he hadn't, but it felt that way. I was angry.

I'd held him and told him that he'd be all right—his pleading gaze searched for reassurance, and I gave it. The few moments we shared together were powerful. Bonding. Or so I'd thought. Now I didn't know what to think. I felt somehow victimized as well as traumatized.

I was becoming nauseated. I didn't want to pass out there. I had to see my doctor. As I turned to go I saw a flash of something white in the street. I was dehydrated and dizzy, but the movement drew my attention. A clean white sheet was being draped over the man in the street.

It had been only a few months since I'd been curled up in a ball while Ava banged on my door. How easily I could have killed her. How close I'd come. For me, the madness soon passed into memory. But this man had acted on his.

What a sight I must have been when I appeared at my doctor's office, covered in sweat, traces of blood on my hands and face. A nurse took care of me, and I got an ice pack for my head and an IV bag full of electrolytes.

An hour later, I returned to the scene. I needed to see it. A small patch of darkened blood had seeped into the asphalt, the only evidence that something profound had transpired on this spot. Another car had parked where the damaged car had been. Cabs honked, families strolled. I stood there like a statue, weak, shaky, poisoned, questioning. I recalled that across the street from my doctor's office, a block away from where the man had jumped, was the Dakota, a grand old residential building, where an assassin had murdered John Lennon just a few years earlier.

I looked at the blood. I felt how tenuous the boundary is between life and its opposite. I felt how limited our span is, and how easily squandered. And I felt the need to embrace life. Put my arms around it.

Doug Donovan

Loving premiered in the summer of 1983 as a two-hour prime-time movie, featuring film actors Lloyd Bridges and Geraldine Page. The ads showed pictures of many cast members and asked: *Who's the victim and who's the murderer?* Out of a large cast, it was pretty easy to deduce who were the one-and-done characters: the stars. Bridges and Page weren't going to go on to do the series; they were bait to attract viewers and get them hooked on the world of the show: the blue-collar Donovan family and the blue-blooded Alden clan.

We started work in the dead of winter 1983. I was one of the last actors hired on the show, and I remember feeling so damn *lucky*. I wasn't Clerk or Cop #3. I had a name and a job and relationships. And I was working with some of my heroes. Commanding Geraldine Page, whom I loved in *Hondo* and *Summer and Smoke* and *Sweet Bird of Youth*. And I'd grown up watching Lloyd Bridges as US Navy frogman Mike Nelson on *Sea Hunt*.

He was so generous. If it was raining, Lloyd would get everyone lunch at the studio. I remember thinking: *WOW. That's a good guy.* I barely had enough money to buy myself lunch, so a free meal made a difference.

Some actors complained about mild inconveniences like early start times, and I remember Lloyd said: Better than digging a ditch. That left an impression on me. He was the star, and he was appreciative. I remember thinking: *That's how I want to be.* And indeed I *was* grateful to be there, and it *wasn't* digging a ditch. After all the restaurant jobs, the security-guard detail, Great Expectations, loading trucks at Roadway (HIGH AND TIGHT!), and all the derisive comments (You're an actor? What restaurant do you work in?), I thought: I'm here.

Being hired on *Loving* as a series regular was the breakthrough in my career. I'd just turned twenty-six years old, and I was a working actor. To this day, that remains my proudest professional accomplishment.

I surprised myself by how prepared I was for this break. What I lacked in formal education I had gained through hard work, through paying attention. I'd worked as an extra, making thirty bucks a day, but I wasn't there for the thirty bucks. I was there to learn the dynamics, the protocol, the jargon of the set. Acting for film and TV has a technical component. You need to know your stuff. What does the gaffer do? What happens when an actor doesn't hit his mark? A "mark" is a little piece of tape they set for you on the floor. Setting a mark ensures that the actor correctly executes the blocking he has worked out with his director and other actors. The camera team bases its work around the marks that have been set. Let's say an actor does a take that's all there. He cries, he laughs, he kills, he hits all the emotional notes. If he didn't hit his mark, it was worthless. He wasn't lit properly. Or he was out of focus. That's not the cameraman's fault. It's on the actor. If the actor screwed it up, that means wasted time, wasted energy, wasted money. I didn't want to be that guy.

I knew it was important for the actor to speak loudly enough so the sound could pick up what he was saying but softly enough to maintain intimacy if intimacy was required. Even though cameras and equipment and people surrounded you, if the scene called for you to be alone with your girlfriend, say, making out on a park bench, you had to find a way to speak in just the right pitch. Private but detectable.

I knew that, on camera, when you walk into a room in your own home, you must know where the light switch is. You can't need to look. Or else it's a lie, which is like giving the audience a pinch of poison.

When you tell a story, you have to take liberties. You compress time. You create composite characters. You jump years ahead or flash back. Art is not life. But if your character has a longtime girl-friend and you're tentative or formal with her, touching her as if she's someone you just met? Another pinch. The audience might not be consciously aware of these little pinches, but if you keep doling them out, they're reaching for the remote, or they're walking out of the theater. They're sick of the poison. They don't want any more. They're done.

They might not even realize they're responding to inauthentic-ity or sloppiness in storytelling. It's not the audience's job to articu-late the reasons. It's their job to feel.

I'm curious from an acting standpoint, so I've never walked out. On anything. I'm always learning something. If an actor is false, I'm looking to see what is making him false and whether he knows it. Is it lack of talent or focus? Does he not believe in his character? Maybe he's judging his character and that's seeping into his perfor-mance. If the play or the movie is horrible, is there someone who stands out from the mess? I'm interested from a professional point of view. But I don't expect general audiences to stay with something that's not true. All that matters where the audience is concerned is: Did it work? Were they moved?

I learned this in dribs and drabs in the parts I'd done leading up to *Loving*, but it all started to click once I was working day in and day out on the show. People sometimes say: You honed your craft on a *soap opera*? Absolutely. I did.

I was Doug Donovan, the son of a large Irish Catholic clan and a professor at the local university. Doug was a nice guy, a good guy. There was one instance, however, when I found out my fiancée, Merrill Vocheck (played by Patricia Kalember), was fooling around on me. That broke up our relationship. Upset in the aftermath, I snapped at my mother, played by Teri Keane. Teri loved it. It gave her something to react to. After I snapped, she was stung. She poured herself some coffee and waited a beat. Then remorse flashed across my face. I saw that I'd hurt her. And the audience could tell I wanted to say I was sorry. Teri let it sit, let it calm down—like a mom.

"Do you want to talk about it, Doug?" she said.

I calmly said, "I don't." We didn't change any of the dialogue, just the way we approached it. Honestly.

"Cut, cut!" The producers insisted I say it nicely, kindly, *like Doug*.

"But it's more interesting this way, more real," I argued.

"But the audience won't like you," the director said. "Doug is supposed to be likeable."

"They'll like me," I said. "They'll like me *more* if the character is honest and relatable—much more than if I'm saccharine sweet all the time. No one is sweet all the time. Doug is not perfect."

In the end, I did it their way. I didn't yet have the clout or the courage to stick with my instincts in the face of an authority saying: "Do it this way." I didn't want to get fired.

Also, that's just daytime television. When you're on the relentless pace of a soap opera, it's tough to take the time to be thoughtful. Got the shot? Good. Move on. Efficiency is everything. You can't debate the integrity of a character or the truth of a moment.

In another episode, the Donovan family gathered for dinner. In the middle of a scene, Lauren-Marie Taylor, who played my sister, knocked over a glass of milk by mistake. Napkins came out. We all moved to wipe it up. "Cut!"

"Cut? Why did you cut? The milk spilled. Milk spills! That's what happens in houses."

"Nope," they said, "clean it up. Let's do it over again."

"Can't we just have a real moment and react to it?"

"No, because how do you get back onto the script?"

"We'll get back on. Trust the actors to figure it out. We'll get back on script. And you'll have an honest moment. The audience will feel that."

Eh. Honesty was a luxury.

On *Loving*, I had to memorize up to thirty pages of a script each day, often four days a week. With 120 pages of dialogue to absorb, it was incredibly difficult to match quality with quantity. It would have been so easy, so utterly defensible to coast. But my fellow actors and I fought to elevate the material, to bring nuance and humanity to our performances. That's why I felt no shame in being on a soap opera. Truly, I felt *proud*. I still do.

Friend

James Kiberd, a barrel-chested, artistic, sensitive guy with an adventurous soul, played my older brother Mike on *Loving*. He introduced me to an acting workshop led by the venerable teacher Warren Robertson. The class was esoteric. Odd. We'd do these exercises: You're an animal. Make a noise. Moo. I tried to be open to it. It's like that great song from *A Chorus Line*: *Be a table. Be a sports car. Ice cream cone.* Okay so I'm an ice cream cone. I'm melting in the heat. I'm a puppy. *Yip, yip.* I'm roaring like a lion. We'd start the class lying on the floor, and then we'd writhe around and paw at each other like animals. Certainly there were skeptics and those who dismissed it or who would only roar halfheartedly. But I thought: *I'm here. Either I dive in or I leave.* I'm a sizzling pancake on a stove. I'm that pancake. Every part of me.

We'd get into scene work, and Warren's philosophy was: drill down on a scene for months and months and polish it to perfection. Almost every week for six months, we'd work on the same scene. I got weary of that and left after about a year. I learned some things from the class, but I felt strongly there was value in letting the imperfection of the work be okay. Wallace Stevens wrote, "The imperfect is our paradise." Something about burnishing that same scene for months on end didn't jibe with my instincts as an actor. I didn't want to drill away every shred of spontaneity and freshness. I wanted to leave room for discovery.

I remember I was doing a scene from a play about artist Amedeo Modigliani. I wanted to know what it was to paint something. James told me to come over to his place and paint. What do I paint? I don't know. Just paint. I took the 7 train over to his loft in Long Island City. He set up all kinds of paper for me. I did a painting, and I didn't like it and threw it away. And then I did another one. And another, and another. I slept and ate at his place and showered and painted and became totally engrossed. I was learning how to get under a character's skin.

James introduced me to art and getting into the process of it and being creative. He also taught me the value of an enriching friendship. I came to understand through him what author Marianne Williamson meant when she said something like: If people don't enhance your life, you have to get rid of them. That may sound harsh, but after Ava and the Suicide Man, I started to feel an urgency and wanted to surround myself with people who lifted me up. James did, and he taught me a lot. And he was fun. He would try anything. He was risk-oriented. He indulged. Sometimes too much.

One time the cast of *Loving* was at a party at the Grand Hyatt.

ABC network brass were there, all of our bosses. James was drinking up a storm. He was staring piercingly at the legendary Agnes Nixon, the creator of *Loving*, like a madman. He asked her to dance and she gave him her hand. He danced feverishly, and at one point, he took his shirt off and wrapped her up in a bear hug. That was all for Agnes, but James was just getting started. He strode up to an amplifier and started humping it. "Bryan, Bryan, feel this," he said. "*Vibrations.*" I was thinking: *He's going to get fired.*

He tried to dance with another young woman, but she quickly got fed up and pushed away from him. Now he was hurt. And remorseful. "I fucked up," he said.

I said, "James, it's a corporate event. All your employers are here. You know, you've got to tone it down." It was a work night. I invited him to spend the night at my place in Manhattan, but he wouldn't come with me. "At least let me get you on the seven train."

"No I need to walk. I need to be alone." He was spiraling. I didn't want to leave him, but he insisted.

"You know where I live," I said. "Buzz me. Come over when you're done with your walk."

He never buzzed me. The next day at work, everyone was saying: "Where's James? He was fucking that speaker last night. Maybe he went home with that speaker? Maybe he went home with Agnes Nixon?" I was calling his pager. Nothing. I was genuinely worried. He finally came in. He looked like shit. He reeked.

"Where were you last night, James?"

"I slept in Central Park." A crazy and dangerous thing to do even now, but in the 1980s? Certifiable.

That was James. He lived in the moment. He taught me a lot about how important it was, for your art, to do that—to tap into that child within and just play. But acting is a business. Through my friendship with James, I learned that the adult within us needs to keep an eye on the inner child.

Before *Loving*, I didn't know I had innate talent. Even when I was enjoying myself working, doubt shadowed me: Could I do this? Was I good enough?

I put myself in the position to see if I had it, and something happened. I showed up and I put the work in and I got a reaction. I made something happen.

Luck also played a part. Any successful actor or writer or artist will tell you that luck is a crucial factor. But the only way to get lucky is to be prepared for luck to find you. Writers write. Actors act. If you're not constantly applying your talents to your craft, no one is going to stop you on the street and say, "Hey, come write this TV show!" Or, "I want you to star in my movie."

Loving was job training; it was preparation. But above all, the show gave me confidence. This whole business is a confidence game. If you believe it, they'll believe it. If you don't believe it, neither will they. Today, when I'm in the position as a director to hire actors, I don't feel entirely comfortable hiring someone who doesn't emit confidence. If an actor comes in, and I feel flop sweat and need from them, there is almost no chance I will hire them. Not because they are untalented, but because they haven't yet come to the place where they trust themselves, so how can I trust they'll be able to do the job with a sense of ease? Confidence is king.

Actors are like athletes in that sense. They have to want to be the one to step up to the plate when the game is on the line. The brilliant actor Shirley Knight taught me that actors need to have an arrogance about them. Not in public or in their private lives, but when they work. Actors have to have that drive, that instinct that says: this role is mine.

Leaver

Agnes Nixon and Doug Marland, who created *Loving*, were nice people. The operating producer, the nuts-and-bolts producer, a man named Joe Stuart, was not. He would make young female actors weep. It was: You're getting fat. You need to do your roots. You're breaking out. But it wasn't just women. Anyone summoned to Joe's office left shaken. Joe rarely showed himself on set or in the halls. You saw him, it was almost always in his office, and it was almost always bad news. He was the grim reaper of *Loving*.

We were in the second week of shooting the show. We'd done eight shows already and I was still without a contract. I'd been featured in the two-hour premiere, so they couldn't easily replace me with another actor. It would be confusing to the audience. So I was in a rare position as a fairly inexperienced actor: I had leverage. And my agents were trying to use it to get me more money.

I finished getting my notes after the dress rehearsal. Seven minutes before they called "places" to shoot the show, I was in the makeup room. Joe appeared in the doorway and asked to speak to me. *Gulp*. He took me aside. "We're having a difficult time finalizing your contract." He told me that the network's upper management was advising him to cut bait and recast the role. I was shocked. He continued, "Do with that information what you will, and have a good show." And with that he turned and walked away.

Have a good show. He was basically holding a knife to my throat. *Have a good show*. I was so intimidated that it wasn't until much later that I realized it was all calculated. He didn't want to pay me a dime more than he had to, so he was trying to get in my head and make me worry about my job security.

It worked. I went to take my place on the set. My heart was

pounding. I didn't want to be fired. I got through my scene distract-edly. I called my manager the moment we were done. "I just got warned," I said. "Close the deal. Wherever you are. Close it. I don't want to have that happen again."

My manager said he thought we could get more.

"Close the deal," I said.

I was on the set, trying to work under duress in the real world. Managers and agents and sometimes writers operate in the theoreti-cal world. The real world is a pressure cooker. I couldn't endure this again. I was sure of that.

I ended up getting $600 per episode and then an automatic bump of $50 per show for the second season—the sweetest deal of any actor on the show. It wasn't because of my talent; it was only because I was hired last. I had leverage.

Joe didn't love that; he resented me for it. But after our run-in at the beginning, I rarely saw him. He never said anything to me. He was not a friendly guy. He didn't speak. He wanted to intimidate and be that man everyone feared.

Every thirteen weeks the producers had an option to renew each actor's contract. In the year and three quarters I was there, attrition was high. We'd see auditioning actors in the hallway with scripts in their hands and we'd try to see the names on the scripts so we knew our fates. If the actor resembled you, it was, *Uh-oh. A look-alike. It's gonna be me next. I'm getting fired.* We got into the habit of calling the show *Leaving* because so many people were canned.

Characters came and went. Patricia Kalember, the gifted actor who played my former fiancée, Merrill, was fired with no warning. I blinked and someone else, some hardworking colleague, had been dumped on the side of the road. No warning. No reason. Just . . . gone. I made it quite a ways. I had one more thirteen-week cycle before my two-year contract was up. My manager, a wonderfully supportive man named Leonard Grant, called and asked what I wanted to do. I said, "I like having a job. I'm enjoying myself. Learning a lot."

"It's velvet handcuffs," Leonard said. "You've got to get out of daytime, or else you'll wake up and it's twenty years later and it's all you've ever done."

He was right. We agreed I'd give notice. After two years I was done. I made a plan to ride out two more weeks and then we'd let them know.

My character was married at that time to Edie, played by Lesley Vogel. Nice woman. Pretty, though in the year we worked closely together I never saw her without makeup. It could have been a complex shoot early in the morning, and she'd show up with a full face on.

On a Friday, Lesley and I got called into Joe's office.

"Have a seat," he said.

We sat.

"We've greatly appreciated your contribution to the show. Story-wise, we're going in a different direction. We won't be renewing your contracts."

He stood up, meaning: *conversation over*. It had been ten seconds, maybe. I looked over at Lesley. Her face was frozen in shock. We stood. We'd barely sat on those chairs before we were up. Because it happened so fast, it was almost as if it didn't happen. I stood there. I shook his hand and said, "Thank you."

It's like if you fall, and someone sees you, and you cover your embarrassment with, *I'm okay, I'm okay*. It's not until later that you really assess the damage—your skinned knee, your bruised rib. In that office, I was punched in the face, and he didn't even bother to close the door first. He fired me, and I actually THANKED him. Damn. I wish I hadn't done that.

I walked into hair and makeup. I hadn't taken my makeup off yet. I saw my good friend John O'Hurley. (We were both married to the same woman, Lesley, on *Loving*.) He was there, munching on an apple. He took one look at me and said, "What's wrong?"

"I got fired," I said.

He dropped the apple. "What?"

I told him what Joe said, exactly. We're going in a different direction. A way of saying, "We're going away from you."

I had tickets to see the Arthur Miller play *After the Fall* that night. I went, but I wasn't really there. When anyone since has asked me how I liked the play, I say: I have no idea. Despite very much wanting to see Frank Langella and Dianne Wiest work, I only heard muffled sounds of actors on a stage. Even the cruel irony of the play's title was lost on me at the time. I was inside my devastation. I wasn't expecting to get fired, but it wasn't *unexpected*. We did call it *Leaving*, after all. But that was lost on me, too.

I licked my wounds in private that Saturday. I was filled with self-pity. Woe is me. I looked out the window, forlorn. I was fired. I thought I was getting pretty good, but obviously I'm not good because I just got fired. I was getting angry. I was feeling terrible about myself. I had a couple of drinks. I brushed my teeth and I looked at my face and frowned and thought: *Poor baby. You got fired . . . poor baby.*

And then I remembered the conversation with my manager. I was going to leave anyhow. Two more weeks and I was giving notice. So why did I feel this way?

It was sort of like I was going to break up with a girl and she beat me to the punch. I didn't want to be the one on the receiving end. I wanted to be the one in control. I wanted to be the one who knocked.

It was my ego. My ego had been hurt.

The next morning I said: *You have to get over yourself, go do something*. I bought fifteen rolls of film and shoved them into my camera bag. I wanted to get out of my head. I walked into Central Park with my Nikon—but barricades were everywhere. The stupid New York City Marathon was under way. And now all these people were in my way and I wasn't going to be able to take pictures of the park!

I started snapping anyhow. The first picture I took was of these two fat cops. They were huge. A sign for the runners was posted above them. It read: MEN THIS WAY, WOMEN THAT WAY. I took that picture. It was a pretty good picture.

The motorcade carrying Mayor Koch and the race organizers and VIPs passed. The racers on wheelchairs flew by, and then the elite runners. A guy with one leg crossed the finish line on crutches. An able-bodied man collapsed twenty feet before the finish line, and a couple of others picked him up and dragged him across. The scene was moving, heroic. I got chills.

I was there for six hours, taking photos of every kind of person. Each one of them had toiled and trained and endured. And finished.

I forgot my troubles. I forgot to eat. An old woman crossed the finish line. She was eighty-three if she was a day. She ran twenty-six miles. Twenty-six miles! That was the distance from Long Beach to Catalina. How could anyone manage that? Let alone dudes in hula skirts and teens in funny antennae and a guy in full clown makeup and a waiter carrying a tray. Triumphant. Amazing.

What the hell? How did they do this? I could never do this.

I could never do this? I heard myself admit failure before I'd even tried. Another elderly runner hobbled across the finish line, arms overhead, victorious. I was twenty-seven. If I put my mind to it, why couldn't I do it?

I couldn't think of a good reason. I vowed to myself, "Okay. Next year I'm going to be in this race." That was that. I set a goal for myself. Without it, I might have pouted for weeks. Now nothing was going to get in my way, except maybe actually having to do it.

I planned to sublet my apartment in New York and go back to LA for TV-pilot season (January–March), the time of year when producers cast new pilots for series that will, with luck, air in the fall.

Before I left New York, I was invited to the *Loving* holiday party, and I went to say good-bye to all my friends from the show.

At the party, I turned around and there was Joe, wearing an expensive suit and a smug look. He was standing there with his wife. He furrowed his brow and said, "Bryan, I thought you'd be long gone by now, back to Los Angeles."

Not: *Happy Holidays.* Not: *Sorry about the way things turned out.*

I said, "Fuck off, Joe." Well, that's what I wanted to say. What I actually said was, "Nope, still enjoying the city! Merry Christmas."

Oh well. At least I didn't thank him.

Murdering Maid

I quickly got cast in a guest-star role on a show called *Cover Up.* The premise was undercover CIA agents masquerading as fashion models. Really.

Prior to my arrival, the show had been on hiatus because of a horrible tragedy. During a break between scenes, late at night, the star, Jon-Erik Hexum, got bored and started playing Russian roulette with what he thought was a safe prop gun. He shot a blank load into his temple, and ended up brain-dead. He died several weeks later. In shock and grief, they shut down the show for a number of months. When CBS revived it, they had a new actor take over for Jon. I was hired for the first show back as a guest star.

I had been told that the female star of the show, Jennifer O'Neill, was nice, and she was. But I think she was still coping with the loss of her costar, so it was tough going at first. I went to shoot an important scene with her, and the script supervisor told me he was reading Jennifer's off-camera dialogue. She was still at lunch. I said, "Get her back. Please." On camera or off camera, you're there for your fellow actor, giving it your all every take. That's my philosophy.

They got her back, and she was not happy. I tried to play off that unhappiness in the scene. I'm not sure it was effective, but I had to play the hand I was dealt.

I had four different roles on *Cover Up*, including a newspaper guy, a blowhard, a mustachioed reporter, and a maid . . . who also happened to be a murderer. I had a skilled Hollywood artist make me up like a woman, and I remember looking at myself in the mirror and thinking, *You are the ugliest woman I have ever seen.*

My manager, trying to raise awareness about my work, put out an ad in *Variety* with pictures of the four characters I played. The text read: *4 your consideration.*

Meanwhile I was auditioning for commercials like a maniac. I ultimately did spots for Excedrin and Preparation H and Coffee-Mate. My mother could never remember if the coffee-whitener product I was selling was Coffee-Mate or its rival brand Cremora. She'd call and say, "I saw your Cremate commercial again! I use that when I don't have cream."

I'd answer, "You like the taste of cremate, Mom?"

"I do!" she'd say. "It's rich!"

When I started getting a lot of guest-star roles, I'd make postcards and send them to casting directors to alert them. Watch Bryan Cranston in *Matlock* this week! Don't miss Bryan Cranston's guest turn as Tom Logan in *Baywatch*! Tune in to *Amazon Women on the Moon* for a special treat: Bryan Cranston stars as Paramedic #3. I knew 99 percent wouldn't watch, but they would see my name. They would see my face. And they would get the message, even if only on a subliminal level. This guy works a lot.

Runner

In my role as Murdering Maid, I brought actor Javier Grajeda, who played a detective, hand towels. We got to talking as they were setting up a shot, and I told him I wanted to run a marathon. It happened he did, too. We lived close to each other, and we were both starting from scratch. We signed up for the New York City Marathon and started training together. The race was in November. We had a lot of miles to run before then to get ready. We started with short jogs in March, and then we got into a running class, which helped. We did long training runs before dawn. No excuses. No I'm not feeling well, I'm too sore, I can't make it today. You knew the other guy was going to be there, so you dragged your ass out of bed. We got into it.

When the time came to fly back to New York for the race, we were as ready as we could be, but at the last minute Javier got a job he couldn't turn down. Good for him. But I wouldn't have a partner to help push me through the race. Oh well. Then I heard from my friend and former on-screen sister from *Loving*, Lauren-Marie Taylor. She was going to run. So we decided to do it together.

At the start of the race in Staten Island, women and first-time runners stood on one side, men on the other. Lauren-Marie and I stuck together and we blazed through the crowd, right up to the front of the line. Today, elite runners are separated from amateurs, but in 1985 everyone was mixed in, and we found ourselves standing in a group of elites, feeling mortal and earthbound next to their sinewy grace, warthogs among a herd of gazelles. Just before the starting gun sounded, an elite runner standing in front of me suddenly pulled down her running shorts and underwear and squatted to relieve herself. We were jam-packed, and I couldn't step away, so I simply straddled her trickling yellow stream as it came toward me.

The gun went off, and Lauren-Marie and I watched the elites blast off and recede into the distance. We ran together for a while and then I moved ahead, wishing her luck. I'd found I could only run consistently with someone who matched my natural gait. Too slow or too fast and I'd burn out.

I got to Brooklyn and I was flying, adrenaline pumping, and I remember hearing the splits as I was running. I was averaging a six-minute mile at mile-marker five. That was too fast. I needed to slow down. Mile ten. I was feeling good! Mile fifteen. Just okay. The course takes you from Staten Island through Brooklyn and Queens, and then back into Manhattan around mile sixteen. Manhattan gave me a boost. Finish line ahead! But "ahead" was actually pretty far away. The course takes you off Manhattan to the Bronx, oh crap, then back into Manhattan. By mile eighteen, I was tanking. I was running in mud. I grabbed Dixie Cups of Gatorade from the side of the road, and I tried to give myself pep talks. Come on, Bryan! I said aloud. I tried to absorb the energy of the crowd. They had inspired me at the outset, but nothing could help me now. I obsessively did the arithmetic—how far I had come and how far I had to go—thinking math might somehow ease the pain.

In a training run just a few months prior, I had hit "the wall," that dreaded wave of fatigue and bodily revolt. I'd ended up splayed on a sidewalk in Santa Monica and had to crawl to a hose bib, lying on the sidewalk with my mouth open to take in a few drops from the spigot. Somehow I revived myself enough to lurch home. I did not want to repeat that experience during the race, so I'd taken every liquid I'd been offered along the course. I didn't quite hit the wall, but I was dragging. The race was becoming an ordeal. I wondered if I could finish.

But just then, I saw the finish line. I don't know if I'd ever experienced such elation. I started dancing. Tears came to my eyes. I caught sight of the exact spot where one year prior I'd leaned against a tree, freshly fired, taking pictures, feeling like a beaten man. I remembered thinking, "I can't do that." Now some other guy was there, taking pictures. Of me. Finishing. I would never again say "I can't do that." That's what I told myself. Never again.

Bad Guy

In the 1980s, if you were a series regular, you were a good guy. Guest stars were either bad guys or victims. I was the bad guy on a CBS show called *Airwolf*, starring Jan-Michael Vincent, Ernest Borgnine, and a helicopter. A helicopter! The helicopter saved the day in every show.

My character was a jilted lover who'd hijacked a sorority reunion aboard the *Queen Mary*. I was the head hijacker and I had a couple of henchmen. One of my victims was Alicia, played by Robin Dearden. I held her hostage at gunpoint. She smelled good! And she was pretty and funny, too.

But I had a girlfriend and Robin had a boyfriend, so dating was off the table. That turned out to be a good thing. There were no expectations. We could relax and flirt without the pressure of won-dering what's going to happen next. The call times aboard the *Queen Mary* were at the crack of dawn, so each long day we did a lot of carefree laughing and bonding.

One of my henchmen was taciturn and suspicious and explo-sively dangerous, and the actor took method acting to a whole other level. In one scene, he was supposed to push Robin against the heli-copter. And rather than making the move *appear* forceful, he actually slammed her hard. He wrenched her finger and bopped her head. An on-set medic attended to her, and she was fine, more shaken than hurt. The guy was inappropriate in his aggression. (A year later Robin was in the supermarket and saw him, and she walked away from a full cart of groceries because she was so unnerved.) As bad as hurting her was, this guy showed no contrition. He was flippant in his response. He said something like, "My character is abusive." That made me mad. Do you not realize you're on a set? You're act-ing. You have to have some boundaries. You have to look out for your fellow actors. When someone gets hurt on the set, it spoils everything. The fun you're having, creating—if someone gets hurt, it all goes away. I was concerned about Robin. I tried to comfort her and make her laugh even though she was in pain, and I suppose that brought us closer. We exchanged phone numbers.

On March 7, 1986, I ran in the first Los Angeles Marathon. It was also my thirtieth birthday, and I threw a party at the merry-go-round on the Santa Monica pier. I invited Robin, but she had a prior com-mitment. She often says if she'd come to that birthday party we wouldn't be married today. I don't quite know why she thinks that, but I believe her.

The next time I saw her was a year later, in 1987. I was in Andy Goldberg's comedy improv class, and she walked in one day. There was instant recognition and mutual happiness. We started getting on stage together once a week. One day, as class was starting, we kissed hello. Actors kiss hello and good-bye all the time, with no lasting consequences. But even for actors, there is an acceptable kiss duration. Any longer than that . . . something is afoot. That day, Robin and I lingered at each other's lips. It was a millisecond too long, and we both felt it. We both swore later that neither of us had planned it. But we both felt it.

Still, I didn't realize how much I liked Robin until I was watching *Letterman* one night with Javier. We'd become close friends since our *Cover Up* days, and he was now my roommate. He was also in my improv comedy class. During a commercial break, he said offhandedly, "I think I'm going to ask Robin out."

"No!" I said. I was surprised at how strongly the word sprang out of me.

He was, too. He said, "Oh, did you ask her out?"

"Well, uh, no," I said.

That was my impetus to get off my ass. Was I going to go through the Carolyn Kiesel experience again? Hell no.

One day after class we were talking and she found out that I'd never been to the Huntington Library, which was close by in Pasadena. It had a great art collection and beautiful botanical gardens. "You should go," she said. "We should go."

Did this constitute a date? I hoped maybe it did.

It was late spring 1987 in Los Angeles, so of course I was wearing white slacks and a short-sleeved shirt with a green floral pattern and mesh shoes. She wore almost the exact same outfit in reverse: a green and white skirt and a white shirt. It worked better on her. We laughed.

We had a beautiful day. Robin drove because I had never been to the Huntington Library before. She knew how to get there.

When she dropped me off, we sat in the car talking for a long time. Then I got out of the car and walked around to the driver's side door and kissed Robin through the open window. I watched as she drove away, thinking: *I hope I get to do that again.*

Punter

That summer Robin was doing an acting program in Oxford at the British American Dramatic Academy, and coincidentally I had planned a hitchhiking trip throughout England and Scotland. "I could stop by Oxford and see you," I offered. We made a plan. As I traveled, I called her from red-box pay phones all around the United Kingdom to make sure she still wanted to see me. Every time I called, she seemed eager for me to get there. But not as eager as I was.

When I got to Oxford, I planned a romantic escapade for us and got lucky with an unusually sunny and gorgeous Sunday. I bought sandwiches and a bottle of wine and decided we'd go punting on the Thames. When I rented the punt—a flat-bottomed boat—and the guy handed me something like a long stick, I realized that in all of my romantic planning I hadn't factored in my total ignorance about what to do with that stick. But how hard could it be? I'd figure it out.

We found our boat and Robin got settled in, facing me, smiling sweetly. We shoved off from the shore. I pushed the stick in, and it hit the soft riverbed. I pulled it up slowly, and water and mud and silt sprinkled everywhere—on my pants, my shirtsleeves. This couldn't be right. What was I doing wrong? I tried to cloak my ignorance about the art of punting with an easy smile; Robin smiled. She must have known, but she was too kind to let on.

On a rare, beautiful day in England, it seems everyone is outside drinking a beer. From a bridge above the river I heard a guy yell, "Hey, Yank, use it as a ra-ah-ah."

"A what?"

"Use it as a RAH-AA-AHHHH."

How does he know I'm a Yank? And a rah-ah? What the hell is a rah-ah? I strained to hear as I soaked myself in river water. Finally I deciphered the code. "Hey, Yank, use it as a RUDDER." Ah, you propel the boat by pushing the stick into the riverbed and then letting it trail behind, so it acts as a *rudder*. Robin didn't hold my punting skills against me.

We docked the boat and set up a picnic under a tree. We talked, we laughed. We made out like bandits.

I was crazy about her. The only hitch was she had a boyfriend. Record scratch.

The girlfriend I'd had when Robin and I first met had broken up with me, but Robin and her long-distance boyfriend hadn't technically split up. They'd been together for years, I think seven, and though they'd been long-distance and drifting apart for some time, she didn't have the heart to let him down.

But now Robin and I had this connection. Emotional, passionate, on every level. I was ready to make a commitment to her. Was she ready to make the same commitment to me? I beseeched her to break up with him. I said, "I want you unencumbered. The sooner you do it, the better for all of us, including him. The longer this drags on, the more painful it will be. Please do it."

We returned to Los Angeles, and he was due to visit. "I'm going to tell him when he comes out," she said. That news drove me to distraction. He was coming to see her with the notion that they were still together. He was going to have . . . expectations. I begged her to tell him. But she couldn't. I think it was probably the most painful decision to that point in her life. So out to California he came.

Robin was so stressed by all this that she got laryngitis. She completely lost her voice. And then to make matters worse, while they were together at Robin's condo, he found a love letter. From one Bryan Cranston. That's how he discovered we were together. He was shocked. She was weeping. And later I was fuming as I listened to her tell me how awful it was for her. She wanted to be with me, but she didn't want to break anyone's heart. That's Robin in a nutshell. She's the most loving, caring person I've ever known.

She'd had lots of dates but only a few real boyfriends in her life. That was part of the reason it was so difficult for her. I listened patiently but then I said a stupid, passive-aggressive thing: "I won't tell you where you went wrong," implying, of course, that she had gone wrong and I was uniquely able to tell her all about it.

That was an early hiccup. But we got past it. And then we were together, rudder in the water, steering for distant shores.

Husband

Outwardly, I am measured. Inside, because of my childhood, a key can turn, and I can get emotional. I wasn't really allowed to express my feelings as a kid. Boys weren't supposed to cry. Also, I was losing my mother emotionally, I'd lost my father physically, and I was too busy figuring out how to survive to cry.

So I have a lot of tears stored up, along with anger and resentment—you know, the good stuff. I didn't quite know how to activate the healing process in my personal life just yet, but anytime I was working I gave myself permission to tap into that store.

And then sometimes that key involuntarily turned on its own.

I knew I wanted to propose to Robin, but I had the overwhelming fear that I wouldn't be able to face her without that key turning, without getting blubbery. I thought I couldn't get through it. I wanted to tell her how I felt, how much I loved her, how I knew I wanted to spend the rest of my life with her, have a family. I'd passed through the gauntlet of a marriage that was not right and relationships that were not right, and now it was time to nurture one that was. If you don't nurture a relationship, it will die. I wanted to nurture ours, but I didn't want to water it with my tears.

One day, it dawned on me: What if I wasn't facing her? What if we could be close and intimate but not be looking at each other? How could I accomplish that?

I thought about it for a while, and then I was in the shower and I had it. A bath! What if we took a bath together? She couldn't face me because the spigot would be jammed into her back. She'd have to sit between my legs, facing away from me. I'd bought a cabin in the mountains with my dear friend from *Loving*, John O'Hurley, and we had a tiny tub there. Perfect!

I brought Robin there just after Christmas. I didn't want to do it on Christmas. The proposal wasn't a Christmas present. But a holiday would be good cover, an occasion to celebrate. So I decided on New Year's Day.

"Let's take a bubble bath," I said.

"Really?"

It's not like we made a habit of hopping into the tub together in the middle of the day. But it was New Year's. I made it an occasion. I got candles. Music. Champagne.

I had the ring. But then—*oh shit*—I had to hide it. But I had to put it within reach—I couldn't jump out of the bathtub midproposal, sopping wet and stark naked, to go searching for the ring. The only thing I could think to do was put it on a digit. I decided on my baby toe.

We got in the tub and listened to music and talked for a while, all as she was facing away from me. It took half an hour to get my courage up before I finally said, "Are you happy, Robin?"

"Yes, I'm happy."

"It's been a great year. You make me so happy. I love you so much. I want to be with you for the rest of my life." I was whispering into her ear. And as she started to realize what was happening, she kept trying to turn around to look at me, and I kept turning her face back around. I needed to get to the question first! I finally asked if she would marry me. It was an instantaneous yes. And then she twisted to face me and we kissed.

Oh, the ring! I hoisted my leg out of the water, and it was covered in bubbles, and at first she didn't see the ring. I shook my leg and some suds floated off, then I bent my knee so my foot was near her. Look! *Oh my God!* She was now charged with taking her ring off my toe, and she gave it to me and I put it on her finger. It was glorious. We called her parents and they were overjoyed, though her dad did give me some ribbing for not asking his permission first.

Robin came from a stable family, so that's what she was familiar with, and I lacked a stable family, so that's what I wanted. We were perfectly matched, and we didn't want to waste time, so we got married six months later on a beautiful Saturday, July 8, 1989, at the Hotel Bel-Air. Reverend Bob, the pontiff of Catalina Island, married us. Robin looked stunning in an off-the-shoulder white dress. She wore white flowers in her hair. I looked as if I was ripped out of a 1980s JC Penney catalog. But damn, we were happy. Both my parents came, and we had to do separate pictures for each of them. They couldn't sit together. There was some tension between them. But nothing could put a damper on our day.

Honeymooner

Robin's parents footed the bill for our wedding, so we were able to afford a monthlong honeymoon in Europe. We were in our mid-thirties, eager to start a family, and we knew this could be our last chance for a long time to see the world.

The travel agent recommended that we take our rental car on a flatbed train from Switzerland to Italy. It would save us hours on the road. And the journey was apparently a rite of passage for newlyweds.

A twinkle in his eye, the agent described three tunnels the train would pass through. The third, dubbed the Tunnel of Love, was fifty minutes long. Plenty of time for . . . you know. The twinkle in his eye started to seem kind of creepy.

Robin and I discussed it. We were both game, and when the day arrived we drove up to the designated train station in Switzerland

and got in line with all the small rental cars. We were instructed to follow the flagman's signal and drive up onto the train's flatbed. One flatbed held three small cars bumper-to-bumper. We were situated between two other cars, my bumper kissing that of the car in front of us, the one behind us kissing mine. Engine off, emergency brake on, a lurch from the unseen locomotive way up ahead of us, and we were off.

It was July, stifling hot, and the breeze created by the speeding train was welcome. We sat in our car, windows open, sighing with pleasure at the cool breeze; when the train got up to full speed, the air whipped into the car like a tornado. The grind of metal on metal of the train's wheels on the track and the creak of the train cars as they flexed their form around the curves created a furious cacophony.

Soon the train was in the first tunnel. The breeze became a wind. We were swept up in the whoosh and pitch darkness. A fantastic sensation.

Blasting out of the tunnel into bright daylight, coming to a stop at another train station, I looked to Robin. "That's one," I said. She rolled her eyes. Perhaps she wasn't looking forward to this escapade quite as much as I was. I peered into the car behind us: two couples enjoying the ride with food and drink. I nodded hello. They waved back.

We entered tunnel two. Again, total darkness. We couldn't see our own dashboard. We couldn't see our hands in front of our faces. Soon, wham! We were out of the tunnel, stopping at another station. "That's two," I whispered to my bride.

At last we were roaring into the final tunnel. We waited for total darkness, and it was go time. I climbed over the stick shift. These European rental cars were tiny, like clown cars, so removing my pants was nearly impossible. For Robin, too. She slid her seat back. I crept forward. My knee pinched her thigh against the console.

Ouch!

Sorry, sorry.

Now, my elbows—where to put them? She groaned. Oops, sorry again. I couldn't put my arms around her, so I just raised them. I misjudged the space and knocked her in the jaw. Sorry, honey.

Robin was ready to give up, but I was no quitter. Focus, I told myself, and her. Failure is not an option. We've come this far. We can do this. Tunnel of Love, Robin. Tunnel of Love.

My eyes slowly adjusted to the darkness. I was able to see Robin's face, in surprising detail. Her expression wasn't one of pleasure. It was one of enduring patience. The sooner this happens, the sooner it's over, that's how I read her. But I also read the contours of her beauty, all the contours, and thought how extraordinary, how really extraordinary, she was. And how extraordinary also is the human eye. I could see her so clearly, all the things I loved about her face were vivid and evident, and then I realized why.

WOOSH! We'd emerged from the tunnel.

The train was slowing and we were coming into the next station. What? How could that be? That wasn't fifty minutes. It was fifteen.

I looked up from my position on top of Robin, perched on the passenger seat facing backward, and I saw the two couples I remembered nodding hello to earlier. The cars were compact, and we were bumper to bumper on the flatbed train, so they weren't more than ten feet away. I waved apologetically. Robin covered her face. But no need. The couples laughed and whistled their approval and honked their horn. *Bene, bene! Motto bene!*

I heard a voice. It was coming from below. Robin. With a tight smile, she was trying to tell me something. Her tone was patient, but her meaning was precise.

Get. Off.

I fumbled back into the driver's seat, pulling up my pants, and looked up. Three small children grinning through the back window of the car in front of us. Even Italian *children* have knowledge of lovemaking—they're probably taught the basics in kindergarten. Like the English with punting.

Robin and I were both red-faced, but we were laughing, too. Well, that last tunnel was not quite the experience that was advertised.

Had the travel agent been mistaken? Or had he set us up on some kind of honeymooners' initiation? We never found out. In the end it didn't matter. It was an adventure. With Robin it's all an adventure.

Robin is my partner in all things. My love. There are a million things I adore about her, but if you pressed me for my absolute favorite thing, it's that from the moment I met her, through the twenty-seven years we've been married, she has maintained this incredible sense of play and wonder. A firefly makes her giddy.

Our marriage has been such a foundation for me. Whenever young actors ask me for advice, I always tell them: get your house in order. Your relationships, your health, your personal life: that's your foundation. If your home life is sane, it allows you to go insane in your work.

Dad

When we met, Robin wasn't sure whether she wanted to have kids. Before we got married, I asked if she would agree to at least one child. I didn't think I could marry someone who didn't want children. She said yes. I said that's good enough for me. We agreed that we wouldn't talk about another kid until the baby was past one.

Robin had a smooth pregnancy, no morning sickness, only an occasional uncomfortable night. But then a month and a half before the due date, our doctor started noticing a drop in amniotic fluid. She ordered Robin to slow down. Then the levels were still dropping and so it was bed rest.

Two weeks before our due date, Robin's fluid levels were still too low, so the doctor said we had to induce.

As the baby was coming out, there still wasn't enough fluid. Robin was fully dilated, and I saw our doctor do this short, worried exhalation. You never want to see your doctor anxiety breathing. I clench up when I feel unnerved. I get tight. But I tried not to show it, because what good would I be to Robin in the delivery room?

Suction. Forceps. Our doctor pleaded, "Robin, you've got to push. You've got to push." I felt so helpless. In my distress, I did the one thing I shouldn't have done. I became the coach. I turned to Robin and got close to her face, as if I were spotting her lifting weights. COME ON, ROBIN! YOU'VE GOT THIS. PUSH! That technique may work on men, but my wife wasn't feeling the burn.

In between deep breaths, she critiqued my method. Shut. Up.

I adjusted my approach. I love you, honey. You can do this. I'm right here with you.

At 7:04 p.m., February 12, 1993, our baby was born. When the doctor finally got her out, it was such a release for me. I wept. And then I freaked. Her head was conical because of the suction and forceps. My daughter looked like one of the Coneheads from *Saturday Night Live*. The doctor, whose worried exhalations had done nothing to reassure, was now wonderfully easy and consoling. "That conehead is normal. That will reshape." Almost immediately it did start to reshape. It was miraculous.

I can, in an instant, recall the depth of feeling for my baby when I first saw her, the utter dependency, the desire to protect her. *Cut the cord, Dad.* I cut her cord. I was a father. I was honored to be the first one to hold her. And then I gave her to Robin, who didn't cry. "Oh, there you are," she said calmly. "You're so beautiful."

They checked the placenta. They needed to do the Apgar test. *Come on, Dad. Hold the baby.* Pinprick test. All good. Length. All good. I put her on a digital scale. It read 6.66. The nurse went to write it down but looked at me first, eyebrow raised. Robin is superstitious, and that decimal point could be missed upon first glance. I put a finger on the scale and nodded to the nurse. It now read 6.67. She smiled and wrote 6.67 on the official paperwork.

Robin started nursing and bonding. When she rested, Taylor would lie on my chest and hear my breathing and feel my rhythms. I'd never felt so connected with anyone.

We stayed an extra day at the hospital because Taylor was slightly jaundiced. They sent us all home with a baby tanning bed; we put tiny tanning goggles on her and lay her under the heat lamps, and she would just fall asleep adorably. At first you hear your baby is jaundiced, and it's alarming. But it's pretty normal. And then she was over that.

A week after the birth, Robin was still struggling. We thought, *Well, of course she is.* She just had a traumatic, emotionally taxing experience. We went back to the doctor after ten days, and her pulse was sluggish, she was anemic, and her blood pressure was way too low. She was hemorrhaging blood.

Right there in the doctor's office I saw Robin's eyes roll back in her head. She collapsed. Seeing anyone lose consciousness is scary.

But to see my wife, who'd just been through so much, go down like that? My heart dropped. I grabbed her before she could fall and we called an ambulance. Even though we were in the Cedars-Sinai hospital complex, she had to get into the ambulance to go two hundred feet to the ER next door. Transportation policy. Bureaucratic bullshit.

We knew something was wrong. They ran the gamut of tests and discovered they hadn't removed the entire placenta after the birth, and that was creating all kinds of havoc. Robin's body was basically treating the placenta like an intruder. They had to do a procedure to collect the tissue from the uterus, and Robin had to stay in the hospital. I brought Taylor back and forth to see Robin and feed. It was stressful, but in a way uplifting, because I felt needed and useful and connected. That bond between a mother and child is so strong that sometimes a father can end up feeling like a third wheel. But I felt so bonded to both Robin and Taylor then. My sister Amy came to stay with us for a while around Taylor's birth, and by that time she was a nurse, and she was incredibly helpful.

When Taylor was two, I brought up the idea of having another baby. I'd started working more, and Robin was working less. I said I think it's fair that you have two votes and I have one vote. The first child was up to us. The second is up to you. What do you think? "I'm good," she said. She didn't want another.

I brought it up again when Taylor was three. Robin said she didn't feel she needed another child. I don't know if the difficult late pregnancy and birth had any influence on her decision. Maybe so.

I'm certain the main reason I thought we should have another child was so that Taylor could have a sibling. Because my parents had been who they had been, I thought of family as siblings. Growing up as I did, I don't know what I would have done without my brother's support and the strong bond we shared. But Taylor would have a much more stable environment than I'd had. So a sibling wasn't a pressing matter. I deferred to Robin, and we stopped at one.

With an only child, it was easier to take her with us, so Taylor has traveled a lot. Also, there's no denying only children spend a lot of time around adults. Taylor was comfortable around adults and adult conversations early on. Her level of comfort around kids her own age took longer to get to, but it came.

Taylor expressed interest in acting when she was extremely young. We tried to steer her into classes and experiences that didn't professionalize her. Of course some children who act professionally go on to be fully actualized adults. Many of them do not. It's a hard road. And we wanted to protect her from that, let her be a child. She'd have a lifetime to work when she grew up.

The great acting guru Constantin Stanislavski said, "Love art in yourself, not yourself in art." I think of that often. I try to live by that. Work, hone your craft, enjoy your successes in whatever doses they may come. But do not fall in love with the poster, the image of you in a movie, winning an Oscar, the perks, the limo, being rich and famous. If that is what you're falling in love with, you're doomed to fail. My father was oriented toward those things. And I wanted to live a different kind of life. And I want a different life for my daughter. Fall in love with creative expression and the surprising discoveries and empowerment it can bring. Be wary of the rest.

When I was nominated for my first Emmy, Taylor was young; Robin and I got a babysitter, and off we went to the award ceremony—a fun, glamorous night. We got home, and I paid the babysitter. The kitchen trash reeked something awful. I mean it was alive. Robin handed it to me, and I held it at arm's length so it didn't drip on my tuxedo and patent-leather shoes as I walked out to the garbage cans outside.

As I was straight-arming the Hefty bag, I smiled. An hour ago it was limos, autographs, flashing cameras, champagne—now, smelly trash.

That's the way life should be. Balanced. Chores. Daily responsibilities. Family. Show business has a natural attraction to charlatans and phonies because it can be superficial. And empty. Sort of like whipped cream. When you dig into it with your fork, there's nothing underneath. You can't build anything on whipped cream. But Robin gave me the bedrock stability that I wanted professionally and needed personally. And when our daughter was born, Taylor gave me that, too. Then it was my job to give my family the same in return.

Confessor

When I attended my twenty-year high school reunion in 1994, I was happily married with a young child. And I planned to finally confess to Carolyn Kiesel and reveal what she meant to me as a young boy. I was now free from that burden, and I'd been open with Robin about how I'd craved Carolyn's attentions and affections, how much tenderness I'd felt toward her, how crushed I'd been when I let my chance slip away, how it had always remained with me, a time-release lesson. Robin was supportive. She encouraged me to talk to Carolyn at our reunion; she was curious to meet her, too.

At the registration table I picked up my name badge, which featured the silhouette of a generic man because my picture had been omitted from the yearbook. I always thought that spoke volumes about who I was then. In some ways, I think it motivated me to leave a mark.

I knew that as active as she was in school, Carolyn wouldn't miss the reunion, and I asked the classmates manning the registration table if Carolyn had arrived yet. They exchanged an awkward look, and then one of them whispered that unfortunately Carolyn was not there. She had died in 1977. A few years after high school. Car accident.

I stood motionless. Finally the classmate asked if I would please step to the side so she could assist others checking in. I murmured thanks for the information and walked away. I relayed the news to Robin, who instantly understood what a loss it was.

You hear of people dying in accidents all the time. But Carolyn? Not Carolyn. I'd barely known her but I'd always missed her, and now I'd mourn her. She died before she got to experience marriage, children, a career. And I'd never be able to express my appreciation for her sweetness. Her generosity of spirit. She'd been so important to me privately, and I wanted the chance to tell her publicly. For days it would dawn on me again and again, and every time I felt both the shock of the new and a deepening sadness: she was gone.

Tim Whatley

When I got the role of Tim Whatley, "dentist to the stars," I was already a big *Seinfeld* fan, and I was thrilled that I'd get to play a small part in one of the best comedy shows of all time. *Seinfeld* was revolutionary, really, in that instead of breaking down the story lines into A-plot and B-plots (major and minor stories), each episode gave all four main characters a major narrative, and somehow all of them intersected. Most other shows use guest stars to inject an element of humor. *Seinfeld* used guest stars to facilitate and spotlight the show's stars. A superb construct.

The first episode I did was called "The Mom and Pop Store," which was kind of an homage to *Midnight Cowboy*. Tim is having a party on the Upper West Side, and Jerry isn't invited. Or is he? Jerry can't tell! George Costanza meanwhile buys a used car he thinks might belong to Jon Voight, the actor. George is really getting off on the romance and glamour of driving around in a car that belonged to a celebrity. But Jerry plants a seed of doubt in George's mind about the provenance of the Chrysler LeBaron. Did it really belong to Jon Voight? Then George finds a pencil in the glove box. It has teeth marks. Kramer tells George: "If you take the pencil to Tim Whatley's party, you'll find a dentist who can match the teeth marks to Jon Voight's bite." Did I mention that Jon Voight had recently bitten Kramer on the arm? As luck would have it, Tim knows Jon Voight! George exults in his good fortune. But then Tim continues: Jon Voight *the periodontist*.

Seinfeld has become a touchstone for so many people. *Seinfeld* superfans, who've seen every episode umpteen times, roam the streets, and when they see me invariably shout out: WHATLEYYYYYYY. Many people think my recurring presence on the show was part of some grand plan. In fact, I appeared in only six episodes, and each one was, for all I knew, the last time I'd be on.

On each episode, I got to see Jerry Seinfeld's legendary comic genius up close. His knowledge of comedy is unmatched. Several times he'd tell me to adjust a joke here or there, and *wham*, the moment was transformed from pedestrian to uproariously funny. But all the major players on the show were brilliant. Going to work was like attending an intensive comedy seminar.

Larry David, the cocreator, an incredible comedian, never put characters first. It was always story first. Then find characters that suited the story. What if Kramer is mistaken for a mentally challenged person? He's drunk. No. What about if he's just come from the dentist? He's got a mouthful of Novocain. Let's bring Tim Whatley back. Thus was born a classic episode called "The Jimmy."

Jerry had a rule about jokes: If you're in the group, you can make the joke. If you're not in the group, steer clear. So Larry David and Jerry said: "We need someone WASPy, who gets under Jerry's skin, to convert to Judaism and abuse the 'in-group' privilege. Whatley!"

Tim converts to Judaism and immediately starts making Jewish jokes. When Jerry looks at him askance, Tim says, "Jerry! It's our sense of humor that sustained us as a people for three thousand years."

Jerry sneers. "Five thousand."

Tim: "Five thousand, even better. Okay, Chrissie. Give me a schtickle of fluoride."

The fact that Tim had been Jewish for a few days, and he was already telling Jewish jokes, offends Jerry not as a Jew but as a comedian. Hilarious.

In a famous sequence from "The Jimmy," Jerry is distressed to see that Whatley has *Penthouse* magazines scattered in his waiting room. It's a dentist's office! Then, with Jerry in the chair, Tim says that his regular hygienist is at Dr. Sussman's. "We find it fun to *swap* now and then," Tim says saucily, sleazily.

Later, as Jerry wakes from the gas, he has a sense that his hygienist and Whatley have molested him. Was his shirt untucked before he went under? He can't remember. Between the *Penthouse* magazines and the untucked shirt, Jerry suspects Whatley is a dental Caligula.

We rehearsed that scene, and then the other actors went on to do another scene. I stayed behind to get comfortable on the dentist's office set. An electrician was adjusting a light, and he called down, "Hey, you know what would be funny?"

I was a bit confused. Was he talking to me? "What?" I asked.

"It would be funny if before you put the laughing gas mask on Jerry, you took a hit off it yourself."

I thought about it and realized he was right.

It came time to shoot the scene. We were rolling, and I said, "Cheryl, would you ready the nitrous oxide, please?" She handed me the mask, and I brought it up to my face and took a healthy hit. Jerry fell over laughing. Larry David was beside himself with joy.

We did a ton of takes. The director, Andy Ackerman, kept saying, "Jerry, you cannot laugh." But every time I took a hit off the mask, Jerry lost it, and then everyone else would have to laugh. Finally we got one take where Jerry wasn't sliding out of the chair. That's the one we used. That's the only take in which he didn't lose control.

In the end, when everyone was telling me what a great idea the nitrous hit had been, I pointed out the electrician who told me to try it. Everyone turned to see who it was. The electrician shrugged sheepishly.

You never know who's going to give you the gift of a good idea.

Lt. Gordon Denton

Brooklyn South seemed like a good job on paper. The show had accomplished writers, smart people, a talented cast. Steven Bochco was executive producing. David Milch of *NYPD Blue* fame was running it. He was a nice man. Extremely bright.

I auditioned with a well-constructed two-page monologue supplied by the show and got the job. My character was an internal-affairs officer. His job was to investigate other cops, weed out the bad apples: Where were you on the night of so-and-so? The cops would reply with uncooperative shrugs. And then my character would embark on a soliloquy showcasing his powers of conjecture and deduction. He had a lot to say. I knew when I got the job that my character was going to be driving every scene. I knew I'd have to put in the hours and prepare.

I called to ask about my script a week before my start date. I was told there was no script yet. Tuesday, Wednesday, Thursday—still nothing. Maybe I'm not working Monday? I called. "Am I working Monday? I need the script."

"Yes, but don't worry about it. We'll send you sides." Sides are extracted scenes. I waited for my sides all day on Saturday. Nothing. Maybe I was going to be filming establishing shots. Maybe I'd be sitting in the courthouse in silent contemplation. Maybe I shambled into the police headquarters and stared into the distance, trying to crack a case.

Sunday came. All day: nothing. Sunday night I was preparing to go to bed early to be ready for my 6:00 a.m. call, and the fax machine started buzzing. This was back in the days you had to take scissors and cut the pages as the roll of waxy paper unspooled. A scene with a huge block of dialogue rolled out. Then another scene—same thing. All my dialogue. All my words. I had to memorize all *this* in the few hours before I had to be on set. Sleep well!

I read the sides. "Hopkins comes down." Who is Hopkins? Another cop? A snitch?? The show wasn't on the air yet, and it was the nineties—before the days when they could just send me a link. I wouldn't have time to memorize the lines or the benefit of understanding what I was saying. I slept with one eye open.

The next morning I woke up bedraggled. We shot the first scene, and a script supervisor read out the lines I "forgot." I was constantly calling, "Line?" It was tough going right off the bat.

I was never comfortable. Never relaxed. No one can do good work if they're not relaxed.

I told Jon Tenney, the star of the show: "I'm dying here. I can't get my nose out of the sides." I think we were shooting episode twelve, and I was supposed to go right to the last episode of their first season, from twelve to twenty-two. I said, "Jon, I can't go on like this. Where is the script?"

Jon said: "We haven't seen a script since episode four."

I met series regulars and they introduced themselves to me. I said, "I don't mean to be rude but I'm just trying to stick to learning your character's name because that's what I need to know right now." That's all I could handle.

I remember driving up to work one cold morning. I came to a stop at the guard shack, an impossibly little box barely big enough to fit a chair and a guy. The guy poked his head out of his window and checked my decal and waved me through. "Go ahead." But I stayed there looking at him for a couple of beats. He was freezing, blowing on his hands to keep warm. I thought: *I wish I were you.* I'd rather be in there than have to go act in this other impossibly little box. I'd rather be a teenager earning $3.85 an hour.

Five days in, I was toast. Robin was worried about me. "You should quit," she said. She'd never said anything like that before. She'd never seen me like this before. I called David Milch's office and asked to speak to him but didn't hear back. The next day I got a call from my agent's office. Milch's office wants to know what this is about. I told my agent what was happening.

The producers called me. "What's wrong?" I explained to them I couldn't do it anymore. I told them that I quit. "No, no, please.

We have you planned to go all the way through the end of the year," they said.

"No, I quit. I'm hating this experience. After this episode, I have to quit." I wasn't under contract beyond the one episode I was doing, so it wasn't as if I was breaking an agreement.

"Bryan, it doesn't show. You look great in the dailies. You're not seeing what we're seeing. Everyone calls for lines on this show. It looks great!"

"It can't look great, because I don't know what I'm doing. I'm only focused on words—not what they mean. Not the character. You're forcing me to come to work unprepared. I've had a headache for a week. I'm not sleeping. I'm a nervous wreck. I can't continue."

This was one of just two times in my career when I was getting no joy from acting. It was painful.

The producers knew all the problems, and they commiserated. I suspect Milch was focused on *NYPD Blue* at the time, and so I think *Brooklyn South* suffered as a result. Whatever the reason, in spite of its promise, the show was a catastrophe. I knew it, and the producers knew it, but they needed to try to keep the show afloat. "Please stay," they said.

"No, I'm not staying. There's nothing you could pay me to do this again."

Then one producer said the perfect thing. He said, "It would screw the show. The other actors. Please, may we write you into one more episode and then we'll kill you off? Otherwise we're left dangling."

I relented. I said, "I'll do it on one condition. Get me the script a week before we start." Deal.

I was emphatic: "One week before we start."

He said, "You'll have it by Monday."

I'd film two more episodes. At least I would hope to prepare for my last one. The penultimate episode was business as usual. My eyes were bloodshot. I couldn't shake my headache. I couldn't even remember simple things. I was going to crack. On the seventh or eighth day, I asked them to give me cue cards. They said, "We've never used cue cards before. I don't think David will go for that."

At this point, I didn't care what David or anyone else thought. Give me the cue cards. Now instead of looking into the eyes of other actors I was giving a speech to a piece of poster board; I was reading dialogue—not acting. I was faking it. I had no choice.

Working in that kind of chaos? James Sikking, another actor on the show, described it well. He said, "Our wings were clipped." Without time to prepare, we weren't able to do much more than remember a single line—if we could even do that.

I finished that episode, and I asked the producer who made me the promise: "Do you have something for me? The script for the next episode?"

He didn't. He didn't keep his promise. He *couldn't* keep his promise. I fault him for making a promise he knew he couldn't keep. I fault myself for being so obtuse and gullible.

Despite the broken deal, I shot the next episode. My last. Fortunately, there wasn't much dialogue. My character was in a locker room alone, and boom. No more locker room. No more Lt. Gordon Denton.

Lance

My dad never gave up. He was always writing another screenplay, another novel, dreaming up another business venture. His dreams kept him alive. To achieve a dream would be great, but what was important was to have a dream. That's where hope came from.

It's more important to have a dream than to achieve a dream. That theme was at the heart of a movie I wrote and directed in 1998. *Last Chance.* I intended the movie as a kind of love letter, a gift, to Robin. I wrote a character I could imagine her sinking into and exploring. I loved the idea of collaborating with her, creating something together. I knew she could give a poignant, riveting performance, and she did.

Robin's character was a woman who felt powerless and without choice in her life. She'd been buffeted by disappointment, so she'd lost hope. She was married to my character, Lance, a high school football star whose best days were behind him, who never made good on his potential, an underemployed, immature man-child. Perfect role for me. They lived in a remote section of the California desert, the fringe of the fringe, and my character always leaned on his small town's lack of opportunity to justify his inability to succeed or move forward. My mom, in part, inspired that facet of my character. She was one of those people always looking outward to find comfort and joy, and excuses, rather than looking within. Mom would point at this boyfriend or that happenstance to explain why her life had ended up in such tatters. Someone or something was always to blame for her disappointments.

Robin's character was a waitress at the Last Chance Café. She worked hard and bore the burdens of waning possibilities with a quiet grace. She didn't see much hope for change, but she was pragmatic: "I don't know what daydreaming does. It doesn't help you get your work done. Daydreaming gives you false hope."

But things changed for her when a truck driver's rig broke down and he had to stay at the motel where she worked. He told her, "I don't believe hope can be false—you either have it or you don't."

That simple message shifted her perspective. And a shift in perspective can change a life. Hope can create possibility. Options are always available to us if we stand back and look at things differently.

I believed in this movie and worked hard to get it off the ground. The shoot got pushed back several times. We had some great actors lined up and then a few had to drop out because bigger jobs came along. We were set to do the shoot in the spring, and then I got a job, a commercial, a big payday, so we moved the dates again. April is tolerable in the desert. July is a bitch. But we couldn't delay it any longer, so at the height of summer we headed to Pioneertown, an Old West motion picture set built in the 1940s on remote, sun-scarred, desolate land in Yucca Valley, California. All the actors stayed at the one motel there, and Pappy & Harriet's Pioneertown Palace catered our meals. The motel and the bar also became our main sets.

We were on the tightest shoestring budget: $300,000. That might sound like a lot of money to some, but it's crazy low to get a movie made if you're shooting on thirty-five-millimeter film. We bought short ends (partial rolls of unexposed film), leftovers from big-budget movies. We'd load those in the camera when we knew the scene was short. We economized in every way we could.

Robin insisted on staying apart from me because she thought it would be good for her character. Plus, given that I was acting and directing and producing, my hours were insane.

Robin's room was immaculate. Doilies. Tea. That's what her character was: orderly.

My room was the opposite. I was grinding, up at all hours of the night, sleeping here and there, completely immersed. I was joyful in chaos. And my personal dishevelment happened to be perfect for the character.

It turned out to be perfect for something else, too.

Patrick Crump

I didn't even have time to shave when I got back from the desert. The clock was ticking. I had a couple of weeks to edit *Last Chance* before I ran out of money. Unshowered, unkempt, I began working around the clock.

Three days in, I got a call from my agent: "I know you just got back. I know you've got a time crunch editing the film. But there's an audition for *The X-Files*. A good part for you."

Robin and I had rolled the dice and put in $150,000 for *Last Chance*. We'd raised the rest from friends and family. I had a five-year-old daughter. I was broke. Of course I was interested.

My agent told me the character was a backwoods anti-Semitic loser. I looked in the mirror. Greasy hair. Badass Fu Manchu mustache. Red-rimmed eyes. I think I can handle that, I said.

I auditioned and got the job. The episode was called "Drive." I played Patrick Crump. The story was this. Besides being a despicable hick, he had a piercing, constant headache, and the only way to ease his pain was to drive west at a minimum of eighty miles an hour. If he didn't keep driving west, his head was going to explode.

Crump's wife had already succumbed to that horrible fate at the beginning of the episode. Mulder (the dryly hilarious David Duchovny) gets into the car with me (I don't remember how that worked without my head exploding) and drives toward the setting sun. Unfortunately for Crump they start in western Nevada, and you know what happens if you keep driving west across America: you eventually run out of real estate. RIP Patrick Crump.

Crump couldn't have been worse company for Mulder. He is racist, abrasive, loathsome. Most writers on television at the time would have sanitized Crump, made him sweet and sympathetic, allowing the audience to root for the series star to rescue the nice man from death. But the writer of this episode imbued Crump with negative characteristics that forced Mulder into a moral quandary: *Is this man worth saving simply because he's a human being?* That question put an emotional and intellectual dilemma right in the heart of the drama, and forced the audience to ask, *What would I have done?*

That was my first taste of the subtlety and brilliance of Vince Gilligan, who wrote that episode.

Vince felt that in order to prevent the audience from completely turning its back on the story, Crump had to retain some shred of humanity despite his odiousness. He wanted to find an actor who could both play a villain and elicit the audience's sympathy when he died. Someone you could, somehow, someway, both love and hate. For whatever reason, he thought that was me.

I enjoyed it. A lot. But my mind was foremost on my film, and the *X-Files* paycheck allowed me to keep the lights on while I finished it.

Vince and I were friendly and expressed our mutual appreciation. But as far as I knew then, that was the last time I'd ever see him. I did the job and moved on.

Auditioner

Many more TV pilots are shot than aired. And even those shows that make it to air stand a high likelihood of getting canceled early. I believe around 65 percent are axed. It's as speculative a business as opening a restaurant. Maybe more so. If you get a job on a new show, you hope the show catches fire, but you never bank on it.

In the nineties I got a job on the *Louie Show* with Louie Anderson, Paul Feig, and Laura Innes. We got half a dozen shows done before CBS canceled us. Diane English was our producer; she'd created *Murphy Brown*, and she'd never missed a taping in the show's eleven-year run. She was absent from the *Louie Show* for half of the six episodes. She and Louie did not get along.

As funny and caring as Louie was, he was troubled, and he wasn't ready to lead a show back then. It was difficult for him, and by virtue of that, it was also difficult for the rest of us. We never got through a scene without stopping. Whether it was rehearsal or taping night, we never got through anything without stopping. Not once. No rhythm, no cohesion—we were destined for the chopping block.

Another show was shooting next to us on the same studio lot; their star dressing room was next to Louie's. Tradition had it that while the audience filed in, the cast would assemble in the star's dressing room and quickly run lines to stay sharp and energized for the show. The other show was on the same schedule as us, so when we were doing our "speed through," so were they. We were halting and tentative with our material—all the while we'd hear their uproarious laughter. We wondered what was so freakin' funny. We were so upset about our own situation that we took to jealously putting the other down. "Who's going to want to see a show about aliens coming to earth?"

The answer turned out to be: a whole lot of people. *3rd Rock from the Sun* went on to become a big fat hit. We did not. I knew we were dead in the water when I read on the front page of the *Los Angeles Times* entertainment section that Louie Anderson didn't like his new show.

I eventually guest-starred on *3rd Rock*, and told their cast how much we used to hate them at the *Louie Show*, all the vitriol we spewed toward them. We had a good laugh. I was happy to finally be able to find the humor in that experience. I hadn't found much joy in the *Louie Show* while it was happening.

That's how it was for a long time. I'd shoot a pilot, and maybe if I was lucky, do a couple of episodes, and then the show would fizzle. Or I'd audition and come so close I could feel it. And I'd lose the part to some other actor.

The process of auditioning for TV pilots is a petri dish for self-doubt. When you test for a pilot at a network, you wait and you wait for them to call your name. When they finally do, it's common to walk into a room and find twenty people in really nice business attire staring blankly at you. A few hellos, and it's show time. Act your ass off on command. Typically, they consider a minimum of three actors for each role, but it can be up to eight. It's nerve-racking, and it's over before you know it. Out you go to wait for the next guy to step to the plate, then the next. When everyone has been in once, you're usually asked in again for round two of the same scene or scenes, but only after sitting in the waiting room, dissecting your audition, thinking about all the things you'd change if you had the chance to do it again. Or maybe you're pleased with the work. But your competition is there, too. By the water fountain. And he seems pleased with *his* work! You sit, trying not to seem nervous. You even smile at your competitors as if to wish them good luck. What you're really hoping is that they break down and confess: I screwed up. I was awful.

But no one says a thing. We're actors. Looking confident under pressure is our stock-in-trade. You look unbothered. Cool, even. Inside, you're wondering: *Am I any good?* You're staring at the door. They're discussing your fate behind that door. It could be five minutes, it could be half an hour before the door swings open and the casting director appears and offers a boilerplate: Thank you. Everyone was very good. You're all free to go.

And just like that, it's done.

You collect your things and go home, your mind racing. *Did they find their guy? Did they think we were all terrible? Will they have to cast a wider net to find the actor they want?*

Ah, fuck it. You may never know. You could get that call from your agent saying, Congratulations! You got it! Or, more often than not . . . nothing.

That's the life. That's why talent alone doesn't cut it. If you want to be a successful actor, mental toughness is essential. Lay your whole self-worth on getting the role, on the illusion of validation, before long you're left angry, resentful, and jealous. You're doomed.

From the time I got back from my motorcycle trip in 1978, I knew I wanted to make my living as an actor. Rejection is part of that living. It comes with it, like rain on the Blue Ridge Parkway. You can sugarcoat it. You can use a euphemism if you wish. But the bottom line is that sometimes they are simply not going to want you. And if they do want you, they may fire you. *We're going in a different direction.* Or they say with what seems like sincerity "Let's keep talking," and then never call you back. Or they tell your agent, in a polite way, that you sucked. Or that you're great. "Wow! Fantastic! Really. He's perfect for this. We'll be in touch." And then . . . crickets. There are a lot of crickets in this business.

Early on, after an audition, I'd wait by the phone, wringing my hands. And then when I heard I didn't get the part, I'd marinate in disappointment and introspection. *Could I have done something differently?*

But about twenty years ago something changed. I'd gotten to a place where I didn't feel any of that negativity. No more post-audition self-laceration, no more competition, no ill will toward anyone else. I made a switch in the way I approached the process. The switch seemed simple enough once I understood it, but it took me years to achieve that understanding.

Early in my career, I was always hustling. Doing commercials, guest-starring, auditioning like crazy. I was making a decent living, but I confided to Robin that I felt I was stuck in junior varsity. I wondered if I had plateaued. Ever thoughtful, my wife gave me the gift of private sessions with a self-help guy named Breck Costin, who was really wonderful with actors and other creative people.

Breck suggested that I focus on process rather than outcome. I wasn't going to the audition to *get* anything: a job or money or validation. I wasn't going to compete with the other guys.

I was going to *give* something.

I wasn't there to *get* a job. I was there to *do* a job. Simple as that. I was there to *give* a performance. If I attached to the outcome, I was setting myself up to expect, and thus to fail. My job was to focus on character. My job was to be interesting. My job was to be compelling. Take some chances. Serve the text. Enjoy the process.

And this wasn't some semantic sleight of hand, it wasn't some subtle form of barter or gamesmanship. There was to be no predicting or manipulating, no thinking of the outcome. Outcome was irrelevant. I couldn't afford any longer to approach my work as a means to an end.

Once I made the switch, I was no longer a supplicant. I had power in any room I walked into. Which meant I could relax. I was free.

In advance of an audition, I'd read the script, suss out what was expected. The character is going to murder his coworker, so there's probably some rage and frustration and fear of getting caught. My job is not just to deliver those expected feelings, but to find something interesting and unexpected, maybe some barely contained glee or mania or righteousness.

I learned to take control of the room. If I felt the scene called for the two characters to be standing, I might ask the casting director to please get up. "What? Get out of my seat? Oh, uh, okay." The casting director gets up, and now we're at eye level. Or if the objective was intimidation, I'd get close. That shift in physicality is visceral. It changes the power dynamic. We are accustomed to keeping a certain distance in professional settings. Cheating that, even if it's just by a few inches, provokes a reaction.

Of course I didn't always get the job, but that wasn't my intent anymore. What was important was I always left that room knowing I did everything I could do.

I had a basket at home. I'd audition and then toss the script in the basket. I'd forget about it. I'd let it go. You can't fake letting it go. You have to really genuinely detach from it.

If I'd get a callback, I'd fish out the script and say, "Oh, yeah. I remember this guy."

In 1999, I tested for another pilot at Fox, and my friend Corbin Bernsen got the part. I was able to say: "Congratulations, Corbin. I hope the show makes it." And I meant it.

Another pilot. It was at NBC. It came down to me and two other guys. I walked into a room of twenty-five people. I did the scene twice. We all did. We waited the wait. In the end the casting director came out and said to us: "We hate to do this . . . but we have to tell you now. We start to shoot on Monday." One of the other guys got it.

I said: Good for him. And I meant it.

Four days after that NBC test, I got a call about *Malcolm in the Middle*. They were looking for someone to play the dad. I read the script and it was excellent, really funny, really smart, but all you knew about the father was that he had a lot of body hair. I'm not hairless, but I'm not hirsute. There wasn't a lot more to go on with Hal. I read it again to see if I could find another way in.

The mother was more fully written. She was an alpha, a sergeant of arms, a lioness. She was fearless, strong, sharp, bombastic. I wrote all those things down. And then, on a whim, I wrote the opposite of all those qualities. *Fearful. Weak. Obtuse. Reserved.* I started to realize I was building a character. I was supplying what she didn't have, which was good for a marriage. Good for a comedy, too. I realized there was a lot of potential for humor in this character. It could be really funny.

I'd learned that if a character wasn't in the script, I had to infer it or imagine it. I had to take it on myself to build it. I came to the audition ready with ideas.

The writer gave me the template in the script, and I expanded that into a multidimensional person. Even in the half dozen lines Hal had in the pilot, I was able to find something. He was distracted by his family—not disinterested. When he was overwhelmed, he took a vacation in his mind. No one wanted to see someone who didn't love his family. But a man who is exhausted by his family? Almost everyone can relate to that.

They auditioned me last-minute; they were already building the sets for the pilot. Because Hal was underdeveloped in the script, they were having a hard time casting him. All of which played to my advantage. But I wasn't thinking of my advantage. I was thinking of giving them Hal. I remember sitting in the office on a folding chair with set construction going on just outside, and Linwood Boomer, the creator of *Malcolm*, falling out of his seat laughing at what I did. I got the part.

After we shot the pilot, I got a call from Linwood. He told me that Fox picked up the show and it was moving forward. What he didn't tell me was that Fox wanted to reshoot the pilot and replace me. The network wanted to go in a different direction with Hal. They wanted to go away from me. I found out years later that Linwood told Fox—emphatically—no. He told the network I was Hal. Linwood fought for me. He believed in me. Everyone needs a champion, and Linwood Boomer was mine.

Composer

I'd been on the show for a year when I got a call from our music clearance office. "Hey, how you doing? Are you a member of BMI or ASCAP?"

"That's music, right?" I said.

"Yeah. It's for composers. Anyone who writes music for film or TV."

"No. Why?"

"Well, my job is to write down every second or half second of music. And every episode, I turn that list over to Fox to make sure we get clearance. "Happy Birthday to You"? Two ladies got very rich off that song."

"Oh, that's interesting," I said, "but, uh, why are you calling me?"

"Well, see, your character hums and whistles a lot. That's technically music, and I have to put it down as music. You might as well get paid for it as the author and performer, because someone else will get paid if you don't claim it. The money will just go to the studio."

"How much does it cost to join BMI or ASCAP?" I asked.

"Nothing," he said.

I called BMI and filled out the application, became a member, and after a few months I received a check for $242. I looked at the stapled connectors. Over the course of two years, it listed all the times I whistled and hummed. In the episode "Reese Joins the Army Part One," I whistled for a few seconds. I read across the page and there was the dollar amount. And then there were dollar amounts from all the countries the episode aired in. I made 49 cents in Bulgaria. For whistling.

Every quarter I would get a check for a couple hundred bucks.

One day, I'd whistled in an episode, and I told the crew, "Hey, you know what? I just made some money. Any time I whistle or hum they pay me."

"Get out of here," they said.

"I'm serious. They pay me." I brought in a check stub and showed them. I said, "Every time I get a check, I'm going to throw a party. Open bar, poker, strippers." All true. Except for the strippers. It was a family show.

The producers said to me: "You're not humming anything we have to pay for? Are you whistling a specific song?"

"Please," I said indignantly. "You think I'd plagiarize? I create my own songs. All original."

A camera assistant friend looked over the scene one day and he approached me and said, "Before Lois comes in the front door, you're under the sink fixing the garbage disposal, and . . . I was thinking. Maybe that's a good time for you to be whistling?"

"Great idea, Jim."

I think he just wanted a party.

Hal

It became a running joke among the *Malcolm in the Middle* writing staff: What won't Bryan do? We already know Bryan will run up and down the street in his floppy tighty-whities. Will he drink a morning shake that consists of raw eggs, raw ground meat, soy powder, and juice? Sure. Will he wear a coat of live bees? Not just a bee here and there, mind you. We're talking a second skin of bees. They didn't want to write it if I wouldn't do it.

So they asked me: are you allergic to bees?

Nope.

Will you do it?

Absolutely I'll do it.

Then the writers worked backward. They reverse engineered the story. How could Hal get himself into that position?

Malcolm and his Krelboyne classmates are entering a battling robot competition. The boys are arguing about what type of robot to build as Hal passes by. His interest is piqued. "Go ahead and play, and I'll get you started here," he says.

"Dad, what are you doing?"

Hal has a lightbulb moment: "We've already had bots with chains. We have never had an empty-cavity robot. *We've never had a robot with . . . bees!*"

Hal is up all night with his creation, tinkering, testing, trying to figure it out. Suddenly he notices a laser pointer on him. Oh no. An army of bees swarms out of the machine and blankets him.

I've always liked bees. My grandfather had bees on his farm. And from that experience I knew that bees are quite docile. Bees will only land on you for two reasons. One: to rest. Two: they mistake you for a flower. So even though I'd have fifty to seventy-five thousand bees on my body, I wasn't scared.

Still, we had to prepare carefully to get the shot. The bee experts made sure that my long-sleeved shirt was tucked in. They duct-taped it at my wrists and then taped my pant waist and cuffs. They taped down my collar from the inside. They put cotton in my ears, so the bees couldn't crawl in.

The queen bee emits pheromones, chemical messages, to her drones, her worker bees. Pheromones bond the drones to the queen; they give the colony a sense of being "queenright." So now with a little eyedropper the beekeeper doused my arms and torso with pheromones, my hair and my ears and my chest. I was a bee magnet. I was their queen.

Once I set a position I wasn't going to be able to change it. Seventy-five thousand bees don't give you a lot of mobility. I picked a comfortable position. Standing. Knees loose. I was ready. The beekeepers were ready. Cameras ready. The beekeeper used a non-toxic smoke to make them mellow. Smoke relaxes bees. He opened the boxes and took out a screen full of bees, and then with a big scooper he gently lifted the bees off the screen and placed them on my waist. The beekeeper instructed me to let them maneuver. Let them find their own route. They did. They crawled up. I was soon covered in bees. The beekeeper warned me to keep my breathing steady, remain calm. It turned out there was no need. I discovered that being covered in bees was like sitting in a vibrating chair at a Brookstone store, warm and rather soothing. I completely let go. I closed my eyes.

In the scene, I had to turn around. As I moved, a bee crawled between my legs. I said, "I think I got stung."

The beekeeper was at the ready, waiting to flick the bee away. "Where did you get stung?"

"In my nuts."

He paused. "Sorry," he said. "Can't help you there."

We got the shot. Everything good. People applauded. The bee expert explained that to get the bees off me they'd reload the pheromones onto the screens, and I was to squat as low as I could and then jump up. When I landed, half the bees would fall off and then follow the pheromones onto the screens and into the boxes. The beekeepers would gently whisk off the rest with a broom. They'd lose a few, but it would be fractional.

I got stung again when they were whisking the bees off. It wasn't too bad. But I knew from the horror on everyone's face how monstrous I looked. After all the bees were back in their boxes, Linwood walked over. "Remember when I said I wouldn't ask you to do anything I wouldn't do?" he said. "I wouldn't do this."

As Hal, I was strapped to the front of a city bus like a bicycle. I spent a hell of a lot of time dancing around in my tighty-whities, including one episode where I sang a song and danced a dance in praise of bacon and its effect on my body. I was doused with water balloons. Fake bird shit plopped on my head. I was covered in blue paint head to toe—everything but my eyeholes. Hal is depressed in that episode, so he takes a painting class, and he paints himself blue—his "blue period"—and splats his body against the canvas. Except for a modesty patch, I was entirely nude, so they turned up the heat onstage. The human body regulates heat through pores. If you close off the pores, you cut off the ability to regulate. Covered in paint in a hot room, I slowly started to overheat and become disoriented. Before we finished shooting everything our director wanted, our producer, Jimmy Simons, called it off and rushed me into a shower to scrub off the paint so my body could regulate temperature again. It turns out painting yourself head to toe is dangerous. Live and learn.

I did roller-skate dancing. I trained for two straight weeks on roller skates—hours upon hours. I could shoot the duck, spin, balance on one leg, all kinds of things. The only thing I couldn't do was leave my feet. I tried a cartwheel once on my own, and my expert skating coach Greg Tallaksen said: "Don't do that again."

I loved *Malcolm*. I loved it. It was always: What's the next script? What do I get to do with this one? It was so much fun. We did 151 episodes over seven years—so much time to explore, to build a character, to develop a kind of symbiotic relationship with the writers. Once, after something happened to Hal, some big achievement, I said Hot-cha! Soon I saw it written in a script. Next thing you knew, the writers were making it a signature expression, a Hal-ism. And then I riffed on what they did. The relationship between actors and writers on a television show can really be a beautiful creative partnership.

Jane Kaczmarek, who played my wife, Lois, was also a creative partner. We had a wonderful TV marriage, a genuine intimacy. When we were in a scene, kissing or cuddling, we could hang out in bed and talk between takes, completely at ease. If you're going to work together over 151 episodes, it's nice to have a connection, a comfort, and Jane and I did. We were lucky.

And my boys were just that—my boys: Chris Masterson, Justin Berfield, Erik Per Sullivan, and of course Frankie Muniz. I shared a significant part of their lives growing up, and they were good kids one and all. And they made it through the gauntlet of life as child actors and became decent young men.

In the last episode of the series, Malcolm goes off to college. The shooting schedule called for filming the last scene last. (It's customary to shoot out of sequence.) When we finished that last take, not one member of the cast or crew had a dry eye. Seven years. We had become a family. And we didn't want to let it go.

Son

My mother was on her fourth marriage. The sequence of husbands was Easy, Joe, Peter, and then George. George was a lifelong smoker, thin as a rail, convivial, but not very bright. After my dad, my mother always chose men who made her feel better about herself. It was as if she wanted to play tennis with someone who wasn't as good as she was. She knew she'd always win if she were playing against a beginner. But in this context, what was winning?

Even decades after my dad split, my mother's anger always felt newly minted. She was angry over being left, angry over losing the love of her life. As a young child, I'd known her as a loving, fun parent; then, without warning, she became a bitter alcoholic stuck in the past.

As an adult I tried to have as much of a relationship with her as I could, but it wasn't easy. My mom dwelled endlessly on the ways she'd been mistreated by life. As for love, she was more about the men in her life than her children. Consequently, I saw her less and less.

George and my mom were living in Hemet, a town in Riverside County, way out in the desert, and they'd decided to move to Saint Louis because George's sister lived there. My sister, Amy, and I went to see them before they left. (My brother was living in New York by then.) We drove out to spend a couple of days and help them pack up their mobile home. We walked in and immediately knew something was wrong with George. His color was bad. He was gray. He said he had a chest cold. My sister, a nurse, shook her head and said, "George, you need to go to the doctor. When's the last time you went to the doctor to check on this cold?"

At the hotel later on, Amy told me. "He's dying."

Meanwhile my mother had severe sciatica. When she was driving, every so often her leg went numb and her foot got heavy on the gas pedal, flooring it. You crossed your fingers no one was in front of her at such moments.

So we convinced them to ship their car and take the bus to St. Louis. We said, "It will be *much* more enjoyable." They agreed, and we made all the arrangements and put up the money.

George and my mother set up house in Missouri. They were there not three months before he was diagnosed.

"It turns out he has *lung* cancer," my mother said, shocked. We were shaking our heads and thinking: *YEAH, he has lung cancer. He's a chimney!*

He died almost immediately, and she moved back to California. She needed more care and a place to live. I found an adult retirement community and moved her into a one-bedroom apartment. We started to notice she'd forget why she was in a room. Everyone does that from time to time, but she started to do it a lot. She was cooking something and forgot about it. She started a fire on her stove. We knew something wasn't right.

I went to visit my mother in her apartment. We were going out to lunch—nothing special—Sizzler or something. She was changing in the bedroom and taking an eon. I knocked. Mom? There was a meek *I'm fine* from behind the door. Finally, worried, I went in, and she had one arm through a twisted pant leg and the pants' waist was stuck over her head. She was trying to get her pants on over her head as if she were putting on a sweater. Here let me help you, I said. Those belong down there.

About the same time, I was asked to raise money and awareness at the annual Alzheimer's Walk. Leeza Gibbons, David Hyde Pierce, Victor Garber, and Shelley Fabares were there. All had parents afflicted with the disease. I got to talking about my mother and described some of her behavior. They said, "Those sound like the beginning symptoms of Alzheimer's. You need to go have her checked." They were incredibly helpful.

She did indeed have Alzheimer's. I called the Motion Picture & Television Hospital, a wonderful medical facility for members of the entertainment industry; actors, crew, production, and so forth are welcome. They had an Alzheimer's ward funded by Kirk Douglas and his wife. They told me they were changing their policy soon because of the demand, the flood of aging baby boomers. Soon my mother wouldn't be eligible.

We went through the channels and applied, and she made it under the wire and got a room. When we first got there, Sandy Howard, who had produced many movies, including *A Man Called Horse* and *The Island of Doctor Moreau*, showed us around the facility. Sandy was informative and gracious; we thought he was a volunteer. He wasn't. He was a patient who still felt the need to be needed.

The facility was beautiful. The patients could wander outside on walking paths and gardens; they could experience the open greenness of nature. Of course the openness was an illusion. Fencing and gates prevented them from walking off. Patients had the sense they could roam freely, but, for their own protection, they weren't truly free.

One day I got a call from the nurse practitioner, Susan. "Your mom is fine," she said. "But a situation has arisen . . ."

"What's going on?"

"Your mother is, well, a friendly person. And she has developed a relationship with another patient." Knowing my mother was the Blanche DuBois type—*I've always depended on the kindness of strangers*—this didn't surprise me at all. "They really like each other," the nurse continued. "It's very rare for Alzheimer's patients to have . . . amorous feelings." She paused. "I know this may concern you, Mr. Cranston," she said, having trouble finding the words. "We have . . . proof that they have . . . consummated their relationship."

"Oh?" I said. "What proof?" And then I thought better: "Forget that. I don't need to know."

"I'm sorry to have to tell you this. It must be very difficult for you to imagine your mother with someone other than your father."

Actually, it was easy to imagine. My mother had had scores of boyfriends. And several husbands.

"I do have one concern," I said.

"What is it, Mr. Cranston?" said the nurse, serious.

"What if she gets pregnant?"

Silence.

Then the nurse started cracking up, and I laughed, too.

"I'm thrilled," I said. "Do they know? Do they romance each other during the day and then forget each other at night? Is it like *Groundhog Day* every day?"

The nurse said, "To some degree, yes. There is a thread of recognition. They don't remember each other's names. But they recognize each other."

I was happy for my mom. She got to have a sweet romance late in her life: two lovers who discover each other anew every day. Every day a new man would pursue my mother. She'd have loved that.

It turned out her boyfriend was Albert Paulsen, an actor who'd been in *The Manchurian Candidate*, among many other films and shows, and I'm sure that his stature in Hollywood would have tickled her had she been still able to absorb such details.

I remember once Robin and I went to visit on arts-and-crafts day. My mother was sitting at a table with the other patients. Everyone was happily crafting away, but my mom had her arms folded across her chest. I could see right away she was stewing. We pulled up a chair next to her. What's wrong, Mom?

That woman in the red is trying to pick up my boyfriend, she said. We looked over. The woman in red was mono-focused on gluing her Popsicle sticks together.

We implored my mom not to be silly. But she insisted: The woman in red was trouble!

A few minutes later, Albert came in, and the woman in red brightened and swooned and called out to him: Yoo-hoo! Will you help me?

Robin and I looked at each other. Oh my God. The woman in red *was* trying to move in on Albert. My mother had lost a lot of her faculties, but not so many that she failed to notice this hussy moving in on her man!

My mother looked back on the years with my dad as her glory days, but I think the two years she spent in the US Coast Guard was the best time of her life. She had purpose, and she was so pretty, and she was making a paycheck.

After that, her aperture onto the world got progressively smaller. She narrowed her focus onto men. The right romance would save her. Through the years there were a lot of paramours. She was seeking a feeling of comfort with each guy. And she'd find it for a time. Then the guy would flitter off. So she'd find another one. She hated being alone. Being with someone—anyone—was better than being alone.

Through the years she had said, "Why don't I see you more?"

During an argument, I stupidly blurted out that the problem was she'd invested her time and energy in men rather than her children. "You got back what you put in," I told her. I regretted that.

She couldn't see or appreciate the love that was available to her. She had three children. All different. All with something to give. Our love wasn't the kind she hoped for, but it was what she had, and it was real, and she didn't nurture it.

Eventually she'd go from the Alzheimer's facility to intensive care and then on to long-term care, where she'd last another year. She died in August of 2006.

But there was a window of peace before everything started shutting down. Because of the Alzheimer's, she couldn't hold on to the pain and the resentment anymore. She got an illness that would not allow her to dwell in the past. And she was released. After she was diagnosed, we never argued again. Our conversations were simple, words you'd exchange with someone you felt comfortable with, but with whom you had no history of misalignment or pain. We'd smell a rose on her walking path. We'd feed the ducks in the pond.

"Look at that one. He's too fat."

"Let's not give him any bread."

Unemployed Actor

Sitting at a bowling alley, cheering on my daughter, I noticed my cell phone ringing. As the ball traced its glacial trajectory, I picked up. It was Peter Liguori, the president of the Fox Television Network at the time. I knew Peter well from my time on *Malcolm in the Middle*. He was smart, a nice guy. I liked him.

At the end of our seventh season on *Malcolm*, Fox told us not to break down the sets, not yet, a strong indication they were contemplating picking us up for another season. I loved the idea of one more year of hijinks as Hal. We knew word could come down at any moment. Then it did.

So now I found myself in a very familiar spot for an actor. I was without a job.

I had recently been offered two comedy pilots—both were for goofy dads. But I had just done seven years of goofy dad.

Taylor's ball completed its journey, nudging down several pins with a quiet clunk. After pleasantries, Peter said he wanted me to rejoin the Fox family. He was offering me a role in a pilot for the upcoming development year. The series was called *Nurses*.

Nurses was a sexed-up version of *Grey's Anatomy*—as if that show needed to be sexed up. Peter was offering the role of the head doctor of the emergency room at a Philadelphia hospital. To conveniently complicate things, my character's daughter was one of the main nurses on the floor. Drama ensued! The show, as far as the pilot script indicated, would follow the trials and tribulations of nurses balancing work and personal life. Oh, and apparently everyone—including my doctor character—had sex in this hospital. A lot of it.

After playing the hapless dad on *Malcolm*, the guy who, while shaving his chest hair with an electric razor, notices his pudgy stomach and breaks into song (*I'm so full of BACON, my body's made for SHAKIN', and when I start to WIGGLE, my nipples they will JIGGLE*), I wasn't exactly a sex symbol.

And now I was being asked to play a skilled doctor, a leader of men and women, a saver of lives, who happened, in the first episode, to have sex with an attractive associate on the desk in his office? At fifty years old, I was offered a role where I got the girl?

I was flattered.

Sadly, the *Nurses* script was, how should I put this? Shallow?

Over the years, I'd developed a philosophy, a way of choosing projects: *Follow the well-written word and it will not fail you.* Good writing is everything to an actor. Give Meryl Streep C-level material, and even at the top of her game, the best you can hope for is she elevates it to a B. Mere mortals might be able to stretch it to a C+.

As much as I appreciated the offer, I knew immediately *Nurses* was not for me. What I really wanted to do was a show called *Breaking Bad*.

My agent had called me about it a week before. He'd asked, "You remember Vince Gilligan?"

"No," I said.

"*The X-Files*?"

"Oh, yeah. I think. I'm not sure."

"He wrote this pilot script."

It had been eight years since my stint as Patrick Crump, but apparently Vince remembered me, and for some reason he felt I had the right ingredients to inhabit the main character of his new show.

I read the pilot script in one sitting. I was astonished. A-level doesn't do it justice.

You meet Walt on his birthday. He rises listlessly at dawn, exercises without enthusiasm on some sad little mail-order machine, chokes down the limp veggie bacon his pregnant wife has arranged in the shape of a "50" on top of his eggs. He goes to work. High school chemistry teacher. People once called him a brilliant scientist. Now he tries in vain to find one kid who might show interest, who might be semi-open to understanding what he's trying to convey. Chemistry is the study of change. *That's all of life.* It's the constant. It's the cycle. It's solution and then dissolution over and over and over. *Transformation. Reformation.*

No one gives a shit.

Walt goes to his second job at the car wash. He took it to pay for physical therapy for his son's cerebral palsy, which his insurance won't cover. Bogdan, his boss, treats him like a simpleton. Walt finds himself applying Armor All to the tires of one of his students. "Hey, Mr. White! Make those tires shine." On the way home, the glove box in the Walt mobile—a Pontiac Aztek painted impossibly flat avocado—won't stay shut.

He grimaces his way through a lackluster surprise party. Hello, hello, how are you? Boxed wine, passive-aggressive sister-in-law, dickish, emasculating brother-in-law bragging about his exploits as a DEA agent.

His wife is kind of neutral to his depression. She gives him the least sexy hand job in the history of mankind. She's multitasking, absently stroking while reminding Walt to paint the back bedroom and monitoring an e-Bay auction. Later she scrutinizes the credit card statement and scolds: Did you spend $15.88 at Staples last month?

Oh God, could it get any worse? It could. It does. Walt collapses at the car wash. Cut to the hospital, where the doctor asks accusingly, Are you a smoker?

No.

You have cancer. Inoperable. Best-case scenario—with chemo—a couple years.

He can't bring himself to tell his wife. He sits in his backyard and lights one match at a time, tossing each one into his filthy swimming pool. There's a chemical reaction that takes place when a match is lit: red phosphorous, sulfur, potassium chlorate. All of life is chemistry. He tosses another match into the water.

(I thought of the mossy green swimming pool of my youth. Mine. Bryan's.)

He goes on a ride-along with his brother-in-law Hank and sees a former student fleeing a busted meth lab. Jesse Pinkman? Huh—easy money in meth. Making drugs is really just chemistry. He could generate enough money to cover his medical bills, perhaps leave a little money for his family. He wants to leave *something* behind. We all do.

That was the first episode of *Breaking Bad*.

I'm not sure I knew what that title meant then, but the script was oh-my-God superb, the best hour-long drama I'd ever read. Great characterizations, complex plots, nuanced story elements, surprises that left you thinking: What on earth is going to happen next?

By virtue of the writing, I began dreaming about this character, this Walter White. I was waking up in the middle of the night with him on my mind. I recalled being back on the Blue Ridge Parkway, marooned by rain. I got so lost in an Ibsen play, the story and the characters, that I forgot about the rain. I can't describe how rare that is to find in script form. I can't explain how an actor longs for that richness and depth and humor and humanity to work with. To build on. This was it. I had no idea where the story was going, but I knew it was gold.

I had a meeting set with Vince the following week. I told my agents: "Make it sooner." I went into the AMC offices in West LA, knowing I was scheduled for twenty minutes, and ended up staying an hour and a half.

"Do you know how he should look?" I asked.

"Uh, kinda," Vince answered, smiling.

I ventured some of the ideas that had come to me since I'd read the script. "He's missed so many opportunities in life," I said. "You can see that in every part of him. He has a mustache that isn't manly. That isn't anything. You look at him and say: Why bother? His skin and his hair are the same bland hue. He wears pale yellow and sand and taupe. He blends into the background. Invisible. To society. To himself. I'm thinking he's doughy. One hundred eighty-six pounds."

I saw this character, this man, so clearly. I knew how he carried himself. Burdened. His shoulders were slumped like those of a much older man. I was imagining a man who carried himself a lot like my dad.

When I asked about his plans for the arc of the show, Vince told me in his genteel Virginia drawl, "I want to take this character from Mr. Chips to Scarface."

"So you're going to take this guy from good to bad?" I said.

He nodded and smiled slyly. "If they'll let me."

I couldn't believe it.

All television, to that point, had been based on stasis, characters you come to know and love. The prevailing thought for most of the history of television had been that viewers want someone they can count on. Archie Bunker. In every episode of *All in the Family*, he's consistently Archie. Jerry Seinfeld, same. Ross and Rachel, you see them in different situations—will they or won't they?—but they're invariably Ross and Rachel. Even the characters we've known to break new ground, like Tony Soprano. As genius and game-changing as that show and performance were, you didn't see Tony change a whole lot from the beginning to the end. Tony Soprano is Tony Soprano. Don Draper may change a little, but he basically remains Don Draper until the show's meditative finale, and even that's debatable. Some argue the workaholic adman was meditating not on the here and now, but on the creative for a Coke commercial. Classic Don.

Vince was proposing to blow up the model of a successful show. Walt would truly change. By the time the series ended, he'd be unrecognizable to viewers, to himself.

"You're really going to do that?" I asked again.

"That's the plan," he said, laughing.

"Do you realize that no one's ever done that in the history of television?"

Vince shrugged. "We'll see if it works."

I didn't know if it would work, either. But I knew I wanted in. I had to have it.

At home, I handed the script to Robin and I said, "Before you read this, know that it shoots in New Mexico." Whenever I really consider a role, if it's going to change our lives, Robin is a part of the decision-making process. If the show moved forward, I'd be away from home a significant portion of the year.

Robin read the pilot and saw what I saw. "Shit," she said. "You have to do this."

The network wanted to bring in five or six guys to test for the role. I was one, thanks to Vince. I heard the list also included Matthew Broderick and Steve Zahn. Walter White was a Jekyll and Hyde character. As talented as Matthew Broderick is, I'm just not sure that he has a Mr. Hyde within him. Steve Zahn? Yes, I can see that.

Vince was convinced I was the one. The network and studio said: "Bryan Cranston? The goofy dad from *Malcolm in the Middle*? I don't think that's what we're going for. Let's keep talking."

Vince said: "He's an actor. He can do different roles. That's what actors do." He sent the execs the Crump episode of *The X-Files*, and they saw I could be a different guy. I don't know if they fell in love with me, but at least they saw I wasn't a one-trick pony. They opened up to the idea of me.

Nevertheless, they implored Vince to please be reasonable and allow them to conduct a proper test, march a half dozen actors through auditions for a room of twenty-five people. They would certainly include me in that test, but also most likely they'd include Steve and Matthew, along with possibly Christian Slater, Paul McCrane, Adam Godley, John Carroll Lynch, and Henry Thomas.

If necessary, of course I'd do the test and try to earn the role. But it was a risk. Even if you knock a test out of the park, you never know who might come in there and hit it harder and farther. Or who might already have the edge because of past relationships. And then the role just slips out of your hands. It happens.

The actors I was up against were very good; any one of us could have gotten the part. I allowed myself to fantasize: *God, wouldn't it be great if they just offered me* Breaking Bad? *No test. No competition.*

And then I had a crazy idea.

I called for a meeting with my key agents at UTA, Brett Hansen and Kevin Stolper, and I said, "Is it possible to somehow float the information out into the Hollywood rumor mill that I have been offered the Fox pilot—*Nurses*?"

My thinking was that maybe, just maybe, if Sony/AMC heard that I had an offer on the table for another pilot, they would launch a preemptive strike and immediately offer me *Breaking Bad*. Maybe they would scramble to keep Vince Gilligan's first-choice actor. It was worth a try, right?

Brett and Kevin pondered for a few seconds and then said they knew a few people they could leak this to—*in confidence*. Wink. Wink.

That was on a Thursday. The casting director for the *Nurses* pilot informed UTA that I had until Tuesday to give them an answer. If I said no, they would need time to pursue another actor. A very reasonable request. I had five days before time ran out, but that included a weekend, so the clock was ticking. Friday came and went. No word. Was I too optimistic thinking gossip could travel that fast? This was before the explosion of Twitter and Facebook. Monday came. Silence. *Damn*. Tuesday arrived, and still nothing. *Oh well*.

I asked Brett and Kevin to call Fox at the end of the day and politely decline the *Nurses* offer. As nice as it was having my ego stroked by the offer to play a stud, *Nurses* just wasn't something I could look forward to getting up for every day at 5:00 a.m. It was a pass.

I turned toward preparing for the impending test for *Breaking Bad*.

And then, late Tuesday afternoon, Dawn Steinberg, the head of casting at Sony, called and offered me the role. No test. *Breaking Bad*, thankfully, unbelievably, was mine.

I never found out what happened, why they decided to forgo the test, whether my ploy had worked. I didn't really want to know. The role was mine. That's all that mattered.

I thought back to my movie *Last Chance*. Had I pushed the shoot even one more week, I wouldn't have been in town to audition for *The X-Files*. Had my character in *Last Chance* not looked pretty close to what they wanted for Crump, who knows? Had *Malcolm* been renewed for an eighth season, someone else would have played Walter White.

So many twists of fate and accidents of timing that seemed, in the moment, insignificant or unfortunate or even like rotten luck, and they all led me to this part.

Walt

They had an assortment of tighty-whities laid out for me in wardrobe. For seven years on *Malcolm*, I wore tighty-whities. I was determined not to wear tighty-whities on *Breaking Bad*. I didn't want to have a shtick.

I voiced my concerns to the costume designer Kathleen Detoro. Tighty-whities were in the script, but sure, no problem, they could get me some boxers, she said.

Then I paused. Vince wrote it for a reason. I called him. "Vince, do you remember why you wrote Walt in tighty-whities?"

"I don't know," he said. "I just thought it was a funny image: a man driving an RV in tighty-whities. Tighty-whities are funnier than boxer shorts."

Tighty-whities *are* funnier. That's why I'd chosen to wear tighty-whities in *Malcolm*. I happened to follow some of the boys' wardrobe calls, and they had kids' tighty-whities laid out, and Hal was just an overgrown boy after all, so it made sense that he'd wear boys' underpants.

I chose them for Hal. But Walt wasn't Hal. So why would I wear the same underwear?

Choices—even seemingly minor choices—matter. Details matter. Now I thought about Walt, and I realized tighty-whities were the right detail, the right choice, but for a different reason than for Hal. A grown man in tighty-whities can be funny; it can also be pathetic.

Building a character is like building a house. Without a solid foundation, a base, you're screwed. You're going to collapse. An actor needs a core quality or essence for a character. Everything rises from there.

I had a hard time figuring Walt out at first. I couldn't find a way in. It was frustrating. Sometimes that happens when I first approach a role. A character is outside of me. And then I go to my actor's palette—which is comprised of personal experience, research, talent, and imagination—and the base begins.

Pretty immediately, I had Hal's base. It was fear. Oh, he's everything Lois is not. He's afraid of being fired, spiders, heights. When something was wrong, Hal would show you what was wrong. He was easier to get. Once I had his core, the floodgates opened. Everything else came to me.

Walt was tougher. Walt was laconic. So it took longer.

I started to ask more questions of Vince. "Why is he a teacher?" Vince responded: "I don't know. My mother was a teacher. My girlfriend is a teacher. I just thought it would be the right thing for him."

I thought about it. Walt was brilliant. He was raised with everyone around him telling him: Sky's the limit. Straight As. Well liked. His teachers, his parents, his fellow students all said you're going to go far. You can write your ticket. You're going to be making seven figures. You could discover the cure for cancer.

Why didn't he? Why did he quit Gray Matter Technologies, the company he cofounded with his friend Elliot Schwartz, a company that could have made him rich? Did he fear failure? What if everyone you knew growing up said you were destined for greatness, you couldn't miss, and then you missed? That's not just failure. It's collapse. It's catastrophe. Maybe Walt was afraid of that. Maybe he just got cold feet. Maybe he got the yips.

And then I thought: How sly of him to teach. Why? That profession is unassailable. He could get away with saying: "I didn't want the corporate world. I wanted to give my passion to the next generation. I had a calling." Teaching *is* a calling for many people. But not Walt. He was hiding out. Had he become a truck driver, people would have criticized him. But a teacher? Untouchable.

What you're not given as an actor you must provide. So I started filling in blanks, and that led me to the why of it all, Walt's foundation. He was depressed. That's why I had trouble finding his emotional core. He had shut it down. He wasn't fearful. He wasn't filled with anxiety. He wasn't anything. Walt's foundation was that he was numb. His depression had deadened his feeling.

Of course there is a massive amount of literature on depression. I wasn't going to become an expert. I'm an actor, not a psychologist. But based on some research and thought and observation—I believe both my parents probably suffered from depression—it seemed to me that there are generally two ways depression can manifest.

One is externally. Your emotions spew everywhere. In the form of apathy: *I don't give a shit.* Or anger: *My ex-wife screwed up my life.* Or anxiety: *My boss is going to fire me.*

The second way is to go inward. You go silent or become antisocial or self-medicate. Or you implode. That's what happened to Walt. He imploded and then, *poof*, he became invisible. He was living a traceless life.

Once the character appears to me, everything else can blossom. Everything else becomes clear. The character is no longer outside.

He's within. When wardrobe asks me questions—"What about this jacket? These sunglasses? These shoes?"—I know all the answers. Hand me a Ralph Lauren shirt? No. No labels. This guy is Kmart all the way. Target is a treat. So let's get that sensibility.

Most costume designers want to work with nice materials. They want their actors to look good. I imagine there are a lot of actors who want to look sharp, not knowing or realizing that's not who their character is. But it's ridiculous to have a middle-class character walking around in Louis Vuitton. Fortunately, our costume designer, Kathleen, was right with me on that.

I'll shave my head, I'll be naked, it doesn't matter. It's far more important for me to be honest in the character I'm playing than to preen.

So I sank into Walt. I dressed badly. I gained weight. Every aspect of Walt was an expression of the fact that he'd given up. The chinos, the Members Only jacket, the Wallabees, the pathetic hair and mustache. Tighty-whities fit into all that. As the series progressed and Walt gained confidence, we went into other underwear and darker clothes in general. But at the outset, tighty-whities was it.

Though I knew the contours of Walt's journey, good to bad, Mr. Chips to Scarface, I never dreamed how riveting, how majestically compelling the show would be as it unfolded over the next six seasons, how it would change—everything.

And I never dreamed how hooked people would get on the show, how obsessed. But looking back, that was part of Vince's grand design.

The hook was set at the very beginning. Walt had gone to seed, but he was a family man, doing his best, living paycheck to paycheck like so many people in the world. At the outset, he was no more a murderer than you or me. He just wanted to do something for his family before succumbing to the cancer. He wanted to go out on *his* terms.

You were rooting for him to succeed. And then all of a sudden rooting for him to succeed meant you were rooting for him to make and sell crystal meth and get away with it. And then—*oh God*—he killed that guy. But that other guy was going to kill him. Of course he defended himself. You'd do the same.

By the time he let Jesse's girlfriend, Jane, die, you were fighting to spit that hook, but it was too late, it was set too deep. You were making excuses for him. You were equivocating, saying: "What else could he do? Kill or be killed." You were headed toward the abyss.

It's easy to take the high road when it's hypothetical, but Walt was dealing with excruciating questions in real time, and you the viewer were privy to his predicaments. You were inside. So you felt for him. You forgave him—even as he crossed the line, even as he was overtaken by a lust for money and power. Even as it became clear that he was being driven not by concern for his family's future but by ego.

Sometimes we were giving you more line, making you feel more sympathetic toward him. Other times? We were just reeling you in. By the time Walt poisoned a little kid, the moral gray area was gone, a dim memory, and the audience, had they been in their right minds, should have said: "Fuck this guy. He's nuts. He's evil." But it was too late. The allegiance had been built.

I heard so many people say—I still hear them—"I love you, but I hate you." Or: "I hated you. *But I couldn't stop rooting for you.*"

Keeping the audience off balance, rooting and hating, required meticulous thought, discussion, and design. That scene where Walt lets Jane die? That was not how Vince Gilligan first conceived it. He originally thought of Walt as a more active, aggressive murderer.

John Shiban wrote the episode, and Vince sent it to the studio and network. Walt looked with pure contempt at Jane for getting Jesse hooked on heroin.

BREAKING BAD #212

"Title TBD" WRITER'S DRAFT 9/17/08

EXT. JESSE'S DUPLEX - NIGHT (LATER)

Walt pulls up in front. Donald helped him change his mind; he's come back to talk some sense into Jesse. He knocks on the front door: *Open up, I want to talk to you!* No answer.

Walt goes around back and peers through the bedroom window - Jesse and Jane, lying on the bed, back to back on their sides, passed out high. So much for "positively no more drugs." Walt shakes his head, *Of course.*

INT. JESSE'S DUPLEX - BEDROOM - CONTINUOUS

Walt reaches in through the hole he made when he busted in at the end of episode 211. He opens up the door and comes inside. He sits down on the edge of the bed. He looks over at the duffel bag of money.

Now what? Take the money back? What if this girl's crazy enough to call the cops on me? Or do I just leave the money and go once and for all?

Next to him, Jane starts to cough, COUGH-COUGH, spit-
ting up some vomitus onto the bedspread. (NOTE: she
will remain unconscious.) Walt looks down at Jane. His
face clouds as he realizes: there is a third way. He
reaches over and softly touches her shoulder. A tender gesture, we might assume that he's comforting her.
That is, until he ever so gently . . . *pushes Jane onto
her back*.

Walt stands and steps away. Gravity does the rest as
Jane's vomit spills back into her trachea.

Guck-guck- GACK . . . guck-gack. . . . GACK! GACK! . . . GACK!

As she continues to suffocate, we RACK TO:

WALT THE MURDERER, backed up against the bedroom's
farthest wall, looking on.

END OF EPISODE

When I first read the script, I was shocked. There would be no
turning back after this. Walt had killed in the past, but his brushes
with violence could always be ascribed to self-preservation. Killing Jane would make him a murderer. Worse. Jesse was more than
Walt's partner, he was something like a son. And Jesse loves Jane. If
Walt pushes Jane onto her back, to her death? That would be the
most diabolical betrayal. I worried we'd lose the audience. It would
be hard to continue to root for the kind of man who'd do that.

I wasn't the only one shocked. The studio and network viewed the scene as a critical turning point in the devolution of Walter White, and they were concerned that at so early a stage in the central character's transformation—we were only in the second season—this murderous act would turn the audience against him prematurely and jeopardize the show. Too much too soon. They expressed their concerns to Vince, and he listened and came to agree. He devised a slightly less damning way for Walt to be involved in Jane's death.

Studios and networks have a reputation for diluting the creative process with their notes. Decision by committee. Conservatism rules. But extra eyes on a story line can actually be useful and generative, and throughout the run of *Breaking Bad* our studio and our network helped us make the story better.

Walt wasn't a cold-blooded killer—yet. He was a bystander. He had the chance to save Jane, but he didn't act. He hesitated. And he was shattered. That moment I saw my daughter's dying face.

One of the things that made the show so compelling was this lack of bright moral lines. No indisputable turning points. No easy answers. We put the moral burden as much on the audience as it was on Walt, implicitly asking: What would you do if you had two years to live? How would you do your life?

I'd been introduced to Vince's nuanced understanding of morality back on *The X-Files*. *Breaking Bad*, however, was a whole new level. Viewers had to decide for themselves what was understandable, given the circumstance, and what was flat-out reprehensible. And most likely it wasn't a specific moment but rather a series of moments that shifted allegiances and sympathies.

For me? Walter's moral decay doesn't begin when he watches Jane die. Killing Mike, Walter's onetime partner, doesn't mark a turning point, either. For me, the seed is sown in the very first episode.

Walter is dealt a bad hand. He's been living inside a kind of emotional dead zone, and, faced with a definitive prognosis—two years to live—he lets it all burst from his core: pity, anger, desperation. As time wears on, those initial feelings burn off and leave a toxic residue, a sludgy fuel that allows him to act with recklessness and hubris, to compromise everything he holds dear, to endanger the people he loves most: his family.

Character is both formed and revealed when we are tested, when we are forced to make decisions under pressure. That test can either make us stronger or it can highlight our weaknesses and crack us into pieces. Walt fails the test. I understand why—temptation, humiliation, wanting to feel like he'd really lived, like he'd really been a man, a desire to go out on his own terms, to control his own destiny.

But whatever the reasons, he fails.

The question for the show and the challenge for me as an actor was: How could we legitimize Walt's trajectory, make it believable and relatable? Walt couldn't suddenly go from meek depressive to heartless bastard who happened to poison a little boy.

The answer was to go slowly. We had to move with consideration; we had to sequence carefully. We had to take baby steps.

That's why serialized TV was the perfect format for the show. In a movie, we would have been forced to take great leaps, compress time, and truncate story lines. That cramming would have strained credulity. The audience would have rejected it.

The pace of *Breaking Bad* was deliberate. We incrementally pushed and tested you more and more. Did we lose some people? Maybe. You can't keep all of your viewers over the course of six seasons. But so many people were with us the whole way through. The show's numbers grew exponentially over the years, and they grew all over the world. Brazil and Germany and Australia. When we started, we were a cult favorite; at the end we were a juggernaut. They were selling Heisenberg hats, the uniform of Walt's dark alter ego, in stalls of souks in Morocco. They were hawking throw pillows stamped with his silhouette in São Paulo. In New York City you could buy rock candy dyed a lovely shade of aquamarine to resemble Walt's signature product, blue meth. In Albuquerque someone started a successful business touring *Breaking Bad* locations. For a long time, fans went by the "White household" in Albuquerque to throw pizzas on the roof, as Walt had done in one episode. Vince actually had to issue a public statement asking people to stop bothering Fran and Louis, the poor couple (who'd been so kind and accommodating to the whole cast and crew) who lived there. "There is nothing funny or original or cool about throwing pizzas on this lady's roof. It is just not funny. It's been done before. You're not the first."

The mania the show inspired was unlike anything I'd seen. The show wasn't for everyone, but I've rarely heard of anyone who watched casually, intermittently. Fans binged. The advent of streaming services like Netflix created the opportunity for people to shoot *Breaking Bad* right into their veins. Each episode seamlessly flowed into the next, and before people knew it they'd watched an entire season of the show in a few days. At a certain point, it felt like a whole *Breaking Bad* nation was wide awake at three in the morning, saying to themselves: *JUST ONE MORE*. People spent weeks glutting, gorging, and many, sleep-deprived, went a little crazy. The show put the audience in an almost Heisenbergian state. Out of control.

When Vince told me he was going to take the central character from good to bad, to be honest, I wondered whether audiences would go for it. In the end, they didn't just go for it. They were addicted.

Actor

Each episode of *Breaking Bad* was slated to take eight days to shoot. When you're employing a giant cast and crew and paying for locations by the day, you bleed money, and going over that time allotment is even more costly. Some shows go over their allotment because they're just starting up and don't have a routine yet or they're too loose in scheduling or they're dealing with setbacks or actor changes or weather issues or the sudden loss of a location. Shit happens.

But the reasons we went over our eight-day allotments on *Breaking Bad* were almost always story-driven. For instance, in the last season, we shot a complicated, visually powerful sequence in which Walt and his cronies rob a train. That episode took ten days. Shooting the train itself took two or three days. It wasn't a CGI train or a miniature train we made look big on screen. It was a real-deal behemoth locomotive. Resetting a train takes a lot of time.

TV shows are complicated—so many people involved, so many ways you can veer off course. Even your run-of-the-mill show is a beast. Trying to make a show that does something different, that takes chances, that ups the ante while remaining on schedule and within budget? Good luck trying to do all that and keeping everyone happy.

Scripts are written and shot at breakneck speed with very little room for error. If the people running the show are disorganized or if a member of the cast or crew is uncooperative, everyone's job becomes impossible. The chaos of *Brooklyn South* comes to mind.

Breaking Bad could have been the same way given its vast complexity and ambitions. It could have easily been a disaster, logjams and difficulties at every turn. But Vince assembled a masterful team. The organization was phenomenal, meticulous. And in the countless, countless hours of production and preparation that went into manufacturing the sixty-two hours of television that eventually aired, I had issues only a handful of times.

Early in the third season we were doing a scene. My wife, Skyler, had kicked me out of the house, and I was missing my kids, yearning to be with my family again, so I made the decision to move myself back home. When we rehearsed, Skyler entered the house, and instinctively I went to the baby.

The director and writer of that episode said: "No, no, we can't have you go to the baby." I was to have direct contact with the baby in subsequent episodes, and they didn't want to cannibalize the coming story line.

"That may be," I said. "But it's not what my character would do. No matter my sins and transgressions, in my heart I loved my children. I had been separated from my baby daughter. I was dying to see her. How could I just pretend she wasn't there? It wouldn't be true or honest."

We talked it over and figured out a workable compromise: just as I am going to the baby, Skyler intercepts me. The desire of my character is still there. Skyler's desire to keep the baby away from me is upheld. A good solution. And a good example of how the process can work. Not everyone agrees all the time, but if everyone tries to stay true to their character and what's best for the story, while maintaining patience and respect, a path will emerge.

Some actors come into work and wait to be told what to do. I think of my costar in *Barefoot in the Park* who needed to be told that she should express affection toward the man with whom she is madly in love. I suppose those actors can do well. But I'm not that kind of actor. I have a finite time on earth. I'm not interested in coasting through it. I want to be invested. An invested actor asks questions that may punch holes in the story or highlight contradictions in a character the writers may not have considered. Asking those questions might mean we have to rethink a beat in the script or redo the blocking. It might mean more work. And that might upset people momentarily. But in the end I'd rather do more work and get it right and give the finished product a richness and resonance that will last.

One day, during season three, we were shooting a scene: Skyler is angry with me and nagging me to sign the divorce papers. I delay and delay. I don't want a divorce. I am camped out in the baby's room, and Skyler passes by and picks up my dirty laundry and washes it. Then, she asks me to join the family at the table for dinner. A new development. After *that* I'm supposed to meekly sign my divorce papers? It didn't make sense.

"I'm sorry," I said, "I can't imagine signing these divorce papers. Why would I do that? I'm invited to join the family at the dinner table. *My wife did my laundry*. If the marriage were really over, would my wife wash my clothes? If she's separating my colors from my whites and inspecting my dirty socks, isn't there *hope*? If there is hope, why would I then choose that moment to finally give up? I'm desperate to save my marriage."

I told the writers I understood I needed to sign the divorce papers for plot purposes. I wasn't objecting to signing them on principle—just signing them under those particular conditions. We worked through the problem. The laundry scene was cut. And the writer adjusted the tone at the dinner table so that, yes, I share a meal with my family. But my son, Walt Jr., played by R. J. Mitte, goads Skyler into inviting me there. Skyler doesn't want me. Yes, I'm in the house, and cordial words are exchanged, but when I look at her I see she's hardened. I feel her chill. She's not getting over this. The distance between us now seems unbridgeable.

After those changes I could see waving the white flag. I could imagine signing those papers.

The collaborative process works well when everyone is communicating. That doesn't always happen.

Another time we shot a scene in my attorney Saul's office. Skyler has discovered my secret life and she's meeting Saul (played by Bob Odenkirk) for the first time to discuss the details of the meth empire I've built. Skyler has an accounting background, and she rationalizes: Well, I don't like the fact that this is going on, but if it's going on, I should be involved; I might even be able to help, make sure all the numbers add up.

Saul is perched on the edge of his desk close to Skyler, who's wearing a low-cut blouse. Saul hadn't expected Walter's wife to be so . . . hot: "Walter never told me how lucky he was." Then Saul catches himself—*these are clients*—and goes skulking back to his chair. I see Saul leering at Skyler, and I feel suddenly protective of my wife. Skyler is aware of the situation and gives me a look: I can handle myself.

Working together, the actors and director built this moment. We all felt we'd given the scene as it had been written a little texture while remaining faithful to our characters and the larger plot. We blocked the scene and then went off while the crew began their work.

Unbeknownst to us, as we were working out the scene, the episode's writer was calling Burbank, calling the writers' room. Vince decided he didn't want Saul to be flirtatious or to even come close to Skyler in the blocking. But no one discussed that decision with the actors. When we were summoned to the set to shoot the scene, we were told that the blocking had been changed. No conversation. Just: This is how it's going to be.

They had usurped our jobs as actors. Extremely disrespectful. I was furious and had to blow off some steam on a walk.

The producers came to my dressing room. "Here's the problem," I said. "The writers are making decisions on blocking in a theoretical world eight hundred miles away in California. Meanwhile, in Albuquerque, the actors and directors are charged with taking their words and descriptions sincerely and mounting the scene. We take the theoretical to the practical. That's the actor's job. We bring your words into the third dimension. At a certain point, a writer needs to let go. A writer needs to say: 'I trust the actor to carry the ball forward.'"

We had built that scene into a true triangulation. Each of our characters had something to react to and there was room for discovery and spontaneity and surprise. We liked it and felt we had created a great and legitimate interpretation of the script as it was written. And if it didn't work, that's what reshoots are for.

Had Vince and the writers seen what we had come up with— the fleeting moment that Saul was distracted by Skyler—I honestly believe they would have loved it. But Vince just heard it described secondhand and made a judgment. It also seemed to me that the writers had a basic misunderstanding of our roles. The actor's job is to interpret the script. Instead of letting us do our jobs, the writer acted like a spy, an adversary. The problem was less about the changes to the scene and more about how they came about.

Ultimately, we actors acquiesced. The scene turned out fine— slightly weaker, to my mind—but fine. Perhaps it seems like splitting hairs, but these small decisions are meaningful. They add up. And aside from the end product, I think it's important that everyone on a set understands that everyone brings value. In this case, that didn't happen. I didn't like it, but I let it go and moved on.

And then it happened again. Hank, my DEA-agent brother-in-law (played by Dean Norris), is in the hospital with gunshot wounds, and the insurance won't pay for the expensive physical therapy he needs; the doctors are saying he could end up a paraplegic. I'm in the waiting room with Skyler and her sister, Marie, Hank's wife (played by Betsy Brandt). Skyler says to Marie: "Walt has the money to pay Hank's medical bills." For a minute, I think she is going to tell Marie everything. *Oh God.* A look of panic flashes across my face. But then, to my utter shock and . . . delight, Skyler comes up with an incredibly brilliant and elaborate lie that integrates shards of the truth and explains how we happen to have the tens of thousands of dollars needed to pay for Hank's treatment.

"Even I myself didn't understand the impact of Walt's diagnosis," Skyler tells Marie with wet eyes. "It wasn't just that he was facing death. He was faced with the devastating knowledge that he was going to leave nothing behind for his family. Less than nothing. He started gambling, Marie. He was good. He won. He paid for his treatment. We were suddenly rich."

The writer created a great scene, a powerfully layered emotional triangle. I react to Skyler's lie first with alarm and then shock and then almost a kind of pride that she would go to this length to cover for me. I see my wife in a new light . . . and I like it. Marie is in teary disbelief, grateful and incredulous that meek, quiet Walter is not only a degenerate gambler but also *capable* of raking in that much money. Skyler is in tears, too—the last months have been so taxing and stressful for her; even as she constructs this lie, she's overwhelmed by what she knows to be the truth: her husband has become a drug kingpin. He's become a stranger. The moment marked a milestone for each of these characters.

At first, Michael Slovis, our director, set it up the way it was described in the script: the three of us lined up in a row on a banquette seat, Skyler in the middle and Marie and Walt on either side. We tried it that way, and as Skyler spoke to Marie, she had to turn her head back and forth between the two of us as if she were watching a tennis match. I couldn't catch an eye with Skyler to react to the initial shock of her lie or to help her build it as she went along. Marie had to crane around Skyler to look at me. We all agreed it didn't work as written.

So Michael moved Skyler into a seat across from Marie, and he had me on a chair almost between the two sisters, forming a triangle. Now I could see Skyler tell her tale, and I could shift my eyes to monitor how it was being received, whether Marie was buying the lie, and Marie could easily look at me like, "Gambling?" In my body language and eyes I was able to shrug as if to say, *Uh, yeah*. Once we changed the seating arrangement, the scene became honest. It became fully realized. Off the actors went to allow the crew to do their work.

Wondering what was taking so long to set up a pre-lit hospital scene, I came back an hour later and our first assistant director was outside. I asked what was holding us up. She made a phone symbol with her hand. "They're calling Burbank on this?" I said. "How we reblocked the scene?" She nodded.

Goddamn it. That made me angry. I walked into the producer's office. The group was on the phone with the writers' room. Our director was in there trying to fight for what we had done. I said: "Is this conversation about the reblocking?" It was. I said to our director: "Michael, do you think it's the best thing?"

"Yes. Without a doubt."

"So do all three actors involved. That's the way we're going to shoot it. Let's go. We've got work to do." I was rightly or wrongly usurping control.

Vince was on the phone, understandably a little upset. He said, "If that's the way you're going to do it, there's nothing I can do."

I said: "Vince, that is the way we're going to do it, because it's best for the scene."

As an actor early in my career I didn't have the power or the confidence or the clout to emphatically and honestly state my opinion when I disagreed with the way things were going on set. Now I did. And I felt I did the right thing. The whole enterprise is about discovering the best way to tell the story. It's worth raising hackles on occasion when the integrity of the story is at stake. One disagreement doesn't affect the essential mutual respect Vince and I had for each other. We smoothed things out later in person. Our spat was not unlike a couple's argument. Natural. Predictable. Totally solvable.

Heisenberg

I meet Mike, my onetime business partner, with the intention of getting the names of the informants he's been paying off in jail. I need that list. Those guys are a threat to my enterprise. They have to be dealt with.

Instead of giving up the list, Mike is smug. He badgers me and tries to diminish me as a man. He tells me that my pride and ego have blown up the entire operation. He says everything would have remained good had I not tried to take over control. He says, "You didn't know your place!" He turns to leave.

My place?

The old me would have fumed inwardly and walked away, my pride and dignity shattered. But I've changed. I've become an impulsive, dangerous man. I'm Heisenberg, Walt's dark alter ego. His id. Heisenberg *takes care* of repugnant assholes like Mike.

So many people have asked me: How did you get there? How could you be *so* evil? Jonathan Banks, who played Mike, was so terrific that, in a way, it was easy for me; I had a solid actor to react to. His belligerence lit the flame. I also called on the time I'd been murderous. I conjured the rage and fear I'd felt when Ava was banging on my door. I didn't commit murder, but I believe I was close. It had been decades since then, but it was easy to summon the feeling. When it was time for Walt to kill Mike, I turned that old key.

After he insults me, Mike walks toward his car. I seem rooted to the spot. But then, suddenly, I'm walking. I haven't willed my legs to move; they're at the mercy of some automatic force. I'm standing at the driver's window, staring at Mike's face. Time comes to a stop. I fire. Done.

Mike's car rolls forward and slams into a boulder. Mike manages to get out and limp into the bushes. I follow a trail of blood toward the river and find him sitting there, on the banks of the Rio Grande, gazing blankly into the distance. He's still clutching his gun.

As we were rehearsing the scene, Tom, the writer and director of the episode, said that he felt I didn't need to keep my gun trained on Mike. But that didn't make sense to me. I said, "Mike's a known killer. He could raise his weapon at any time and shoot me."

Tom disagreed. He thought Walt would recognize that Mike was resigned. Mike knew he was dying, so he didn't pose a threat anymore. That argument went against my instincts, so I kept the gun on Mike until I removed his weapon from his hand.

We were working on location, with natural light. We didn't have a lot of time to argue about the script's fine points. When the sun went down, our day would be over. I knew that. But I couldn't help raising another issue. After Walt takes Mike's gun away, the script called for Walt to say, *I just realized that Lydia has the names. I can get them from her.*

"Why do I say that?" I asked.

"It's a shift of audience allegiance away from Walt," Tom said. I knew he was getting irritated with me, and he wasn't wrong. I was taking up time, the one commodity we couldn't replace.

"But you're going to get a shift of the audience's allegiance anyway because I just shot a very popular character. That's enough to sway them away from me." After Walt shoots Mike, he knows he fucked up. Saying he could have gotten the names from Lydia just makes him look like a huge asshole.

I understood they wanted not only to turn the allegiance away from Walt but onto Jesse. When we were together, partners, it was easy for the audience to root for us as a unit. As the rift grew between us, the allegiance was split. By the end of the series, the intent was to sway the audience from Walt to his former student.

But having Walt say to no one in particular, "You know what I just realized, I didn't need the names," that went against the sophistication of the show, the nuance of the character. Instead of savoring another emotionally taut and complex situation, you were left thinking: *what a jerk*. That's not where I felt the character should go. That's not where the *writers* wanted the character to go, in my opinion. I was afraid the audience would scoff, blanche, cringe. Much better to have Walt realize he let his impulses get the better of him, look with horror at Mike, who has collapsed, dead. *Oh my God. What am I going to do?* You'd still have the audience hating Walt's actions, but they'd be ambivalent about the man himself, on the razor's edge. The guy gives into his impulses, his ego. It's horrible, but it's human.

The muddy water of the Rio Grande trickled by. We were losing daylight. Jonathan Banks was getting upset. This was his final scene. He was going to die in this scene. And he was not going to have the time to do it properly. It wasn't fair to him. And it was my fault. I should have brought the issue up earlier. I wish I had. But it just didn't hit me until that moment. I felt I had to bring it up.

Feeling the pressure, I offered a compromise—I'd say the line, but as a function of Walt's anxiety. I still felt uncomfortable saying it even after I made that adjustment. So I wanted another take where I expressed my anxiety by pacing like a caged panther. Tom agreed. We shot the scene, and then I let it go. No hard feelings.

When the episode finally aired, I watched with Robin. We normally watched *Breaking Bad* together—though we mostly watched in daylight. She couldn't stand to see the show before bed. Night-mares.

I'd told Robin nothing of this dispute. I wanted to see how she would react without leading the witness. I trust her instincts. I respect her opinions. And I had a feeling I knew what was coming but I didn't know for sure. I still thought: *Maybe their way is the stronger choice.* But when the scene came up, when I said the line I hated, Robin scoffed derisively, as I worried she would. She turned her gaze from the TV to me, rolled her eyes, and pshawed. *"What an asshole."* Not an asshole for killing Mike, no. An asshole for not *caring* that he'd killed Mike.

It pained me.

But it's such a subjective business. Tom may have watched that episode and thought the beat was perfect. In the collaborative process, sometimes there are differences. Sometimes there are battles. Sometimes you lose.

In all the hours making *Breaking Bad*, I got upset only a handful of times. I think any family would wish for so few arguments. The quality of the writing on the show was so superb, we didn't have to fight. We knew from day one we were all working together to build something of deep quality. So when we did fight, the arguments were always about the integrity of the show and its characters. It was never about early call times or trailer size. It was: "Is this working? Can we do better?"

Difficult. Sometimes actors get that label if they raise a question. As a producer, when I hear someone is difficult, I ask: Difficult how? I worked with Oscar-winning actor Cloris Leachman on *Malcolm in the Middle.* She played the not-so-lovable Grandma Ida—and won an Emmy for her performance. Before I worked with her, I heard rumors that she was difficult. In reality, she was like a bumblebee, vibrating with ideas. She was fun and theatrical and talented and I just loved being around her. She brought so much energy to the set, and it was always about the work. She's also a nut, a certified lunatic in all the lovely ways she can be. One day we were doing a scene and she said, "I gotta pee." Right now? We were shooting. We were on a tight schedule, and she was going to walk off and go pee. She shrugged and grabbed an empty coffee cup and just squatted down in front of everybody, and *tinkle tinkle*. Like she was camping. And then she handed the cup to one of our wardrobe people. "Let's get on with it."

So, yes, she's quirky. But difficult? No. She channels her creative energy to serve the character and the story. She works at it and comes in very prepared. I don't call that kind of actor difficult. As opposed to the actor who comes in and says: "There's no God-damned almond milk!" Or: "I'm not doing the scene, it's too cold outside." Or: "Don't ever give me direction."

That is difficult.

Difficult and creatively engaged are not the same. Having an engaged, invested cast and crew comes through on a molecular level. Even as a casual viewer, you can feel that kind of care. On *Breaking Bad*, the storytelling complex did not end at the writers and directors and actors. The electricians, the technicians, the gaffers, the production assistants were all part of what made the show work. Everyone was all-in, proud to be a part of the show. Stew Lyons, our producer, got calls every day from crew members all over New Mexico and Arizona, who said: I'm dying to work on the show. Our attrition level was really low. Once people got hired, no one wanted to leave. Even guys who were ready to retire said: Not until the show is over.

I remember shooting the scene in the last episode when Walt says good-bye to his daughter. I leaned down over the crib and touched my baby's soft sleeping head. This was the last time I'd see her. This was good-bye. Forever.

As I was leaning over the crib, my eyes welling, I saw Andy Voegeli, the camera operator, who was shooting me from below. He was shaking, trying his damnedest to stay unemotional and hold the camera still—but he couldn't. He was a new father himself. And the moment got to him. He wiped tears away as he was shooting.

We hugged when the scene was over. We all hugged one another often. That was the culture: we showed our love and concern for everyone. It was very sweet. And real. And rare.

Producer

At the beginning of the show, I was told that Jesse Pinkman would not be a series regular. He wasn't going to live past the second or third episode. He was designed to hook me up with the drug culture and then he'd be killed. But because everyone adored Aaron Paul and loved his work, and because he and Walt were perfect foils to each other, Jesse became much more than a gateway into the drug world for Walt. Their relationship became, in many ways, the emotional core of the show.

They had nothing in common: age, values, education, style of dress. As Jesse might put it: *Mr. White is this big homo in tighty-whities, yo.* And Walt thought Jesse was a ridiculous imbecile. Their friction created comedy and a kinetic strange-bedfellows, opposites-attract, father-son dynamic.

When they first became partners, they shared nothing except mutual dependency. But ultimately they came to love each other in their way.

Aaron Paul was a shiny-eyed kid in his midtwenties when I first met him. He was a puppy. He was attentive and playful and honest and present and vulnerable and richly talented. Right from the pilot, it was clear that we had the makings of great on-screen chemistry. And off camera, Aaron and I got along very well. He looked up to me, and I saw something of myself in him: a youthful energy. Hopefulness. As our dynamic within the story line varied and evolved, we became even tighter outside of work. That *Breaking Bad* ride bonded us deeply. He's a friend for life.

Every year, Aaron and I would rent out the Silva Lanes bowling alley in Albuquerque and host the cast and crew and their families. Food, open bar, karaoke, and of course, bowling. In 2011, amid the revelry and silliness, someone whispered into my ear: Osama bin Laden was just killed.

Navy SEALs had crept into his lair in Pakistan and taken him out—more than a decade after 9/11. The day we thought might never happen had finally come.

I was behind the counter, on the public address system, in the process of issuing the next bowling challenge. So I incorporated this news into my remarks. "Okay, there are three announcements to make: First, any kid under twelve who gets a strike wins a plush toy. Second, the Navy SEALs have killed Osama bin Laden. And third, the next adult to get three strikes in a row wins a *Breaking Bad* DVD box set. Good luck!"

A stunned silence. I let the news sink in and I then said: "I'm not joking . . . anyone who gets three strikes in a row wins the *Breaking Bad* DVDs!"

I went for the joke, my default. When the laughter faded, I went back to the PA: "And that thing about Osama bin Laden is also true. They got him."

I'll never forget the energy in the room at that moment. Pride, shock, vengeance, relief. People were cheering, hugging, a few cried. I'll never forget where I was that night. It always comes back to me viscerally: the smell of beer and bowling-alley wax and the disinfectant they spray in the rented shoes, the easy feel of camaraderie among the cast and crew, the looks of raw surprise and elation on the faces in the crowd.

It should have been a happy night. But then there was Steve.

Steve had been trying to get on our crew for a while, and finally in our fourth season he was hired as a production assistant. Steve was effective and professional. He clearly knew his way around a film set, and he caught onto protocol quickly.

Until Bowling Night.

Steve got so wasted that his face went slack. He lurked around the bowling alley, approaching women and commenting on their bodies. His targets included Betsy Brandt and Lauren Parsekian, who would soon become Aaron Paul's wife.

Aaron and I organized those nights to show appreciation for everyone's hard work. We were a celebrated show by that point, and a few names, like Aaron and Vince and I, got the lion's share of the accolades. But the truth was that every single person who worked on the show played a part in making *Breaking Bad* what it was, and that night was meant for us to say thank you, from the bottom of our hearts, to our community, our family. Steve's crude behavior would have been reprehensible on any night. But on this night especially it was a disrespectful affront. It also went against everything we cared about and stood for.

I didn't find out about Steve's behavior until the next day. Betsy told me. "Steve will have to be fired," I said.

"Oh," Betsy said in her compassionate way, "is it possible to just have him work in some other area of the show and not be around me?"

"No, that is not possible," I said. "We can't have someone working on our show whom you have to worry about running into. He's got to go."

I remembered the shame I felt when I got fired from the *Canoga Park Chronicle*. All those newspapers I'd thrown in the Dumpster. I hadn't even known I was stealing, and I felt humiliated by my ignorance, my failure.

And when Joe Stuart called me into his office on *Loving* to say, *Story-wise, we're going in a different direction.* All the times people had said: We're going another way . . . away from you. I remembered feeling crushed. I remembered the self-doubt, and how it lingered.

I had never thought much about what it would be like to be on the other side. I hadn't needed to. Now I did. And I didn't like it. But I told myself: This isn't akin to Joe's hatchet jobs on the set of *Loving*. This isn't the *Canoga Park Chronicle* canning a kid taking shortcuts. This is serious and necessary and just. No question.

I called Aaron. Lauren had told him about Steve's behavior, and he was livid. Of course he was livid. Still, I was taken aback. In the six years of shooting the show, I couldn't recall seeing Aaron Paul angry *one other time*. He was capable of gut wrenching menace and emotion and danger as an actor, but his true nature was gentle and kind.

I'd had no question about how to proceed before I heard Aaron's voice, but now I felt a new urgency. We had to fire Steve immediately.

I called Stew Lyons, our experienced, pragmatic line producer. A line producer handles the business end of the production, the operations, working out the cost of trucks, confirming permits for locations, making sure the caterers are there, and so much more. Stew was ahead of me. He had already dismissed Steve earlier in the day. News travels fast. Harassment, especially sexual harassment, is not tolerated.

Stew told me that he'd urged Steve to seek professional help, not just for his future job prospects but also for himself personally. Later, we learned that Steve was an alcoholic. He'd been spinning out of control, and that night at the bowling alley had been one in a series of nights. I felt for him. I hoped he would get help. But there was no way we could let him be part of what we were trying to do. We couldn't let anyone put at risk this thing we'd worked so hard to create.

Crime Victim

Albuquerque was as central to the show as any person or character. Shooting there, I got to know the place well; its friendly people, stark beauty, and quirky charms will always have a place in my heart.

Even though it's New Mexico's largest city, Albuquerque is a small town, really, set in a wide valley in the high desert, flanked on the east side by the Sandia Mountains. Sandia means watermelon in Spanish, and it's true that the mountains take on a gorgeous watermelon hue when they catch the glow of the setting sun. Sandia Crest is the highest point in Albuquerque, about 10,500 feet above sea level. During the spring and summer, whenever I had a day off from work, I would hike the area. Crisp air, pine trees, strenuous trails. Not what you expect when you think of the desert, but at this elevation the topography changes completely. During winter, there is snow.

I drove up to the top one winter day. An observation platform allows for a 360-degree panoramic view of Albuquerque to the west, Santa Fe to the north, and vast deserts to the east and south. It's a beautiful thing to stand up high and see the great seam where nature and civilization meet. But it's cold at 10,500 feet, so I couldn't stand it for more than a few minutes before it was back to the car. Only when I got inside my warm car—it wasn't so warm.

I noticed bits of glass on the dashboard. I looked over and saw a gaping hole in the passenger-side window. My shoulder bag was gone. I jumped out of the car and looked around. The only people nearby were a family I'd seen earlier taking pictures. Could it have been them? They shrugged and said they hadn't seen anyone near my car. I'd been gone maybe five minutes, and the parking lot was visible from the observation deck, only about forty yards away. I'd been looking in the very direction of my car when it happened.

My shoulder bag was gone. Shit. The contents included my iPad, plus a hard copy of the second episode of our last season.

I contacted Sony to tell them about the script, and the two other electronic scripts on my iPad, and then I drove to the sheriff's station in Tijeras. It was closed. Small town! Taped to the door was a note: "This station is closed during off hours. If this is an emergency, call 911. If this is not an emergency, call [a local number] and leave a detailed message of the incident. Include your name—spelled out—and your contact information, and a sheriff's deputy will return your call soon. Thank you."

As I drove to the dealership to get the window repaired, I called the nonemergency sheriff's line and left my detailed message as instructed. Blah blah blah, my name is C-R-A-N-S-T-O-N. I left my number and hung up.

Then in January 2013 we were shooting a scene in the episode titled "To'hajiilee." Walt pays a visit to Andrea (beautifully played by Emily Rios) to convince her to lure Jesse over to the house so that neo-Nazis can kill him for his treachery. (He'd broken the one rule criminals hold dear: You don't rat.)

It was a bright day in Albuquerque when Ollie, one of the great grips on the show, said to me, "Hey, did you talk to that guy who's working as an extra with us today?"

"No," I said, "why?"

"Because he spoke to the dude who broke into your car and stole your stuff."

I walked over to the guy, who was sitting in his car. That day it was actually his *car* that was the extra, driving up and back on the street during takes. Movies and TV shows always use this technique for filming. Without background people and cars (controlled by the production) the frame would look empty and unreal.

I introduced myself and asked him about what Ollie had told me.

He hesitated at first, but after a few minutes he broke down and said: "We were hangin' at a strip club Wednesday morning . . ."

"Hanging at a strip club on Wednesday morning?"

"Yeah. And the dude comes up and says, 'Hey, I got some *Breaking Bad* stuff—you interested in buying?'"

He told me that he mentioned to the dude that he occasionally works with the show. "And the dude just took off." I asked if he knew the dude's name. After some hesitation he said, "Yes, his name is Xavier."

I said, "Do you know where we can find Xavier?"

He said that Xavier was currently being held at the downtown MDC (Municipal Detention Center) on another charge, and that he thought that "Xavier comes from a whole B&E family. That's what they do."

A family. I thought back to the family I'd seen on the mountain. Was that family Xavier's?

I relayed this information to the sheriff's office immediately. They moved quickly to question Xavier, and charged him, and then the case moved through the system with glacial speed. I don't know that the extra was right about his family, but eventually I heard that Xavier got a year of home confinement for this crime and two others. The punishment seemed light to me, but maybe a brutal stretch of wearing an electronic ankle bracelet would teach him a lesson.

Later, in March 2013, as we were shooting the very last episode of *Breaking Bad*, the break-in story erupted from what seemed like every possible news outlet. Networks, local stations, websites, blogs, everywhere. "FINAL EPISODE SCRIPT OF BREAKING BAD WAS STOLEN!"

Wait, what?

On *Good Morning America*, the hosts sat on the couch discussing this heinous crime, all hoping that the missing script wouldn't be revealed and spoil the ending.

In other news: "The dramatic audiotape of Bryan Cranston's 911 call for help!"

What?! It wasn't a 911 call. I calmly followed instructions from the Mayberry-like sheriff's station to the letter. But the world was told I'd hit the panic button. I even caught flack on social media for tying up the 911 system for a nonemergency. Untrue. Innocent. But guilty, in the court of pop-culture opinion.

Walt

The robbery at Sandia Crest didn't mar its beauty. And early on I said to Vince that it might be cool to shoot something up there. The landscape was so different in look and feel from our other locations around Albuquerque. An image of someone dragging a dead body through the snow came to me. I thought the juxtaposition of the red blood against the white snow would look striking on the screen.

I don't know if Vince remembered me bringing it up, but we did indeed end up shooting there in the last season. When Walt is holed up in a cabin in New Hampshire, we used Sandia Crest as the stand-in for the Granite State.

Walt is taken into the deep woods and told that he'll be apprehended if he leaves the property. Left alone, he's imprisoned in the snowy wilderness with only a barrel of money for company. A fitting end.

Ed "The Disappearer" shows up with supplies. I ask after my family, desperate to know how they are. Ed says that Skyler is working as a part-time taxi dispatcher for money and still has custody of the kids "for the moment." She's using her maiden name, presumably trying to expunge any trace of the name White from her memory and résumé.

Robert Forster played Ed. Of course I remembered Bob from 1979 when I was a production assistant in the special-effects department on *Alligator*. I remembered stuffing plastic bags of fake blood into the cavity of a pretend reptile, and I remembered how excited I was to do it. I remembered sitting in the van with him, shoulder to shoulder, how starstruck I felt. He was a famous actor. I was just a kid. But he'd been so kind to me. I'd never forgotten that. I'd run into him a few times over the years and reminded him of our encounter. He didn't remember—didn't even pretend to, that's not Bob. And I didn't expect him to.

In those last few days of shooting *Breaking Bad* with him, I reflected on the arc of Bob's career. He did it right. He understood the ebb and flow of this business. An accomplished movie star, he now does smaller roles and enjoys every minute of it. He never developed a sense of entitlement. On set he said quite often: *Happy to be here.* He meant it.

In our last scene together, Walt offers Ed ten thousand dollars to stay a couple of hours and play cards with him. He's that desperately lonely. He just wants a little company. Deadpan, Ed doubles the fee and reduces the duration. Walt agrees. The price doesn't matter. What's money to him anymore? Ed deals the cards for five-card stud. The first two up cards randomly come up kings.

The director, Peter Gould, hadn't yelled "Cut," so we both stayed in character and continued playing. Bob improvised and announced the cards: "Two kings." The irony isn't lost on Walter White. For a short period of time, he'd felt like a king. Now . . .

• • •

Aside from Ed's visit, I am all alone in that cabin. Robinson Crusoe meets Scarface. I have a full beard. The cancer has come back. I can feel myself slipping away. Should I just wait for death to take me? Is this, after everything, the sum total of my works and days? A barrelful of money I can't use and can't get to my family? Everything for naught?

I know my family is disgusted. I feel ashamed. I was hoping I could convince my son to find some measure of forgiveness in his heart, hoping I could say I was sorry. I was hoping I could find a way to leave them *something*. Money isn't everything, but it's a lot. My family needs it. There has to be a way to get it to them without the Feds tracing it.

I lay eyes on the box of Ensure meal replacement drinks Ed brought me to help to keep my weight up. I empty it and fill it with as much money as it will hold. I trudge through the thick snow, holding the box tight to my chest. I find a dive bar. I find a pay phone. I call my son at school. I try to tell him: Everything. I was doing it for you, I tell him. I'm sending you the money so the Feds can't trace it.

I tell him once: I love you.

I never want to see you again, he says. I want you to die.

I weep. I feel the waste of my life. My good intentions got derailed by greed and hubris and rage and resentment. I was the danger, all right. A danger to myself. To everyone around me. So much pain and loss. I haven't left a mark. I've left a stain. I am . . . nothing.

I wept as we filmed that scene. When we finished, I was spent. Exhausted and a bit traumatized. It was also my birthday.

We shot *Breaking Bad* on thirty-five-millimeter film. Few shows, if any, do that anymore because of the expense. And the technology has improved so much that you can get similar quality on digital. We shipped the film to the lab back in LA as we shot it. Each day, we knew exactly when the flight that was carrying the film was leaving, and we'd have to "break" the film, box it up, and get it to the airport. A courier then picked it up at LAX and took it to the lab, so that the next day the digital copies were ready. The assistants loaded them up so our editors could see what they had. That way, if there was a problem with the film—say, a scratch—we could still reshoot before we were long gone from that location.

While the film of that wrenching scene with my son was being shipped from Albuquerque to LA, it fell off the back of a luggage cart. Then one of those tanklike tows that push and pull airplanes to the gates ran over the film cans. The film didn't just get exposed. It got pulverized. Ruined. The insurance company covered it, but we would have to go back and shoot the scene again.

When I first heard that some film got ruined, I thought: *Oh please, let it be the something like the scene where I walk into a store and put the milk down on the counter. Or a scene where I'm driving my Aztek. Not the scene where I hear from my son that he wishes I were dead.*

But of course.

The day I had to reshoot that scene was challenging. I felt myself reenacting, rather than acting. I remembered what I did the last time and tried to extinguish that from my mind, but it was hard. I needed to find a new path back to those depths, and I couldn't.

But it had to be done. So we did it again. And again and again.

As an actor, you have to be able to endure repetition without losing emotion or energy. You're hysterical? Do it again. You're experiencing the most piercing loss? Do it again. And again. How to be honest and true and feel all of those feelings on command? Then repeat? You just do. To get through, to communicate, to move your audience regardless of the problems, that's the job.

So I wept. And I wept again. And I found a new path.

• • •

Walter White was more alive in the last years of his life than he had been in the previous fifty. He went from utter failure to great power. In the final episode, Skyler says: Give me a break, you didn't do it for your family.

"You're right," Walt answers. "I didn't. I did it for myself. I did it for me. I liked it. I was good at it. And I was really—I was alive."

He was. I don't agree with the decisions Walt made or the actions he took, of course. But I feel for him. If you have two years to live, you don't let them cut your balls off. You go out fighting. That's what he did.

He was alive.

And when I was doing the series, so was I.

Saying good-bye to *Breaking Bad* was incredibly difficult. Doing the last episodes, the characters were all dying or driving off into the sunset. Walt was saying good-bye to Skyler, and from a distance he was watching his son get off a school bus, he was exchanging a final, meaningful look with Jesse. They both knew it was good-bye.

And we knew, too. I was Bryan saying good-bye to Aaron, and to Anna and Betsy and Dean and R. J. This was likely the last time most of us would work together.

I suppose you could be on a terrible show and still feel loss when it ends. But to be on a show that was so respected, not just by us but by the world? And to feel so intensely connected to one another? We all knew we might never have that feeling again. But we had to move on.

Good-bye, Lydia.

Celebrity

I've seen *Breaking Bad* T-shirts in cities and little outposts all over the world. People dress as Walter White for Halloween. They dress their children and dogs in hazmat suits and Heisenberg hats. People have shaved my face into the back of their heads, they've inked it on their backs, their forearms, their legs, their asses. I'm the permanent resident of some guy's left butt cheek. Next to Larry and Moe. I suppose I've taken the place of Curly, the third Stooge. It's a little . . . odd to have your face tattooed on someone's backside. I did not see that coming when I lied about my ability to mountaineer in order to get a Mars bar commercial.

I didn't even see it when we were shooting the pilot. A lot of people around us were raving: Profound, they said, groundbreaking. We have a hit on our hands. Something very special and rare.

But all I knew at that moment was that we were doing something daring and we were having a good time. Nothing more.

People tend to think that actors or writers or directors know when something is going to be a hit. We don't. We can guess. We can hope. We can do the work. But that's all. No one can know with certainty if a movie or a show is going to work, even if it's damn good. There are so many outside variables: marketing, music, timing. Competition also determines if something succeeds or fails. Sometimes there's another movie about giant man-eating grasshoppers coming out the same weekend as your grasshopper movie. Social mores are another part of it. Sometimes a show is ahead of its time. Or maybe it's just a little bit behind. You just don't know. You keep your fingers crossed. But you don't know.

The audience embraced *Breaking Bad* beyond anyone's wildest imagination, and that changed my life. I'd been a working actor for nearly my entire adulthood, and now, suddenly, in my fifties, I was a star.

That's never what I aspired to be. I wanted to act. I wanted to work. Being an actor and being a celebrity are different things altogether. For a long time I had a real ambivalence toward fame. And praise. Whenever someone gave me a compliment, I would downplay it. Which would then have the unintended consequence of prompting the person giving the compliment to reiterate: You were great.

No. I appreciate it, but, no, I was okay.

No, no, no, you were really great!

Well, I don't know. Thank you.

I said thank you more as an apology than a genuine expression of gratitude or appreciation. I did that all the way through my thirties. Maybe I felt that because I didn't have a formal education, who was I to get these jobs? Who was I to receive this praise?

I remember I bristled the first time someone called me a television star. No, no, I'm just an actor working on a show. The show could end at any time.

At a certain point I gave in. I realized I was spending a lot of time and energy pushing away fame. I realized how taxing it was. I realized I could just say thank you. And appreciate it. And once I realized that, I got out of my own way. I had to come to terms with what was happening in my own life.

Undeniably I've benefitted from fame. Many, many opportunities have come my way because of the insane success of *Breaking Bad*. But there are downsides, too. As an actor you need to be sensitive, to be open, to be able to observe people and study human behavior. I don't want my character to be me—but with a hat! I have my Bryanisms, and I study people to help me get away from those tics. But as a celebrity I am no longer the observer, I am the observed. I am not the one who knocks. I am the one who ducks and covers.

People who sell celebrity autographed material find out when your plane is landing, where you're staying, where you're eating, and they lie in wait, and they shove paraphernalia at you to sign. Many of the guys are aggressive; they bark at you. If you sign, they tell others: "He'll sign." And then you're mobbed by even more people. And your time and energy get drained this way. And it's like you're going out there handing them money. And when you don't hand them money, they get upset at you. (Of course it couldn't be more different with real fans who just want to shake your hand and say that your show or film really touched them. I love that.)

I've become hyperaware of the catacombs, the secret exits, how to escape from any given place. I choose a hotel because I know it has a good back-door situation. At an airport, if I'm not in a lounge, I'll look around and find old people and sit facing them. They're far less likely to know who I am. If there happens to be a conversation, I can count on a normal exchange. It's really cold outside. What time are we boarding?

I go to a restaurant with my wife and daughter, and I sit with my back to the room so fewer people can see my face. When Taylor sees people whispering and pointing she says, "Dad, you've been made."

People rush up to my wife and me. OH MY GOD, IT'S WALTER WHITE! They hand my wife their cellphones. Would you mind? She's gracious, always. But it's uncomfortable at times. She'd never say anything. She realizes how lucky we are, what incredible gifts we've been given. But it's hard being a plus one. It shouldn't be that every invitation reads Bryan Cranston plus one. It shouldn't be that photographers wave her aside to get an unobstructed shot of me. I don't want her to feel unimportant. She's the opposite of that.

• • •

I love work. I even love work on my birthday—especially my birthday. It's like a gift I give myself. I've always believed in work. But because *Breaking Bad* ushered in an avalanche of new opportunities, my workload since the show ended has been enormous. Part of that is my nature. I want to do as much as I can while I can. I know that my career will slow down eventually. That's the natural cycle of things. When that happens I want to have no regrets. I want to know that I took full advantage of my good fortune. Even if I make mistakes along the way. I'd rather fail than regret.

The other reason I work so much is that my work life is more protected than my nonwork life. I asked Robert De Niro about it once. We were both at a hockey game at Madison Square Garden, guests of the New York Rangers. We'd never met before, but between periods we were hustled into a green room, a protective area, which is easier for security to guard. Otherwise people constantly come down to say hello or get an autograph. We got to talking. I mentioned at some point that it seemed he worked nonstop.

He said, "I just feel more comfortable when I'm working."

If he's not working, it means he's stepping outside of his apartment, walking down the street, being pointed to and stared at. He's Robert De Niro! How can he have a normal day? Ever?

As a celebrity, you can easily create your own kind of self-imprisonment. I think of the Alzheimer's ward where my mom spent her final years. You have your gardens and your walking path and your illusion of freedom, but you don't go beyond this wall. You're not really free.

We were shooting the film *Contagion* in Chicago, and I was on the street with Laurence Fishburne. We were done working for the day and we wanted to get a bite to eat. I commented it was a nice night. It would be great to walk. But then I said, "I guess we should get a car, so we don't have to deal with the public attention."

Fish said, "No, we can walk. You can deal with it, just don't stop moving."

"What if there's a stoplight?" I said.

"Just keep moving. Wave. And then find a way around."

And we did.

Slowly, I came to understand why celebrities make celebrity friends. Because you can be yourself. Tom Hanks doesn't need anything from me. I don't need anything from him. We can relax in each other's company. After I saw his work in *Captain Phillips*, I told him his performance was so heroic yet deeply vulnerable. I told him it really affected me. It's not adulation or fawning. It's collegial appreciation, on a human level.

Since I became famous, my personality has changed. I tend to leave my house less. If I leave my house I'm in a hat and sunglasses, and when I'm walking down the street and I pass by a group of people, I'm looking down at my phone, pretending to be absorbed in it. If I don't happen to have my phone with me I'll pretend to wind my watch or wipe dust off my sleeve. Head down. Louis C. K. told me he feels the same things, but he fights it. He tests himself, pushes himself out. But he always feels vulnerable. Armorless.

Every time I feel claustrophobic or hemmed in by my fame, I remember the first time I was nominated for a Golden Globe for *Malcolm in the Middle*. I was so excited and greatly honored. At the Beverly Hilton they'd cordoned off the hallway that led from the ballroom to the parties. Once the ceremony was over, security would escort everyone out of the hallway and into the party rooms. Plenty of people on both sides of the rope would be asking for an autograph. We were told: please don't stop. If one actor stops and another one doesn't, the one who doesn't is going to look bad. Please just nod and say hello and move into the party.

Robin and I did as we were told. We walked the long gauntlet, waving and smiling but ignoring all the requests. But about half-way through the lobby we hit a bottleneck. The procession came to a dead stop. We were standing just a few inches away from two thirteen-year-old girls.

"Please, please, please!" They were leaning over the rope, begging me, almost crying. It was like Beatlemania.

"I really can't. They told us not to."

"But PLEASE. PLEASE."

I looked around. The line wasn't moving. I said, "Okay, but don't tell anyone."

I surreptitiously took their autograph books, and as I was about to write my name, one of the girls said, "Who are you?"

Robin and I burst out laughing.

I wrote: *With love, Tom Cruise.*

Visitor

Not too long ago, I visited a teenage boy, a huge *Breaking Bad* fan, at the Children's Hospital in LA. Not long to live, I was told. The doctors couldn't do much more than make him comfortable.

To be honest, I was dreading it.

What could I do? I wasn't a doctor or a healer or even a speaker with a positive message. I was just an actor. I didn't know how I could help him or his parents.

I was stressed. I wanted to be on time and yet I didn't want to go at all. Robin and I parked the car and hurried toward the elevator. "Can you come in with me?" I asked. I needed support.

"Of course I'll come," she said.

But as we walked down the corridor toward the kid's room, it started dawning on me: my dread and stress were selfish. This wasn't about me, about how I felt. This was about Kevin. It was my responsibility to do whatever small thing I could for Kevin while I had the chance. I needed to get out of my head and focus on the boy. I took a few deep breaths. I had the same feeling I have when I'm standing backstage, before I make my entrance. I'm filled with nervous anticipation, but once I step on stage it dissipates. And that happened the moment I entered the room. It was all right.

I walked in and said, Hi, Kevin, casually, and he responded in kind. We exchanged ideas and thoughts, and I challenged him. I took the contrarian point of view. He said Walter White was evil. WHAT? I said, pretending to be angry. You like Jesse? WHY? Oh, you're crazy. That's insane. I started pacing, pretending he was driving me mad. The fact that he was ill did not come into the conversation. Except I told him he looked like Walter White with his bald head. He thought that was funny. You need to grow a mustache and goatee. Can't you grow any facial hair, kid?!

For a moment it wasn't about his illness. It wasn't a doctor giving him more bad news or a nurse drawing blood. I was this guy on his favorite show, and we were together, alive in that moment.

Statistician

Toward the end of *Breaking Bad*, I was deluged with scripts, and I had to devise a way to sift through, a system to evaluate them. In order of importance I weighed: story, script, role, director, and cast.

Here's what the system looks like:

EVALUATION GRADE	STORY	TEXT	ROLE	DIRECTOR	CAST/ MISC	TIME (+ OR – 1 POINT)
A	6	5	4	3	2	
B	5	4	3	2	1	
C	4	3	2	1	0	
D	2	1	1	0	0	
F	0	0	0	0	0	

21: Perfect score.
18–20: Must do.
15–17: Seriously consider.
13–14: On the bubble.
Below 13: Pass.

Here's how several projects scored: *Argo*: 19. *Trumbo*: 17. *All the Way*: 20. *The Infiltrator*: 15. *Why Him?*: 14. *Godzilla*: 15. *Wakefield*: 16.

The baseline is always the story. Good storytelling is timeless. It's the essential human art form. Civilians might look at a script and see a monologue of several pages and be scared by it. I could never memorize that. An actor reads it differently. Actors feast on challenging language. We are nourished by words. Role and director are important, of course, but story is essential. If the story isn't compelling and the writing isn't well constructed, it doesn't matter how great the character is. A legendary director like Ridley Scott is helming a project? But the story is eh? Might be a no. Although that combination would be rare. Great storytellers know great scripts.

The criterion of cast/misc is a catchall. How supportive is the studio? Do I have a history with anyone attached? Is there someone involved with whom I've always wanted to work? So many things can and do come into play.

One criterion not on the scale, however, is money. I figure my agents are incentivized to make the best deal they can, so whatever they're happy with, so am I. Money is simply not a key factor in choosing projects. I never want to make a creative decision based on financial need. I keep my lifestyle within my means so I don't have to do that.

Of course, every now and then, an offer comes up that's too good to refuse. Like the Super Bowl in 2015.

I was asked to shoot an Esurance commercial that would have a one-time airing during the game and then never be played again on television. A woman comes in to see her pharmacist and instead she encounters Walter White behind the counter. It was funny, and it paid a lot. A ridiculous amount. I thought I would be a fool not to take it. Accepting a commercial like that makes it possible for me to do super-low-budget passion projects.

I've been dead broke, and I've been rich, and rich is better. But now that money is less of an issue for me, I'm mostly about the quality of the work and the experience.

Once, Warren Buffett visited the *Breaking Bad* set to tape a sketch that would be played at his annual gathering of stockholders. The financial guru played a version of Heisenberg opposite Aaron Paul and me. A funny bit. On a break, I asked the same question that everyone asks Warren: What's your secret? Oh, it's no secret, he said in his affable homespun way. Just make more right decisions than wrong ones and you'll be fine.

The Cranston Assessment of Project Scale—CAPS, if you like—embodies that principle. I'm going to make mistakes. But the idea is to give myself the best chance to make more good decisions in the face of an overwhelming number of choices.

Nephew

I heard from my aunt Sunday most often by snail mail. Postmark: Woodland Hills. A nice community close to my childhood home in Canoga Park. She and my father's brother Eddie had no children, no pets, no great friends. Aunt Sunday's adventures were vicarious ones she took on her La-Z-Boy recliner. Every time I was mentioned in *TV Guide*—"Agent #3," "Obnoxious Dinner Guest"—she got out her scissors. An inveterate clipper, she sent me every clipping, carefully folded into an envelope. I appreciated the thought. Which didn't stop me from throwing the clippings in the trash. I can't bear clutter.

I didn't see much of Sunday, nor of Uncle Eddie. My brother ran into Eddie at the Motion Picture Hospital when my mom was in intensive care. But Eddie wasn't there to visit Mom. If he hadn't bumped into Kyle, I don't think Eddie would have known or thought to ask after his former sister-in-law. That was 2006.

Three years later, I'd wrapped a season of *Breaking Bad* and was back in Los Angeles. It was late at night and the phone rang. "Your dad," Robin said.

My dad still had stars in his eyes, but they were different stars. Not acting stars. Producing stars. I remember he produced a variety show. *The New Sounds of Country!* He had six or seven country music acts. They were pretty good. One fresh face popped and he sold that show into syndication. And many years ago, he came up with a precursor to the Country Music Awards. His version didn't stick, but the CMAs did. He was ahead of his time. Over the years, he sold one or two things, but it wasn't enough. He was constantly behind. Money was a daily struggle.

I hated that whenever he called I assumed he needed something. I always braced myself for the inevitable question: "Hey, buddy, do you think you can loan me a few grand?"

"I'm here in Woodland Hills," he said, his voice shaking. I knew right away it wasn't about money. He told me it had been a few months since he'd heard from Sunday and Eddie. For weeks he'd been calling. Nothing. They had a Winnebago and used to travel a lot, so it wasn't unusual for them to be gone for stretches.

He went over to their place to check on them and the yard was overrun with weeds. He knocked and knocked. Nothing. He got spooked and called the police. He had a bad feeling.

The police found two bodies inside, one male, one female. Approximately my dad's age, in their eighties. The lady was next to her walker in the living room. The man was in the bedroom. The description fit. Eddie and Sunday were dead.

The police told my father, "We have to call the coroner and

do an autopsy because of the rather . . . odd circumstances and the length of the time they were dead."

My dad said fine. And he said he didn't want to see the bodies. The police told him to go to a coffee shop and come back in an hour. He called me from the coffee shop.

The next day I picked my dad up and we drove to Woodland Hills. The bodies had been removed and the evidence gathered. My dad had somehow forgotten that he owned a set of keys, and he gave them to me and said he'd wait outside while I got the lay of the land. For a pugilist who saw plenty of blood in the ring, my dad was squeamish.

I unlocked the door and tried to push it open but it barely moved. Drifts of mail on the floor were blocking it. I shoved the door open enough to slide in. And right away there was the smell. Oh the smell. Not only rancid and putrid but chemical and toxic and sickly sweet like rotten fruit. A cocktail of decay. I held my breath as best I could. The room was pitch black. My eyes adjusted: stacks and stacks and stacks of stuff—stuff from QVC, stuff from yard sales, stuff from Christmases gone by. Clothing, furniture, newspapers neatly wrapped in twine, piled almost to the ceiling. I knew from infrequent visits years ago that there was a sliding glass door at the other end of the living room. I had to get there and open it and let in some air and light. But how? It was an obstacle course of garbage. I passed by a walker and a large rectangular cutout of the carpet and padding where Sunday had been found.

I hoped she hadn't suffered, but I saw the stain on the plywood subfloor and I knew from my limited police studies that she probably had. A body doesn't secrete fluid (other than urine) if it's only dead a few days. Full-body decay: she had been there a while.

I saw two beat-up La-Z-Boys with doilies on the arms. I saw a half-finished crossword puzzle on a soiled chair. I saw a nightstand in between the chairs, with an electric clock radio, blinking. Across from the chairs were three TVs stacked on top of each other. The broken sets on the bottom propped up the working one. I saw a gooseneck lamp on the nightstand and I went over to turn it on. A tangle of extension cords all led to one dusty, overloaded power strip.

With a little more light I managed to make my way to the glass doors. Boxes fell. I pulled the drapes. They hadn't been touched in years. They were brittle. Eons of dust and dirt showered down on me. But no light came through the glass; a wall of cardboard covered it. I ripped the cardboard off.

I was sweating now. My pulse raced. I needed air. I tried to open the glass door, but a wood dowel was in the track. I got the dowel out. The latch was jammed from years of disuse. I found a brass lamp and used it as a hammer. Slowly the latch slid. Now there was a screen door, caked with dirt, and as I tried to force it open, the dirt cascaded onto me and stuck to my sweat. I felt buried alive. I was wiping my eyes, panicking.

At last I busted down the screen door and stepped into the backyard. Close to passing out, I found a hose and poured water on my head and drank and drank and drank. It had taken me half an hour to hack through this hoarder's maze—it couldn't have been more than twenty-five feet across.

I went around to the front and got my dad and told him what to expect. He was aghast. He hadn't known. No one had. I imagine no other person—except for maybe a pizza deliveryman—had peeked into the house in the last twenty years. We saw Eddie and Sunday on some holidays. They'd always say, "We'll meet you there." *We'll meet you there.* We never thought twice about it.

My dad didn't want to go in, but we needed to know: Was there a will? Was there a safe deposit box? I'd described how hard it was to squeeze through the door, and my dad suggested we try getting in through the garage. It was so full of junk that they could *just* wedge their car in. I flashed on my mom's garage full of old furniture and dusty, cracked dinnerware, and boxes of other people's discarded clothes. We shimmied alongside the car and went in.

My dad retched. I told him to keep going. I wasn't doing this alone. In the kitchen, the fridge was filled with mostly condiments. The stove was dust-covered and stacked with papers and knick-knacks. The oven was a storage locker for still more junk.

Empty bottles of champagne were strewn about. The microwave was caked with food.

I opened up the freezer. Towers of frozen dinners.

In the second bedroom, another cutout on the floor. Half a man's length, probably about four feet long. Eddie. Oh, poor Eddie.

Boxes and boxes covered their bed. They must have slept in the La-Z-Boys out in the living room. I went to the window and I saw a glow of light through the pull-down shade. I pulled the shade down and let it roll up. There must have been fifty flies crawling on the windowpane, trying to get out. I knew how they felt.

Covering our mouths, my dad and I grabbed whatever papers we could easily find and loaded them up to examine later, elsewhere. They weren't ultimately the papers we needed, so we would have to return. Meanwhile, the autopsy results came back. Eddie and Sunday both had alcohol in their systems. Prescription drugs. But nothing illicit. No foul play. Eddie died of blunt force. We were told he was found with one trouser leg on, one off. He was trying to put on his pants and fell and hit his head. Sunday, we guessed, was trying to get to him with her walker. She fell and broke her hip. Probably lay there for three or four days before she died.

We finally found a will. Handwritten. We were all mentioned, as was a guy named Dale with a Texas number. I called. "Who are you, Dale?"

"I'm her son," he said.

Her son?

It turned out Sunday had a son from a previous relationship. Who knew? Certainly not my dad or any friend or relative. Sunday was a devout Catholic. There must have been a scandal seventy years ago when she'd been a teenager. She must have given the child up for adoption.

Dale said: "How do I know you're being fair about this?"

"Excuse me?"

Dale continued: "How do I know you're dividing the assets up fairly?"

"You're *welcome* to take over," I said. "I *invite* you to take over."

He didn't, but to safeguard his interest, he called the county. They then took over the estate and sold everything that was worth something, including the house, taking 5 percent as a fee. Before we learned the county would take over, we did a search to make sure we'd found all the important papers. We found a box labeled *Empty Arrowhead Water Jugs*. We opened it to find four empty Arrowhead water jugs. Taped, closed, stored. Madness.

My sister Amy found a paper bag neatly wrapped in twine. Attached to the twine was a label that read: *Two Bras Too Small*. Amy pulled the neat bow off and opened it up. Two bras Sunday must have outgrown. Truth in advertising.

Robin found a box labeled: *Eddie's Old Underwear*. Inside? Sure enough.

Another bag was labeled: *Keys to the Old Cars*. None of the keys fit the car in the garage or the abandoned vehicles parked on the dead grass in the backyard. So. They kept keys to cars they hadn't owned in years.

All of this felt like the end point toward which all clutter leads. The end point to which all disordered thinking and living lead. And it struck me how sad their lives were at the end, how dark and chaotic, how devoid of reason. I spent weeks and weeks trying to put those images from my mind.

And just when my own life seemed so good, so full of light.

In a way Sunday and Eddie had not only caused their deaths—they'd *staged* them. But why? I'd spent my life puzzling over human motivations, and I had trouble cracking this mystery. What is it that makes a person want to *keep* and *curate* garbage? Is it some kind of security blanket? Some hedge against time and loss? Some notion that the past might be resurrected—through things? That those old cars might be driven again?

My brother said: "It was mental illness."

Dad said: "Nah. It's just nuts."

Stepson

My dad never had time to analyze the present. And the past was the past. He was all about the future. Full steam ahead.

He was a dreamer. You could say he hoarded dreams. But they all revolved around the same goal. He was going to be a star. Nothing short of stardom would do.

Of all the side roads and jaunts and harebrained ideas, of all the distractions and detours, he probably had the most success with his magazine, *Star's Homes*. He would find the addresses of stars and take photos of their houses and publish them for tourists. "Here's Jimmy Stewart's home! There's Lucille Ball's mansion! Hey look it's Robin Williams's place!" He'd list his own name and home in the magazine. Joe Cranston! Hollywood producer. Well, would ya look at that! "Joe! You have a place on the beach in Malibu?"

Sly grin. Why sure.

My dad lived in a condo in Studio City. He felt a blurb about his imaginary beachfront mansion somehow gave him credibility—and he also thought it was hilarious. Behind the laughter was the hard fact that he'd never have a Malibu address.

When I was just getting my career going, I worked for him. The business was mostly mail-order then. I went to the PO box in Hollywood and got the checks and cash. I stuffed the magazine in envelopes and mailed the envelopes to subscribers. And then the business evolved. Dad made his money at point-of-purchase, at all the places they sell Hollywood memorabilia, like the world-famous Grauman's Chinese Theater. The shops would take the magazine on consignment. They got a piece, he got a piece.

At the end of the magazine's run, he still had the big names of yesteryear, but very few relevant stars of today. He needed to update his list, get more current stars, and that was beyond him. I was one of the few current actors pictured in *Star's Homes*.

"Would you look at that, Bryan," he'd say. "You made the cut."

He was trying, in his way, to help me. It wasn't so different from the way my aunt Sunday clipped my name from the weeklies. My dad was proud. He was trying to show it.

But I always felt there was a hidden agenda. He was continually trying to get me to promote and produce his screenplays. He'd hold up a script. *Do you think you can get this to Tom Hanks?*

At twenty-five, as soon as I was steadily employed on *Loving*, I started loaning him money. Small, manageable sums to start. Then we graduated to larger amounts. I covered his utilities and his rent on occasion. And then I paid the funeral expenses for his mother when she died.

I'm sure Eddie loaned my dad money and never saw it again. Uncle Eddie wasn't rich, but he had a job; he worked as a gaffer in Hollywood for thirty years and made investments. He might have ended up a hoarder in the end, but he didn't squander what he'd earned.

Dad came to me fairly regularly. A few times every year. It felt like a role reversal, like he was my son, asking his dad for a loan. I didn't cherish the feeling, but I couldn't spend my time being angry. He didn't much like it, either, but he was often desperate; he was often the recipient of pink-hued caution bills from the gas company or departments of water and power. He was always on the verge of losing service.

I came to accept that he relied on me financially, but that I couldn't rely on him emotionally.

One day, he asked to see me. Something very pressing. I sighed, knowing that the "in-person" request always meant a big check.

Sure enough, he asked to borrow $30,000.

"Thirty grand?" I said. "Wow. Why do you need $30,000?"

"I can't tell you."

"We're not going to play this game, Dad."

He hesitated. "Cindy is sick," he said. "But you can't tell her I told you."

Cindy was my dad's wife of thirty-five years. The woman he left my mother for, the woman he stole from the husband he'd knocked out cold in the courthouse corridor when I was a boy. In spite of their rocky beginning, Cindy and my dad were actually well suited. I'd gotten along fine with them ever since she and my dad quit drinking. At our wedding Robin moved to give my father a hug, and Cindy, already seriously drunk at our afternoon ceremony, said, "Get your hands off my husband."

I took my dad aside and I said, "She stops drinking, and you stop drinking, or I'll never see you again." I meant it. He knew I meant it. And that was it. They stopped. And they both became born-again Christians.

Now Cindy was facing cancer. Two kinds of terminal cancer, in fact. She didn't want chemo. She wanted to cure herself naturally, and she found some doctor in Mexico who had promised recovery to patients by "cleaning the blood."

Robin and I checked out the website. Very shady-looking. The process was illegal in the United States, so the doctor had set up an operation in Tijuana.

I talked to a board-certified oncologist, who told me that there was no hope. *One* of those conditions was a death sentence. Two? With 100 percent certainty, she had maximum of a year to live.

But my father begged. It's going to save her life. He was desperate.

Robin and I discussed the matter and we agreed. We knew this transfusion wasn't going to save her life. And yet Cindy and my dad believed it. I said to Robin: "You know what this is? This is a $30,000 Get Well Soon card." We gave my dad and Cindy the money, and they were extremely grateful and ventured into her treatment with hope.

Cindy died the following May. Almost exactly one year after her diagnosis.

Son

The whole family was at a Japanese restaurant, celebrating Taylor's high school graduation. My brother was out from New York with his girlfriend Greta. After we'd returned from our motorcycle trip in 1978, Kyle had gotten a theater degree from UCLA, but he didn't give the acting life long before he moved to New York to live on an ashram. He now buys and sells college textbooks and lives happily on Long Island with Greta, an actor as well as a hairdresser.

In 2011, Kyle was visiting me on the set of *Breaking Bad*. Greta was there, too, visiting her brother Steven Michael Quezada, who ably played Steve Gomez, Hank's solid DEA partner. I think that was the first time on set for both of them. Kyle and Greta basically took one look at each other and *whoosh*—they were in love.

Both Kyle and Greta are talented, and both wanted to get back into acting, but they needed a reel to showcase their work, a project to get things going. A flash went off. With the newer cameras we could make a movie so much more cheaply than in the *Last Chance* days. Now, on Taylor's big night, I turned to my dad and said, "What if you wrote an eighty-to-ninety-page script? Something contained, not big in scope. Something we could get done. I'll put up the money—thirty, forty thousand dollars. We can get a fresh-out-of-film-school director, someone talented and eager and hungry. We'll put together a crew of people I know. Kyle and Greta will both have good roles in it. Let's make a movie together. What do you think?"

Odds were the film wouldn't be a box-office success. It probably wouldn't even break even. I knew I'd probably never see that money again. But it wasn't about that. It was about the experience, working together as father and sons—and Greta. A personal success, something we could be proud of. Something that would bring us closer. I was excited.

My dad smiled wryly. "No."

No thinking or mulling. Just a no. He had zero interest in such a puny passion project. He only wanted the Holy Grail. He mentioned one of the scripts he'd been working on, a project that would require around $15 million to produce. "I'm going to get that made."

"But we can do this now," I said. "While you're working to finance your other one."

Again, he politely declined.

My dad was only interested in the home run. Early in my career, I'd learned how to hit singles. He spent his whole life swinging for the fences. Until I knew I could hit a single, I didn't go for moon shots.

No matter how many times I butted up against the hard fact of who my father was, and wasn't, it always hurt. There's so much dark territory between fathers and sons. My dad and I could never bridge that distance. We never reached each other. We never met.

I was shooting *Trumbo* in New Orleans in the fall of 2014, and I talked to my dad on the phone. He'd had a pacemaker put in the previous Saturday, and his voice sounded weak. He was now ninety, but that was the frailest I'd ever heard his voice. That was the last time I would talk to him.

Robin called me before dawn the next morning to deliver the news.

Months later, we were at my dad's condo, packing up his belongings, and my daughter Taylor found a scrap of paper. It was dated just three days before he died. In his shaky handwriting, it read: *The highlight of my life was when my children forgave me.*

I'm glad he knew. He'd blown such a hole in our lives when we were kids, and I'd never truly understood why, but I didn't need to grasp it intellectually, and I *had* forgiven him. I had let it go.

Sibling

After Dad was gone, my sister Amy suggested that the three of us siblings go to therapy.

I see a therapist from time to time when I'm feeling edgy or anxious, and Robin and I have been to a couples' therapist periodically. We have an agreement. If either of us feels like going, the other can't object. I suggested this system to her before we were even married, and it's worked for us over the years.

So I said yes to Amy. Sure. Why not? Kyle was in, too.

We hired Robin's therapist (female), and mine (male), to be in the room with the three of us. The Cranston kids. We talked for a while and then the therapists gave us their sense of things.

"This is quite normal," they said. "Pretty bad childhood. Not as bad as some. Worse than others. You each found a way to survive. You each found a way to cope. That's perfectly understandable, perfectly acceptable, perfectly right at the time. The problem is those same coping mechanisms that you used to survive a less-than-perfect childhood will cannibalize your life as an adult and prevent you from growing to your full potential."

"Amy," they assessed, "you came into the family when things were starting to go south. You never got proper love and nurturing. Your veneer is you're perfectly fine without love. You adapted and learned to do without it."

Amy is six years younger than I am. She was five when my dad left. So no stringing lights for Christmas. No homemade Halloween costumes. None of the good stuff. She only knew my mom lonely and drunk and consorting with unambitious, trying-to-get-by-with-the-least-amount-of-responsibility men. Amy had zero guidance, zero assistance or support in seeking an education. She left high school at sixteen and got her GED; then she moved out on her own and began to support herself, taking college classes at night.

Amy became a licensed vocational nurse and then went on to get her bachelor's degree. Next was a master's in education. Now she's the administrator in a school system with a doctorate in education. Given her history, she looked destined to struggle. And now she has a doctorate. I really don't know how she did it. She's a miracle.

But when the therapists assessed her, she recognized herself immediately.

"Yep," she said. "Yep, yep. That's me."

"Bryan," they said, "you take your pain and you divert it. Instead of working through it, you deflect it. You use humor when you get embarrassed or vulnerable. You use performance to exorcise the demons. You use acting to sort through your emotional baggage. You get love from your work. It's therapeutic for you. Cathartic."

"Yep. You're right."

It's true that I use humor to deflect. And it's true that in acting, there's safety in vulnerability. It's the character crying, not Bryan. I found a channel—a use—for the anger and resentment and feelings of abandonment that came from my childhood. I flush those feelings through my system in my work. Is that always enough? No. I check in with my therapist when I hit a rough patch. I go for a run when I need a release. I've found multiple ways to cope. But acting has been my great salvation.

"Now Kyle," they said, "you're still holding it, brother. You think it's your fault. You're still feeling it."

"Yep," Amy and I said.

But Kyle looked at us quizzically. He couldn't see it. He was still inside of it.

I thought of the ninetieth birthday party we'd thrown our father—just a few months before he died. Amy didn't make any remarks because she didn't really know my dad. I said something jokey—like a pretend eulogy—diverting my feelings, true to form. Then Kyle got up and did this whole long, elaborate tribute. He put a lot of time and effort into it.

If you had been in the audience and didn't know our history, you'd say: "How lucky were these three kids to have a dad like that?" Amy and Robin and I were looking at each other and wondering: Who is Kyle talking about?

In my dad's later years, Kyle talked to him every day. To the end, he was the dutiful son, attempting to mend the damage that years of absence had wrought. At times, it seemed to Amy and me that Kyle was trying to reinvent a perfect father-son relationship. My brother is a sensitive, thoughtful, compassionate, and hardworking man. He was generous and faithful to the relationship with my dad. He wanted to make it work.

I said to Kyle at one point: "I don't think Dad is capable. He's already done all he can do. Think about the movie we offered him! A chance to work with his sons in his chosen field. He was not willing to make it, even to discuss it."

But Kyle had his own truth. His own memory.

My brother is two and a half years older than me. In our early lives, our experiences were very close: I think of our McNulty Avenue Garage productions. I think of how we supported each other as we stocked other people's junk and odds and ends to sell. How we clutched each other as our dad went to beat the man who'd cut him off in traffic. How together we were jolted out of our lives and into the country, charged with killing chickens. I think of the epic motorcycle trip, those days we spent riding with no plan, no sense of obligation, the future and the road endlessly open in front of us. We were as close as brothers could be. But there were underlying differences—always. Kyle knew our dad longer while our family was still intact. He knew two and a half years more of the happy times. So Kyle, who was always the most emotional of the three of us, who always felt things more deeply, felt them longer, felt the blow of the loss of those happy times most.

I always thought of my brother at the bow of his ship getting battered, getting the brunt of the storm, and I was in the boat behind him. I had Kyle to guide me and show me the way through. He did things first, and I watched him, and then I did them. And that's how I learned.

In so many ways, my brother is my savior. I love him. And I owe him a great deal for how my life turned out.

Dad

Robin and I felt that the best thing we could do for our daughter was to let her figure things out and even get into trouble now and then. So long as she always knew we would be there.

When something moderately bad happened to my daughter, outwardly I was always saying: "Oh, honey, I'm sorry." Inwardly I was shouting: Yes!

You've got to fail, or risk failure, to learn, to succeed. You've got to be hungry. It seems to me the job for parents is to console the failure but nurture the hunger. That's how you create independence in children, give them the tools they need to be functioning adults. Our goal, Robin's and mine, wasn't to raise a well-adjusted child; it was to raise a well-adjusted adult.

And she's become just that. Taylor is an actor. And, thank God, she's good. And she's refining her craft daily. She just received a major break in her young career, a co-lead role in a TV series. Her modesty and desire for privacy stop me from boasting further. Taylor is fully aware that this is just one job—albeit a good one on a well-written show—and no one can predict its success. Her work ethic and sensibility fill me with pride. After she learned she got the part, she kept her survival job up until the last minute. That's my girl.

We talk often about acting and storytelling, but we rarely talk about each other's work. My number one role is to be her father—not her acting coach. All I want to do is support her passion. When we discuss acting, it's usually about someone else's work, a play's merits.

But I suppose some of what I've tried to share with my daughter about life has applications in acting. I always encouraged Taylor to wander, to feel it's okay not to know exactly where you are. Figuring it out builds confidence. Of course I don't want her to be risky to the point of being dangerous. But go ahead, get lost. It's okay to be afraid. Being afraid can actually be a sign you're doing something worthwhile. If I'm considering a role and it makes me nervous, but I can't stop thinking about it—that's often a good indication I'm onto something important.

Fatherhood has been such a part.

And it's been my favorite one.

LBJ

I needed to let Walter White die.

And I thought the perfect way might be a different medium: a play. I asked my agents at UTA's New York office to look out for something great, and I got a call right away. "I found it, Bryan. The character is on par with Walter White, only on stage. But it's different. It's like King Lear."

The thirty-sixth president of the United States. Lyndon Baines Johnson. In a play called *All the Way*. Huge role; huge risk. The play would run nearly three hours, and I'd barely have the chance to take a breath. I'd be offstage for about fifteen minutes total. And the character, the man, was big. LBJ was brilliant and cruel and restless and funny and visionary and angry and ambitious and insecure, and more. It could be a tour de force if done right. Or it could be a big turd. Professor Flipnoodle on a national stage.

I read it through, and one scene toward the end of the play stuck with me for days. Johnson is getting ready for bed and he laments, "I have a genuine desire to unite people, but my own people in the South are against me and the North is against me and the Negroes are against me and the press sure doesn't have any affection for me.

"I could drop dead tomorrow . . . and there wouldn't be ten people who'd shed a tear."

His assistant tries to comfort him. "That's not true, Mr. President."

"The hell it ain't," Johnson snaps.

"People turn on you so fast. When my daddy lost everything, people who'd been glad-handing him treated him like dog shit. Humiliated him to his face in public. And my mother, the way she would freeze him out; that's what killed him. You know what I think it is? People think I want great power but what I want is great solace; a little love. That's all I want."

He was reliving his pain, his father's embarrassment. His mother's cold demeanor.

I could imagine it. I could see myself on stage, allowing myself to sink in, letting the audience witness that moment, that pure vulnerability. I could see myself conjuring up that pain. The need. That neediness was at the root of everything LBJ did, everything he was: his quest for power and his flaws and his great gifts.

I thought of my own ego-driven father, my brokenhearted mother. If I did this play, they'd be on stage with me, too. I could imagine tears coming to my eyes. And I could feel the energies and sympathies of the audience. I felt them crying, too.

Then, after I gave the speech, I could imagine myself abruptly changing. Embarrassed, I'd almost slap myself to get rid of the tears. Fuck it. I'd try to cover. Pain is vulnerability for a man—especially a man of that generation. I'd give the audience a glimpse of Johnson's soul, how he truly felt, then slam the door.

I imagined myself, on my feet, close to the audience, so that I was able to talk very quietly, so quietly that they'd have to lean in. They'd want to lean in. They'd yearn to be close. And with a few words, I'd make them feel more alive.

On stage, you and the audience, it's like sonar. You give them something, and it all washes back to you. Especially with the right part.

And what a part.

This was *the* part.

It was my part.

I knew I wanted in. But I also wanted to meet the director and writer to make sure they wanted me. And to make sure we were a good fit.

Bill Rausch, the director, and Robert Schenkkan, the playwright, came over to my house. The agency is fond of saying: *It's not an audition.* But in truth *every* meeting is an audition. I'm sure Bill and Robert wanted to see if I was in the ballpark of what they had in mind for LBJ. And, in truth, I wanted to know: Is this going to be a director who is rigid about everything I try? A writer who thinks his every word is chiseled into stone? I don't work well with that kind of domineering, my-way-or-the-highway type of director or writer. I work better in collaborative environments. Everyone respects each other, challenges each other, and works toward a common goal. The best idea wins.

As part of the storytelling complex, as an actor, I have to be able to know I can ask questions and be heard. I wanted to know if Bill and Robert would allow for that kind of exchange.

In the protocol of theater, there's far more respect for the writer than there is in film and TV. A history of reverence and laws protect the text; you're not allowed to change lines without the playwright's permission. You can't even cut text unless authorized. No rewriting allowed. In film and TV, you respect the text, but it's a blueprint, not a bible. Changes are common, especially when stars insist on them. In the theater your director and your writer (if you have the luxury of a writer being present, if he or she is cooperative and not dead) are giving you notes through the previews; they change lines and blocking and make adjustments.

But after opening night you're in what they call a *locked show*.

In my view, that is the antithesis of what creativity should be. As long as actors and audiences are showing up, nothing is locked. How can it be?

With any play, moments can get bigger or smaller. They evolve from night to night. Sometimes I change for no other reason than to see how it feels. I twist the reading of a line. It may result in a much bigger laugh. It may not. Then I try it another way the next night to see what happens.

I'm part of the creative triumvirate: writer, director, actor. I listen, I respect, but I don't lock anything. That works for computer programming—not acting.

I think you run a tremendous risk of getting complacent if you don't keep looking for changes. You should never be too at ease on stage. Get too rehearsed, too relaxed, you lose focus and slip into autopilot, and then you're not listening. Someone could drop a line. You have to work out of that problem, react to it. *He skipped ahead, so I need to clarify that point for the audience.* Otherwise, they're completely lost.

Some actors panic; some assimilate mistakes and correct course.

If you're paying attention, if you're present, more often than not you can rise to the occasion. Or sometimes your castmate will rise to the occasion for you. I know I've been bailed out many times. But you can't bank on someone else coming to the rescue. You have to be open and present and willing to adapt.

If you tell me a play is locked at opening night and there's no room for exploration or change, I'd say I'm probably not the best actor for your play. If every night you gesture here, put your hands on your hips there, if every night you sip your drink on exactly the same line, your consciousness will pop out of your body. You'll be a casual observer of yourself, going through the motions. Once that happens, you're dead. You're a robot. Every performance needs to have its intimacy, its difference.

Every night, a new audience is sitting out there in the dark, waiting. And you're new, too. You're a day older. Maybe you're hoarse. You drink some hot tea. Then you're on stage and you have to pee like a racehorse. Note to self: ease up on the tea. Maybe you didn't eat as much as you did last night. You're hungry. Use that. You caught a cold. You have a sinus infection. LBJ is dealing with these same maladies on stage, blowing his nose, hacking away. You bring everything you are on stage with you. And you see if it can fit into the character. If it doesn't, you need to note it and make an adjustment.

Bill and Robert and I sat down for coffee in my guesthouse in California, and I wanted to know: Were they open? Or were they "lock it" people? Were they going to say "the play is the play"?

We talked for a while, and then I suggested we read some passages.

They were delighted. Since it wasn't an audition, it would have been awkward for them to ask me to read. But I'm sure they were wondering: Can this guy pull it off?

Together we found out. Robert picked out a scene. How about this one with Hubert Humphrey? I read. They listened. I experimented with putting LBJ's voice in my body, and suddenly I felt more attached to the role.

At the end of the meeting, we all knew. They liked what I had done, and I liked them. They were not rigid. Nor were they pushovers. I had the strong feeling we'd make a good team. And I could see myself in the part. This could work.

We got the agents involved, signed a deal. We'd open in Boston in the late summer of 2013.

I dove into the research. The literature on Johnson is wide and deep, and I got lost in it. I devoured Robert Caro's masterpieces. I listened to the LBJ tapes that Michael Beschloss edited and put into historical context. I read LBJ's memoir, *The Vantage Point*, as well as books by Doris Kearns Goodwin, Joseph Califano, Taylor Branch, and Mark Updegrove. I also visited the impressive LBJ library in Austin, Texas, and soaked up everything I could.

Lastly, and most importantly, I leaned on the brilliant, powerful text in front of me, Robert Schenkkan's *All the Way*.

I arrived in Cambridge, where we'd be mounting the play at the American Repertory Theater before taking it to Broadway. We gathered for a table read of the play, and it was me me me me me me him. Me me me me me her. Oh my God. Of course I'd read the play a few times before, but I'd been reading it objectively, not from a logistical, elbow-grease, what's-it-going to-take perspective. I'd been looking for a deeper understanding of the story, the man, not thinking, *Look at all these lines I need to memorize*.

At the end of the reading, we got the schedule. Four weeks. We had four weeks before our first audience. The first week we'd rehearse Act One. The second week, Act Two. The third week we'd put it all together. The fourth week would be a technical rehearsal. Costumes, lights, makeup, sound. That wouldn't really count as time for the actors to prepare.

So basically we had three weeks.

Holy shit.

What had I done? Or more appropriately, what had I not done? I thought if I could show up in Boston with the character nailed, I'd be in good shape, but I got lost in the joy of the research and neglected the nuts-and-bolts work. Memorization.

It was as if I'd been planning a feast, and then a few hours before serving it I realized I hadn't shopped. The table was set, but the main thing was missing. The food.

Usually, preparing for a part, I memorize alone. But I knew this time I'd need help. I contacted my old friend Bill Timoney. When I was on *Loving*, he was on *All My Children*, playing Alfred Vander-pool. We were on the same network, right around the corner from each other in New York, and we became fast friends.

Now I hired Bill to come to Boston to be my right arm: to be my coach, to run lines with me, to help me with the daily stuff, power me through. He knew what that would entail. And I knew he knew. Bill is bright, personable, perceptive. I could count on him.

I'd never had problems with memorization before. Over the years I developed a habit of doing margin work, writing notes to myself in the margins of the script. That helps me memorize or "bone" lines as well as developing the character. I write a sentence's verb in the margin (a trick I learned from Jane Kaczmarek), and the active verb works like a gatekeeper to the rest of the sentence's meaning. As I'm familiarizing myself with a speech, I can test myself by reading the list of verbs in the margin to trigger each sentence.

Pretty soon, I've memorized a page. Then repeat the process for the entire script.

But this part was so big, and I had so little time. The amount of dialogue I had to memorize was mind-boggling. Too many verbs! *Do the work*, I told myself. Just do the work. There are no shortcuts for doing the work.

But I soon started to feel the amount of work I had to do would crush me. I've loved work and thrived on work my whole adult life, but I was just dizzy with how many words I needed to stuff into my brain.

Within a week I had serious doubts about whether I was going to be able to pull it off. My uncertainty affected everything I did. My mind was heavy. My chest was heavy. Even my legs felt heavy when I went for my run. Each day was so crammed with input that I thought the wiring in my brain might short-circuit. By night, the morning was a distant memory. Before bed, I'd call Robin. "I don't know if I can do this," I told her.

"Sure you can," she said.

"I need more time."

I thought: *I have to be in a place where my body can support this effort, this stress.* I tailored my whole existence around the role. I ate oatmeal and vegetables and fish with a squeeze of lemon. No sugar. Few carbs. I pounded water. Every meal, I sat with the script. Every night, homework. Seven days a week, I worked. I needed every minute.

We'd finished blocking the first act and were on to Act Two. A couple of days into that second week, I was feeling desperate and asked for a meeting with the director and writer. Off-site. I didn't want to talk in the theater. Too close to home. I took them across the street to a park in Cambridge.

"I'm drowning," I told them. "I'm dying here."

They exchanged a curious look. "What are you talking about?" they said. "You're in great shape."

"I don't feel that way. I don't have enough time to be ready."

"No, no. You're on track. Keep going."

Every day I willed myself out of bed. Sit-ups, push-ups, push-ups. A run every other day. Oatmeal. And then into the play. I'd see how well I remembered what I did the day before and then I'd go further. I'd memorize more. By 10:00 a.m., I was at the theater rehearsing. At dusk, I'd go outside with my script just to get some air. I'd eat dinner, then read more sections of the play. I'd go to sleep with the play on my chest and wake up with pages scattered all over my bed.

Except for bike rides with Bill on Mondays and *Breaking Bad* on Sunday nights, that's all I did. The play, the play, the play. I stayed on it. The other actors would shoot the breeze, talking about their days off: dinners, day trips. What about this new movie? Did you try that new restaurant?

I was envious and resentful of their freedom. For a minute. And then I went back to work. As we rehearsed, per equity rules, we took periodic fifteen-minute breaks. I'd get some oxygen and do a stretch and then back into the play, reading, rereading, making notes, memorizing. I was never without it. Even when I was going for a run, I was working out how I'd deliver a line, when I'd punch it up, when I'd hold back. The play was always with me.

"I don't think I can do this," I said to Robin, more and more urgently. We were nearing the end of the second week. "I'm adrift. I'm at sea."

"You can do it." She hadn't heard me like this, other than when I struggled through *Brooklyn South*. I was doubting, but I heard no quaver of uncertainty in her voice. Her counsel was soothing. She believed in me.

"Trust the process," Bill Rausch said. "It's amazing what the brain will allow you to do. You open your brain and fill it with words, and close it and let it rest. You have to rest. And then the next day you'll be able to stretch and fill it with more. I wouldn't say this if I didn't see it working every day. You have to trust the process." Bill was a wonderfully open and generous director, supportive and smart. I wanted to believe him.

And I did, intellectually, but it wasn't resonating. Easy for him to say. He wasn't going to be on stage forgetting lines. I nodded along, but I was steeped in doubt.

By the end of the second week, I was feeling my sanity at risk.

For the first time in my life I was having the classic actor's nightmare. I was on stage, doing the play, and then—blank. I couldn't remember my lines. I felt naked, defenseless. I gave pleading looks to my fellow actors, but they couldn't help. I was on my own. The audience was looking at me with sympathetic embarrassment. If I was lucky, I'd wake up from the awful dream before too long. But then I couldn't go back to sleep, because there was too much adrenaline running through my system. Bad sleep? Good luck with the memorization tomorrow.

I'd had moments of insecurity and doubt before in my career, but never the standard anxiety dream, never The Nightmare. Now I'd had it a few times. It would shadow me into the morning hours. It was hard to shake.

When I was feeling overwhelmed, on my walk to work, I would concoct these elaborate victim scenarios. Morbidly reassuring daydreams. What if I got hurt? What if I got injured just badly enough so that I *couldn't* do the play? Then it wouldn't be my fault. I couldn't be blamed if the play was delayed or canceled. I started imagining a Tonya Harding-type situation. Could I pay someone to kneecap me with a baseball bat, put me out of commission? Not a permanent injury. Just enough to sideline me for a couple of weeks. No one would blame me if I had to bow out because of a shattered kneecap!

And then it was out of my reverie and back to the play.

Bill Timoney said to me, "Here's the bottom line. Come the first night of previews, *you will be* on that stage. You *will* perform. So work backward. Trust that you'll get there. Don't stop working. We won't stop working. We'll get you there."

Yes. I just had to trust the people around me and the process and keep working. Never stop working.

With one week to go, the play suddenly began to open up. It began to come to me. Everything I'd done in my life seemed to have prepared me for this moment. Collecting eggs and killing chickens at my grandfather's farm. Watching my mother gather junk to sell at swap meets—she didn't give up. Announcing that Abraham Lincoln was going to write one of America's greatest speeches as soon as he returned to the White Front—that failure and embarrassment was with me somewhere, too.

Opening night, I stood in the wings as the audience got settled. The script called for the other actors to fill empty seats on stage, and then for the lights to cut to black. That was my cue.

Downstage center. Right in front of the audience. That empty seat at center stage. That was my seat.

Two weeks earlier, it looked like an electric chair.

Now, opening night, it looked like a throne.

Standing in the hushed darkness, I smiled. Oh. That's why I went through this. The monastic life. The doubt. The work. The pain. It was all part of it.

It was all so I could have this feeling. It was so I could live this moment.

I took three deep breaths. I shook those breaths into my body. And then I relaxed. I let it go.

And I went to take my place.

Acknowledgments

Shannon Welch. For your superb talents in orchestrating, contributing to, and editing this book. Your guidance and support in taking charge made this collaboration an enriching experience.

Bill Timoney. For your counsel on this project, and helping me get through a difficult time.

John O'Hurley. For your support and suggesting that I do this book.

Mrs. Waldo and Mrs. Crawford, my fifth- and sixth-grade teachers, for encouraging me to take chances toward a creative path.

Vince Gilligan. For giving me the role of my life—that also changed my life.

My grandparents, Otto and Augusta Sell. For taking me in and teaching me tough love and discipline.

Joe and Peggy, my parents. For teaching me, in their unique way, the person I should become.

Thank you:

Jodi Gottlieb, Lindsay Shane, and my team at Independent PR.

Sarah Clossey, Jeremy Zimmer, and my team at United Talent Agency.

Leonard Grant, the Baral family, Mickey Middleton, Linwood Boomer, James Kiberd, Reverend Bob, Stewart Lyons, Brett Hansen, Kevin Stolper, Mark Subias, Chris Highland, Ivan Markota, Break Costin, Shirley Knight, Diane Galardi, Taryn Feingold, Georgette Reilly-Timoney, Kris Chapman, James Degus, Kirsten Jacobson, Andy Garcia, Dan McVicar, Raymond Fitzpatrick, Bill Rausch, Robert Schenkkan, Richard Pine, Jeff Widener, Louis Rego, Javier Grajeda, Carolyn Kiesel, Reuben Valdez, New Mexico, Daytona Playhouse, and

All the great people I've met on my path who had an influence on my life.